ON THEIR OWN

WHAT HAPPENS TO KIDS WHEN THEY AGE OUT OF THE FOSTER CARE SYSTEM?

MARTHA SHIRK & **GARY STANGLER**
With a Foreword by **JIMMY CARTER**

BASIC
BOOKS

A Member of the Perseus Books Group

Copyright © 2004 by Jim Casey Youth Opportunities Initiative
All Photos © 2004 by Gale Zucker

Hardcover first published in 2004 in the United States of America by Westview Press, 5500 Central Avenue, Boulder, Colorado 80301-2877, and in the United Kingdom by Westview Press, 12 Hid's Copse Road, Cumnor Hill, Oxford OX2 9JJ.

Paperback first published in 2006 by Basic Books, a member of the Perseus Books Group

Books published by Basic Books are available at special discounts for bulk purchases in the United States by corporations, institutions, and other organizations. For more information, please contact the Special Markets Department at the Perseus Books Group, 11 Cambridge Center, Cambridge MA 02142, or call (617) 252-5298 or (800) 255-1514, or e-mail special.markets@perseusbooks.com.

Library of Congress Cataloging-in-Publication Data

Shirk, Martha.
    On their own : what happens to kids when they age out of the foster care system? / Martha Shirk, Gary Stangler ; with a foreword by Jimmy Carter.
        p. cm.
    Includes bibliographical references and index.
    HC: ISBN-13 978-08133-4180-4; ISBN 0-8133-4180-9
    1. Foster children—United States—Case studies. 2. Problem youth—United States—Case studies. 3. Youth with social disabilities—United States—Case studies. I. Stangler, Gary J. II. Title.
HV881.S55 2004
362.73'3—dc22

2004007735

The paper used in this publication meets the requirements of the American National Standard for Permanence of Paper for Printed Library Materials Z39.48–1984.

Interior design by Lisa Kreinbrink
Text set in Palatino Light

PBK: ISBN-13 978-0-465-07766-3; ISBN 0-465-07766-8

10   9   8   7   6   5   4   3   2   1

CONTENTS

FOREWORD
by Jimmy Carter

In our travels around the globe, Rosalynn and I have seen the debilitating effects of poverty on some of the world's most vulnerable populations. Our hearts have been wrenched by the faces of the many children and youth who have been marginalized and left to a life of want.

Unfortunately, these images are not confined to the developing world. Here in the United States, amid the greatest wealth the world has ever known, too many young people are trapped by poverty, by lack of education and opportunity, and by hopelessness. And as this book demonstrates in compelling detail, there is probably no group of young people in America more at risk than those who have "aged out" of foster care.

With the world's biggest economy, billions of dollars a year of government spending on education and social services, and outstanding public schools and universities, Americans expect that our young people can all realize their dreams and become productive citizens. For most children who grow up in healthy, supportive families, little stands in the way. But for the half-million children and youth who inhabit our nation's foster care system, the reality is more complicated, the future more in doubt.

Most of these children eventually return to their parents after they have overcome the problems that caused their children to be placed in foster care. Thousands more find love and support with new adoptive families. Still, every year as many as 25,000 young people reach the age of majority while still in foster care and abruptly lose the support of the state. In the words of Martha Shirk and Gary Stangler, they are "on their own" in a world for which they have been ill prepared.

In recent years, our newspapers have been filled with heartbreaking stories of young children who have been poorly served by our nation's foster care system. But rarely have we been asked to reflect on the special challenges that older youth face as they prepare to leave a system that has fed and housed them and seen to their medical and educational needs. In most states, when these children turn eighteen, social workers close their cases. The assumption is that they are ready to be independent. But once they are "emancipated" from the system, many seem simply to melt away into society's cracks.

Recent polls indicate that a majority of Americans believe that most people don't achieve full-fledged adulthood until age twenty-six. Our own experience as parents bears this out. How many times do our own children, well past the age of eighteen, seek us out for advice, for money, or for a soothing word? What kind of a message do we send, as a society, if emancipation from foster care means no second chances, no room to learn from mistakes, no helping hand?

The reality is that young people who leave foster care at age eighteen are no more ready to become independent than our own children. In fact, most are probably less ready. Many youth in foster care do not benefit from normal growing-up experiences, such as holding down a part-time job, watching a parent balance a checkbook, or learning the meaning of household responsibility by performing daily chores. Without basic life skills, youth who leave foster care often have difficulty negotiating more complex tasks like finding safe housing, getting and keeping a steady job, staying healthy, and avoiding financial or legal trouble. Too few undertake the education and training necessary to compete in today's economy. In fact, four years after leaving care, only one in five former foster youth is fully self-supporting.

Our government has not been deaf to the needs of these young people. In 1999, Congress passed and President Clinton signed the Foster Care Independence Act, also called the Chafee Act, which expanded transition services for older youth leaving foster care. Although the new government mandates and funding are welcome, they are far from suffi-cient. Ensuring the safe passage of these young people into adulthood will take more creativity and cooperation than has been mustered so far.

In their arresting and important new book, *On Their Own*, Martha Shirk and Gary Stangler put a human face on this invisible population. *On Their Own* provides an intimate and often gripping account of the struggles and triumphs of young people at critical turning points in their lives. I was deeply moved by the experiences of those young people. Al-though I was troubled to read how bad decisions could so quickly lead them into crisis, I was also gratified to see that perseverance in the face of adversity usually paid off. And I was particularly pleased to see how the presence of a caring adult at the right moment could make a differ-ence in their lives. In the end, these stories gave me hope.

On Their Own offers specific recommendations for how we can help youth leaving foster care become healthy, independent adults. Not con-tent merely to describe the problems, Martha Shirk and Gary Stangler suggest improvements at the national, state, and local levels. Their ob-servations cut across a number of policy domains, including workforce development, housing, education, health care, and personal and com-munity engagement. They also point to the need for greater youth en-gagement in designing their road maps to independence and for greater cooperation among community organizations, child welfare agencies, charities, and business leaders in supporting them. Many individuals and groups are doing good work, but they have not worked closely enough with one another.

I commend coauthors Martha Shirk and Gary Stangler and the Jim Casey Youth Opportunities Initiative, which supported the creation of this book. The authors have created a vitally important addition to the literature on child welfare, foster care, and youth development. *On Their Own* is a must-read account not only for students of American social policy but for all Americans who care about children.

The question we should ask ourselves is this: If we willingly give our own children the benefit of our support as they struggle to become inde-pendent, productive adults, why do we tolerate the abrupt withdrawal of support for youth who are aging out of care? These young people go to the same schools, experience the same adolescent pressures, and yearn for the same successful futures as other youth in our communities. Their only "crime" was being born into homes where, because of abuse or neglect, they could not remain safe. Obviously, the state is no substitute for a caring family. But in the absence of family support, we as a nation *must* do better for children whose custody we have assumed.

I have long believed that how we treat the most vulnerable members in our society is a measure of the greatness of our nation. *On Their Own* makes clear that the current system leaves young people aging out of care with few educational and job resources, and with a lack of life skills and practical experience. Without support from caring individuals, many of these youth are making unwise and unhealthy decisions today that will affect them for years, if not the rest of their lives.

We should dream of and plan for a day when fewer children require foster care. But until that day comes, we have a moral responsibility to prepare young people leaving foster care for their journey into adulthood. Our communities must commit themselves to a common goal of helping these young people to become whole adults who can fulfill their potential and build bright and promising futures.

As I told the audience in Oslo when I accepted the Nobel Peace Prize in 2002, "God gives us the capacity for choice. We can *choose* to alleviate suffering." I know that throughout America, tens of thousands of passionate and caring people stand ready to help so that these young people need not become a permanent underclass.

ACKNOWLEDGMENTS

We are deeply indebted to the young people who welcomed us into their lives to help the American public gain a better understanding of the challenges young people face as they age out of foster care. It takes great courage to share your hopes and dreams with strangers. We wish them all well.

We are also indebted to the many people around the country who helped us find our subjects or fill in the blanks in their personal histories. In New York, they include Candace Rashada, director of Work Appreciation for Youth at Children's Village, Keith Hefner, director of Youth Communication, and Jennifer Nelson and Gessy Nixon of Voices of Youth; in Massachusetts, Ginny O'Connell, at Casey Family Services, and JoAnn Villiard, one of Patty's foster parents; in Texas, Scott Ackerson and Liz Cruz, at Casey Family Programs, and Victoria Bernal, at Stepping Forward; in California, Anne Stanton and Sam Cobbs at Larkin Street Youth Services; in Kansas, Brenda Chamberlain of the Kansas Youth Advisory Council and J. D. Kerr, at O'Connell Youth Ranch; in Iowa, Ray Benter, Mitch Henry, Eve Hickman, Diane Martin, Howard Matalba, and Jena Sigler, all of Youth & Shelter Services, Pat Glassell of the Des Moines public schools, Clark Kauffman of the *Des Moines Register*, and Deb Thompson, of Golden Circle Behavioral Management; in Florida, Bernard Perlmutter, Joanne Manees, and Elizabeth Messer of the University of Miami's Children and Youth Law Clinic, and Marilyn Dillon and Theresa Salazar, Alfonso's angels.

The board of trustees of the Jim Casey Youth Opportunities Initiative has shown unstinting support for both the Initiative's mission and this project. We are grateful to cochair Douglas Nelson, Oz Nelson, and Calvin Tyler of the Annie E. Casey Foundation, and cochair Ruth Massinga, Gary Severson, and Richard Ford of Casey Family Programs. We also want to express our sincere appreciation to the staff members at the Jim Casey Youth Opportunities Initiative who have informed our views on the issues and provided assistance, as needed, on tasks both mundane and weighty: Sherry Amen, Toni Cooke, Shawn Huff, Kate Lee, Carla Owens, Rita Powell, Liz Squibb, Gary Stangler, Jay Vazquez, and Karen Yavorsky. Consultants Ed Hatcher and Greg Michaelidis of The Hatcher Group also provided valuable counsel. We are particularly indebted to Kate Lee, Rita Powell, and Greg Michaelidis for their close readings of the manuscript. Robin Nixon, director of the National Foster Care Coalition, provided valuable insights into the challenges facing youth leaving care.

We were lucky to find a photographer, Gale Zucker, who approached her assignment with enthusiasm and empathy and produced photographs that reveal the essence of each of the young people who are profiled. At Westview Press, Jill Rothenberg saw the promise in our book proposal and shepherded the project to publication.

Our spouses, William Woo and Beth Stangler, were unfailingly supportive of the project. And finally, our sons—Tom, Bennett, and Peter Woo; and Dane, McKay, and Connor Stangler—provided us with more insights than they can ever know into what young people need as they head out into the world. Each time one of them seeks our advice or approval, we're reminded of how important it is for all young people to have caring and responsible adults involved in their lives.

INTRODUCTION
On Their Own in a World of Unknowns

For most children, turning eighteen is an important milestone. At long last, they eagerly step through the doorway into adulthood. It is a time of ritual and celebration, of high school proms and graduations, going-away parties and senior trips. It is also a time of apprehension and excitement, as these children, now legal adults, start full-time jobs, move into college dorms, or head off to boot camp. Friends and family shower them with checks and best wishes for success in the "real world," as their parents proudly suppress tears, remembering them as babes in arms.

When we send our own eighteen-year-olds out into the world, it's with the tacit understanding that they aren't *really* on their own. We're as close as the nearest phone, ready to provide counsel about how to cope with unexpected emergencies of the everyday variety. When they're playing in a game or a concert, they know they can count on someone being there to applaud them. And for mundane achievements and joys, they know someone who will be proud to share them. Besides their parents, they have the backing of other family members and friends, and even friends of family and friends, not to mention coaches, teachers, and clergy, all of whom provide a collective safety net.

For as many as 25,000 other children who reach their eighteenth birthdays each year, the emotions are similar. But there is a defining difference. These are young people who step through a doorway into a world full of unknowns, without the connections and supports that other children take for granted. Something has happened in their lives that forever makes them different: Usually through no fault of their own, they were taken away from their families and placed in foster care.[1] They entered a bureaucratic system peopled with strangers who had complete control over where they lived, where they went to school, and even whether they ever saw their families again.

The supports in their lives were not people who loved them, but people who were paid for the roles they played—caseworkers, judges, attorneys, and either shift workers in group homes or a succession of often kind, but always temporary, foster parents. In most states, on the day that a child in foster care turns eighteen, these supports largely disappear. The people who once attended to that child's needs are now either unable or unwilling to continue; a new case demands their time, a new child requires the bed. There is often no one with whom to share small successes. And with no one to approach for advice, garden-variety emergencies—a flat tire, a stolen wallet, a missing birth certificate—escalate into full-blown crises.

Try to imagine that you have just turned eighteen and have been put out of your foster home.

You may have amassed some savings from a part-time job and received a one-time "emancipation" grant, but you don't have a job. You have no idea where you'll sleep tonight, let alone next week or next month. Your belongings are packed into two plastic bags. Your family is unable to help, and may even have disappeared.

Further clouding your prospects are your educational deficits and a history of trouble with the law. You read at a seventh grade level. You were held back a grade, and you have a police record.* What kind of future would you predict for yourself? Can you cope with:

---

*The most recent research on youth about to age out of foster care found that they are more likely to have been held back a grade, suspended from school, or expelled than most other youth. At age seventeen, they read, on average, at a seventh grade level. They were also more likely than a representative national sample to have been in trouble with the law, with more than half reporting an arrest. Mark E. Courtney, Sherri Terao, and Noel Bost, *Midwest Evaluation of the Adult Functioning of Former Foster Youth: Conditions of Youth Preparing to Leave State Care* (Chicago: Chapin Hall Center for Children, 2004), http://www.chapinhall.org/PDFDownload_new.asp?tk=1002275&ar=1355&L2=61&L3=130.

- Sudden homelessness, at least temporarily, while you wander through the referral maze?
- Difficulty finding a job, since you don't have a permanent address or even the basic documents you need—like a birth certificate and a Social Security card—to fill out a job application or a W-4?
- An interruption in your education, not just because of the cost, but also because of complex eligibility requirements and your inability to document your school record?
- The pressure to engage in unhealthy or even illegal behaviors as a means of survival?

Whatever you are imagining as your fate, the reality is much worse for many youth who age out of foster care. Data from several studies paint a troubling picture. Within a few years of leaving foster care:

- Only slightly more than half of these young people have graduated from high school, compared with 85 percent of all youth eighteen to twenty-four years old.
- One-fourth have endured some period of homelessness.
- Almost two-thirds have not maintained employment for a year.
- Four out of ten have become parents.
- Not even one in five is completely self-supporting.
- One in four males and one in ten females have spent time in jail.[2]

On Their Own tells the stories of ten young people who stepped through the doorway to adulthood without the support that most children in America take for granted. We hope that you will be inspired by the tenacity, resilience, and perseverance that these young people display in the face of numerous obstacles. But we expect, too, that your heart will ache as you read of the lingering effects of abuse or neglect and their bewilderment about how to navigate a complex world for which they have been poorly prepared. Their stories reveal the mix of positive and negative outcomes that await young people who "age out" of foster care without being returned to their birth families or adopted.

Who Are These Young People?

Between 1980 and 2003, the number of children in foster care in the United States grew from 302,000 to 523,000.[3] Ominously, the rate of placement nearly doubled, from 4.7 per 1,000 children to 7.7, which means that a higher proportion of children than before are spending time in foster care.

Children are generally placed in foster care for one reason alone: their protection.[4] Those placed in care are most often victims of some form of neglect—failure to provide the basics of life, such as food, clothes, and housing, or failure to supervise—and in the vast majority of cases (nearly 60.5 percent), these are failures of the parents, with poverty, ignorance, and alcohol and drug abuse being contributing factors. In a minority of cases—35 percent—the reasons for removal are physical abuse, sexual abuse, or severe emotional abuse. In these cases, too, a parent is the most likely abuser, but sometimes the abuser is a parent's partner or a relative.[5] (Legally, harm by a person who is not in a caretaking role is not considered child abuse.)

The process of removal typically starts with a call, often anonymous, to a child-abuse hot line. A social worker comes to investigate. If assessment shows that the child cannot safely stay at home, the social worker petitions a court for a removal order. If a judge agrees with the assessment, the child is removed, usually by uniformed police officers, and often suddenly. The psychological trauma created by the removal, combined with the neglect or abuse that preceded it, leaves the child forever changed and forever different from other children. "The policeman held my hand and walked me across the street," Raquel Tolston, one of the young people you'll meet in the following pages, remembers eighteen years later. "I remember looking back and seeing my mother standing there crying. I didn't know why."

Only a minority of child-abuse reports result in a child being placed in foster care. In FY 2003, there were 2.9 million reports of suspected maltreatment, of which about one-third—906,000—were substantiated.[6] Less than one-third of these children—297,000—entered foster care.

After removal, a child is taken to what is euphemistically called an "out-of-home placement." The first placement is rarely the last. It may be in an emergency foster home or an emergency shelter, both designed to meet the child's immediate needs for just a few days, or in a foster home or group home licensed both for emergency placements and for longer stays. In theory, removal immediately sets in motion a process to determine a goal for "permanency": reunification with the family, adoption, placement with relatives, long-term care, or independent living. In practice, permanency is usually a long way off. Nationwide, the mean stay for children who exited foster care in 2003 was just under twenty-two months, and the median stay was just under a year, though both indicators vary widely among states. Nine percent of children who left in 2003 had been in care five years or more.

Although Hollywood commonly portrays children in foster care as toddlers clutching teddy bears, nearly one-half are eleven or older. And about one-fifth—103,500—are sixteen or older. Although the rise in overall numbers has made it increasingly difficult to find family settings for all ages of children, this is especially true for teenagers. They are by nature rebellious and difficult to work with, so relatively few foster families are willing to try. As a result, only 60 percent of children fourteen and older live in foster or pre-adoptive homes, compared with more than 90 percent of younger children. In the group homes or large residential institutions where many teens live, their caretakers are often poorly paid shift workers; despite the low wages, care in these settings costs taxpayers up to ten times the cost of family foster care. Over time, many teens experience stays in both settings.

The longer a child stays in foster care, the more placements, although this varies by state. In Maine, for instance, 92.5 percent of children in care for four years or more experience more than two placements, compared with 1.3 percent in Puerto Rico. In 2002, states reported a median percentage of 72.8 for long-term foster children with more than two placements.

Although white children and African American children land in foster care in roughly equal numbers, African American children are disproportionately likely both to enter foster care and to remain there until they become adults, a troubling phenomenon. African American children account for only 15 percent of all children in the United States, but they accounted for 27 percent of those entering care in 2003 (the last year for which national data are available) and 35 percent of those in care.[8] The reasons for this high rate aren't fully understood, but the higher poverty rate of minority families is a major factor.

In 2003, 281,000 children of all ages left the foster care system. Fifty-five percent returned to their families, and 11 percent went to live with a relative or guardian; 18 percent were adopted, 8 percent "emancipated" (left the system generally because they reached the age of majority), and 4 percent 10,700—entered gardianships.

The young people with whom this book is concerned are those who are neither reunited with their families nor adopted—that is, those who emancipated and departed from foster care directly into the world of adulthood, with little or no family support.[9]

Aging Out

Each year, between 18,500 and 25,000 teenagers "age out" of foster care by virtue of reaching the age at which their legal right to foster care ends (21,720 in 2001).[10] Another 4,000 or so run away from foster care before they formally age out. Of those who age out, most are eighteen. In a few states, youth can voluntarily remain in care until reaching twenty-one.[11] However, relatively few choose to. Even more than our own children, they are eager to take control of their own destinies.

Generally, the teens who age out of foster care entered care as teenagers, although many have spent much of their lives in the system. (Forty-one percent of the teens who emancipated from foster care in California between 1992 and 1997 had spent five or more years in the system.)[12] Children who enter foster care at age twelve or older are more likely than others to age out rather than be reunified with their families or adopted.

A substantial number of older youth in care are concentrated in just a few states. California, New York, and Illinois account for almost 40 percent of emancipating youth nationwide. Twenty-two states report fewer than 1,000 teens in foster care in the sixteen-to-eighteen age bracket and only a few hundred aging out each year.[13] The relatively low numbers in each jurisdiction may account for the system's disinterest in this segment of the foster care population for so many years.

For most of the child welfare system's history, most states did little to prepare the children in their custody for life in the real world. The federal government offered no financial help to the states to assist emancipating youth until 1986, when for the first time, Congress passed a law authorizing limited "independent living" efforts. Over the next fifteen years, about two-thirds of older youth in foster care received some sort of assistance in building independent living skills, ranging from a thirty-minute course on résumé writing to an eight-week course in household management. But most state child-protection agencies were reeling under the burden of providing foster care to the increasing number of younger children who were being removed from their families because of crack cocaine, so youth on the edge of "aging out" got little attention.

The 1986 law was seriously flawed because it only paid for skill-building services to youth between the ages of sixteen and eighteen. That meant that states could not use federal money to help those age fourteen or fifteen begin to plan for independence or learn necessary life skills. Nor could they use federal money to serve youth *after* they turned eighteen, a period of critical needs.

In 1991, Congress gave states the option of providing independent living services until age twenty-one but appropriated no additional funds, which meant that few age eighteen to twenty-one actually received help. The law also prohibited the use of federal funds for housing support for this group of young people.

For fourteen years, the federal financial commitment to independent living was frozen at $70 million a year.[14] In 1999, after years of complaints by children's advocates and youth in care about the inadequacy of the government's effort, Congress approved the Foster Care Independence Act, which doubled federal funding to $140 million per year and expanded eligibility to include young people from age fourteen to twenty-one.[15] President

Bill Clinton signed the bill into law on December 14, 1999. The law is commonly referred to as the Chafee Act, in honor of the late Rhode Island senator, John H. Chafee, a longtime champion of children's issues.

Among other provisions, this law requires states to identify teens who are likely to remain in foster care until age eighteen and to help them prepare for self-sufficiency. It also requires that states help young people who have aged out of care by providing career exploration, job placement and retention services, and vocational training. And it permits states to provide assistance with room and board, up to a maximum of 30 percent of their federal allocations, and to extend Medicaid coverage for those eighteen to twenty-one who were in foster care on their eighteenth birthdays. Of particular importance, it increases state and federal accountability for what happens to young people after they leave foster care.

Although the Chafee Act represents a major improvement over the past, neither the funds appropriated nor the state and county systems charged with spending them are adequate to the challenge. The total available funding amounts to less than $1,000 a year for each young person in the target population—all those between fourteen and eighteen who are moving toward emancipation, plus those between eighteen and twenty-one who have already aged out.

Despite the Chafee Act, many youth in care are still being sent out into the world with little more than a list of apartment rental agencies, a gift certificate for Wal-Mart, a bag full of manufacturer's samples, perhaps a cooking pot, maybe a mattress. The additional federal dollars aren't likely to make a huge difference in future prospects for young people who age out of care unless the foster care systems attract new partners to the effort.

Listening to the Stories

In 2001, the Jim Casey Youth Opportunities Initiative, headed by Gary Stangler, asked journalist Martha Shirk to find young people whose stories could help bring to life the otherwise numbing statistics on what usually happens to youth who age out of foster care.

Through contacts with public and private agencies and individuals who work with children in foster care, Ms. Shirk talked with dozens of young people who had aged out of the foster care system and selected the ones you'll meet in the following pages for in-depth interviews. Beginning in December 2001, Ms. Shirk spent up to a week with each of the subjects (except the two who are deceased) and then kept in close contact by telephone, mail, and e-mail through April 2004, when this book went into production, and each story, by necessity, came to an arbitrary end.

As you're reading the stories, bear in mind that these are still lives in the making. Except in two cases, the real end to the stories is not yet known.

Ten lives. Ten stories of young people who made the transition from dependency on the foster care system to living on their own. Ten individuals from diverse backgrounds, from the tough neighborhoods of Brooklyn to the plains of Kansas, from the melting pot of Miami to the cities of Des Moines, San Antonio, Boston, and San Francisco. Hispanics, whites, and African Americans. Boys and girls on their way to becoming men and women. Ten sets of hopes and dreams. The stories that follow are meant to help you understand what opportunities and supports young people need to make successful transitions to independence.

Sometimes, the challenge for an individual is to overcome what he or she has been through, often including violence and abandonment. Sometimes it is to overcome a tendency to make poor choices—in friends, in effort, in planning, in spending. Yet again and again, the resilience of the human spirit comes through, even when we reach a story's end and understand that disappointment and even disaster may lurk around the corner.

These stories bounce from heartbreaking to heartwarming, sometimes within a page or two. As you enter them, we hope you'll be alert to three themes:

- The importance of a permanent family or family-like relationship.
- The importance of preparation for independence, especially in financial matters.

- The inherent potential for engagement and leadership in each individual.

As members of the society that took guardianship of each of these children in a crisis, the challenge for us is to figure out how best to promote the resilience that will allow them to make successful transitions to adulthood. How do we compensate for the deficits in parenting they have endured? How do we provide them with opportunities to develop "constructed families" and social networks? How do we provide them with opportunities to learn the skills of everyday life, the skills needed to hold a job, manage money, and make their way in the world of modern America?

The Importance of Family and Social Networks

We already know from research in many fields that a connection to a knowledgeable and caring adult is the single most important contributor to resiliency in youth. These individuals' stories prove it beyond a doubt.

What do we mean by "a knowledgeable and caring adult?" For most children, that means a parent or close family member. However, young people stepping into the doorway of adulthood from foster care are uniquely deprived of this, by legal fiat. Yet no matter how badly their parents have treated them, and even when they've found nurturing substitutes, many children keep going back to their parents, hoping that they will have changed. The pull is incredibly strong and persists even in the face of constant rejection. "Despite all that's happened between us, she's still my mom, and I can't stay away from her," Monica Romero tells us.

When a connection can't be found within their families, the most enterprising children try to find it somewhere else. With wisdom belying her age, Holly Moffett of Boston set out to build a "constructed family" comprising a former foster family, a longtime caseworker, and her boyfriend's family. Another of our subjects, Giselle John of New York City, forged a close personal connection to an English teacher who encouraged her to take more challenging courses, found her opportunities for personal growth, and took her to church, where Giselle built a larger support network. "She took an interest in my life, and I felt special," Giselle says. "I had found someone who thought I was valuable." For Lamar Williams, the connection was with his counselors at the institution where he spent his teen years. Lamar remembers, "They really believed in me, which is one of the most important things anyone can do for a youngster."

Unfortunately, for many children in foster care, the raw material for a substitute family is often lacking, the potential surrogates undependable, or even worse. All too often, these young people look in the wrong places. Until she found focus for her life in motherhood, Monica Romero looked to drug users and partyers. Discharged from foster care to a homeless shelter, Reggie Kelsey looked to the disaffected youth who live under Des Moines' bridges and in its abandoned warehouses. Jeffrey Williams looked to the streets of the Crown Heights section of Brooklyn. "I wasn't getting love at home, so I looked for it on the streets," he said. "They were our surrogate parents."

In the child welfare field, this yearning for family, for connection, is well known. What is not well known is how, in the absence of a supportive family, we can help young people leaving foster care compensate. Government cannot mandate relationships; friendships cannot be forced. The challenge for us is to promote permanent relationships that extend beyond foster care rather than simply to rely on a young person to make a chance connection with a caring and knowledgeable adult.

The Importance of Preparation

The second theme that emerges from these stories—the importance of preparing youth for the transition from care—cannot be overstated. For several of our subjects, the lack of preparation is especially pronounced for social skills and financial literacy, skills generally honed in family settings. For a young person who may have experienced thirty-seven different living situations over the previous four years, the norm for those in care for four years or more, where would such learning and role modeling have occurred? The challenge is to provide young people in foster care with not just book learning but opportunities to practice life skills.

Over and over again in these stories, you'll see that money poses big problems for youth leaving foster care. They either have too little of it, or manage what they have poorly, or try to get it too easily.[16] Although many youth in care receive some financial education in living-skills courses, until they suffer the consequences of bad choices, the lessons often don't take. Lamar Williams received education in money management at his group home, yet he concedes that he "didn't really understand what credit was all about . . . it didn't really sink in" until credit problems forced him to defer his dream of buying a home.

For others, financial aid for education sometimes goes unused for lack of guidance in applying for it and the inability to present the necessary documentation, such as school records, a birth certificate, and a Social Security card. One of our subjects, Casey-Jack Kitos, of Lawrence, Kansas, lost a $2,500 scholarship because he missed a deadline for notifying its donor that he was enrolling in college.

Independent living skills—what Alfonso Torres calls "house skills"— are often lacking in youth who age out of foster care. Raised mostly in group homes and juvenile detention facilities, Alfonso never had the opportunity to learn to prepare even simple meals. He didn't understand how quickly the collect calls he accepted from a friend would add up to $200, where he could get a check cashed, how to mail a letter, or even how to dress appropriately to apply for a job. Many youth in care never see an adult pay bills, fill out income tax forms, arrange for car insurance, or undertake the dozens of other mundane tasks required to run a household. Although most children receive medical care while they are in foster care, few know how it is paid for and what they have to do to get it once they are no longer wards of the state. How to get from one place to another is also often a mystery. While their friends are getting their driver's licenses, most youth in foster care aren't, since they generally have no one to teach them to drive or the money for insurance or driver's education, let alone access to a car.

Nature has programmed teenagers to push for independence from us, even as they reluctantly return time and again for help. Because the most effective learning comes with experience, teenagers generally require many, many opportunities to succeed. They also require opportunities to fail. Good judgment develops from learning lessons from mistakes. One of Raquel Tolston's caseworkers tells us, "She had basically failed out of a lot of programs. We set up various jobs for her, and she failed a couple of times. But we provide a safety net here, so we just tried other things. She didn't believe she could do it. But we kept after her, like a protective parent would."

Unfortunately, many youth leaving foster care experience many more failures than successes, because the state—their legal parent—has not prepared them for independence in the same way we prepare our own children. They have not acquired the skills and knowledge to make it on their own, and the real world isn't always patient enough to stick with them through their many stops and starts, like a protective parent would.

The Importance of Youth Engagement

For many youth in foster care, the lack of control over even minor aspects of their lives creates a dependency on others that disables them after they age out. They have had little opportunity to make decisions about their lives, with the courts and social workers deciding where and with whom they will live (and even whether they can attend a sleepover) and with congregate care staff or foster parents making decisions about practically everything else. "While they were in care, they got away with a lot of stuff," Raquel's caseworker says, explaining the difficulty experienced by youth who have aged out of care. "The ramifications of their actions didn't really sink in because they were underage, they were protected. Their caseworkers tended to hold their hands too much."

The desire of the system players to maintain control is understandable. Social workers and court officers are acutely aware that their primary legal responsibility is the safety and protection of the minor, as opposed to the minor's empowerment. They know they can be held accountable—perhaps even publicly and criminally—for any decision they make about a young person's life, a prospect that understandably leads them to exercise maximum, minute control. (As director of social services for Missouri for eleven years, Gary Stangler was legally responsible for 12,500 children in foster care, which meant he was vilified by editorialists, and often sued, whenever something terrible happened to one of them.)

Failing to involve youth in making decisions about their lives leads to predictable, sometimes tragic consequences. Monica Romero ran away for seven months and missed a semester of high school rather than stay in a foster home in which she felt she had no say over the rules. "I think if they would have listened to what I had to say, and let me have more space to grow, I wouldn't have run away," she says in retrospect. When the system's control over the minutiae of daily life ends abruptly, as it does when a young person emancipates from foster care, the results can be very serious. As his eighteenth birthday approached, Reggie Kelsey told a school social worker that he sometimes thought about killing someone, because at least in jail he would "have a place to stay and three meals a day." After three months of homelessness, his life ended in a logjam of fallen trees in the Des Moines River.

Numerous studies have demonstrated that the quest for leadership is a manifestation of resilience, and it is striking how often the young people profiled here demonstrate leadership. Lamar Williams shows it in football and his workplace, his brother Jeffrey, though incarcerated, through his involvement in peer counseling and prison service organizations. Casey-Jack Kitos advises school officials about how to help special education students make the transition to independence. Giselle John writes about the experiences of youth in foster care, and then parlays that experience into a full-time job as a youth organizer.

Not surprisingly, the leadership roles these young people choose often involve helping other youth in similar situations. But as youth move toward emancipation from the foster care system, it is crucial to engage them in the larger community as well.

Our Goal for This Book

When we send our own children into the world, we worry about all of the things that could befall them, even when we know that they have the support of caring family members and connections to other adults who can be of periodic help. And we certainly don't expect them to make the transition to adulthood overnight.

A national survey in 2002 by the National Opinion Research Center found that most Americans believe the transition to adulthood is not complete until age twenty-six. A majority expressed the belief that the most important hallmark of adulthood was completing an education, and they put the age at which that could normally be expected at 22.3 years. Other important hallmarks of adulthood were financial independence, which a majority expected at age 20.9; not living with parents, at age 21.2; full-time employment, at age 21.2; able to support a family, at age 24.5; marriage, at age 25.7; and parenthood, at age 26.2.

Put another way, Americans expect it to take a youth 5.3 years from reaching the first milestone—financial independence—to the last—parenthood, or eight years past the age of eighteen, the age at which we send children from foster care out on their own.[17]

Each of the young people profiled in *On Their Own* has a distinctive story. However, read as a group, their stories provide a fairly complete picture of the range of challenges that youth face after they leave care, as well as the typical outcomes. We hope that the stories will help you better understand the hurdles that stand in the way of youth leaving foster care and the critical importance to their success, however it's defined, of permanent family or family-like relationships; of preparation in life skills, and of youth engagement. By understanding what forces have shaped the lives of the young people who are profiled here, we can begin to develop a repertoire of responses to the thousands of other young people who move from foster care into adulthood each year. We can make sure that they are no longer on their own.

Lamar Williams

Jeffrey Williams

Jermaine Williams

A TALE OF THREE BROTHERS
Jermaine, Jeffrey, and Lamar Williams,
Brooklyn, New York

While growing up together in the Crown Heights section of Brooklyn, the three Williams boys were thick as thieves. Born just one year apart, they did everything together, from playing catch in the street in front of their apartment building to snatching candy from the corner store to seeking refuge in the local police station when their mother's boyfriend beat them.

Although they were in and out of foster care throughout childhood, they were usually lucky enough to be placed in the same home together. And when one of them began missing his mother, it was a signal to all of them to run away and head back home. "Our childhood dream was to live together as adults in a three-family house, with each of us having our own floor," Lamar Williams, the youngest brother, remembers.

In 1987, a judge sent all three boys to Children's Village, a home for abused and neglected children in Dobbs Ferry, a bucolic suburb in Westchester County. Lamar settled in, but Jeffrey and Jermaine rebelled. And as they moved further into their teens, the brothers' paths diverged.

Jermaine and Jeffrey ran away repeatedly from Children's Village, returning to Crown Heights to earn easy money selling drugs. As a result, neither of them benefited from the preparation for independent living that Children's Village offers to its older residents. Instead, each was in prison when he formally aged out of foster care.

Lamar, however, stayed at Children's Village through his teens and voluntarily retained his foster care status until he turned twenty-one, a right granted by just a handful of states. He had as normal an adolescence possible for a child living in an institution, attending a nearby public school and winning acclaim as a football star. By remaining at Children's Village through high school, he also reaped the full benefit of the institution's highly regarded Work Appreciation for Youth (WAY) program, which helps residents make successful transitions to adulthood. A mentor taught him asset-building and money-management skills and helped him through the college application process.

Lamar's prowess on the football field won him a partial scholarship to Pace University, and Children's Village provided continuing financial and moral support through his college years. Lamar graduated in 1999 with a bachelor's degree in management information systems and went to work almost immediately for a major national firm.

By the end of 2002, Lamar was earning $72,000 a year and counting the days until he and his wife could move into their new $320,000 home in a Long Island suburb. Jeffrey was serving the tenth year of a twelve- to twenty-five-year sentence for armed robbery. And Jermaine was dead.

Three brothers, three different paths out of foster care.

"Everything Went Downhill"

In the late 1980s and early 1990s, the Crown Heights section of Brooklyn was not a pleasant place to come of age. Unemployment was endemic. Drug-related violence made the streets unsafe. And the crack epidemic was sending record numbers of children into foster care.

Until Lamar was four or five, his mother was a strong presence in the household, he says. (The boys' father wasn't involved in their lives.) She took pleasure in dressing her three boys in identical outfits and delighted when people mistook them for triplets.

Then a new boyfriend arrived on the scene. "I can still remember the first day she brought him home," Lamar says. "From then on it seemed everything went downhill. She started using marijuana, and then cocaine, and then crack, along with a lot of alcohol. The abuse wasn't far behind. It trickled down to us, and there was nothing she could do about it. If she stood up for us, he hit her even more."

The boys' mother periodically fled with them to a shelter for battered women, but she always took them back home after a week or two. Sometimes, when things got really bad, the boys sought protection themselves. "We'd run to the police station, and they'd place us in foster care for awhile," Lamar says. But after a few months, the brothers always ran away from the foster home and returned to their mother.

When the brothers were living at home, they basically ran wild. "I must have gone to all of a week of third grade," Lamar admits. "We'd just hang out on the streets, and steal from stores to sell things for money. We'd get caught and taken to the police station, and my mom would come and pick us up. We'd get a beating, and then the next day we'd back out stealing something else."

When Jermaine was twelve, a family court judge sent him to a children's home in Pleasantville, in a suburb of New York City. After a while, he was allowed to come home every other weekend. His brothers couldn't believe his transformation. "Just looking at him, you could see that he wasn't stressed any more," Lamar recalls. "He was eating good food instead of junk. He was doing sports and going on trips to places like Great Adventure and parks and stuff. And when it was time to go back after the weekend, he was OK about it. He said it was fun there."

Jermaine eventually moved to another group home, Children's Village, just a few miles from Pleasantville, and he liked it there, too. The next time their mother's boyfriend beat them, early in the summer of 1987, Lamar and Jeffrey knew where they wanted to go. "We ran to the police, and when we appeared before a judge, we told him we wanted to go to Children's Village," Lamar recalls. "Sure enough, in the next day or two, we were there."

Jeffrey and Jermaine Rebel

Children's Village, founded in 1851, is the largest children's treatment center in the United States. The 445 residents, all male and most African American, like the Williams brothers, range in age from five to eighteen. They live in several dozen cottages spread across the facility's 150 suburban acres, staying an average of two years, during which they attend school on-site and receive regular therapy.

When the two younger brothers arrived, Jeffrey joined Jermaine in Rose Cottage and Lamar moved into Bradish Cottage, just across a private street. Each cottage housed between twelve and fifteen boys and was staffed by shift workers. All three boys attended the on-site school, where every classroom is classified as special education.

Lamar adjusted easily to life at Children's Village. "My particular cottage was a good place to be because the staff offered different incentives to get you going," he remembers. "My favorite was the Breakfast Club. If you were up on time and you had your bed made and your area swept, you'd get to cook your own breakfast—waffles, bacon and eggs, pretty much anything you wanted. The laggards just got toast and cereal. I was a regular member of the Breakfast Club."

"Then there was something called 'Boy of the Month.' Once a month someone from each cottage was chosen to go out to dinner at a nice restaurant. I got chosen a few times."

Jermaine and Jeffrey had less positive experiences in their cottage, where the residents were older and tougher and the staff sterner. "I didn't like the staff," Jeffrey says. "They brought their problems from home and took them out on us. They wanted to treat us like we was their children, beefing us. There was nobody I bonded with there. I was always in trouble."

About seven months after their arrival at Children's Village, Jermaine and Jeffrey started running away. Typically, they'd make their way home to their mother's apartment in Crown Heights, and a few days later she would make them return. When they got back to Children's Village, there would be consequences, which would make them dislike it even more, so they'd run away again.

In retrospect, Jeffrey says, "I was a knucklehead for running away. I guess I was homesick. I wanted to be home with my mother, to make sure she was all right. I realize now that it wasn't the right thing to do, but I was living in a fantasy world. I was already in the fast lane."

The next to last time that Jeffrey and Jermaine ran away, they made their way to Pittsburgh, Pennsylvania, where they'd heard that they could earn more money selling crack than in Brooklyn. "The money was great there," Jeffrey recalls, "way more than in New York. We were pulling in close to $1,000 a day."

While in Pittsburgh, they got involved in a shoot-out. No one was hurt, but they were caught and held in a juvenile detention center for two or three months. They somehow beat the charges and got sent back to Children's Village.

But a few weeks later, they ran away again. "From then on, we were more or less on the streets," says Jeffrey, who was fifteen at the time. "They were our surrogate parents. You know that old saying, 'Wherever you lay your hat, that's what you call home'? Well, that's how it was. We partied and went out with girls and drank beer and smoked a little weed. I wasn't getting love at home, so I looked for it on the streets."

For a while, Jermaine and Jeffrey split up, with Jermaine staying in Brooklyn to try to jump-start a rap career and Jeffrey moving to Philadelphia to sell drugs. "Selling drugs was not the lifestyle I longed for, but I needed to survive, and so I did," he says in explanation.

In the year after leaving Children's Village, Jeffrey and Jermaine were each arrested a few times and sent to juvenile facilities. Within two years, they were both locked up at Rikers Island, New York City's largest correctional facility, while awaiting trial on first-degree robbery charges stemming from a holdup on a train. They were surrounded by some of New York City's most violent criminals. "I was scared, to tell you the truth," Jeffrey says.

Early in 1991, they negotiated plea bargains that resulted in prison sentences of two to six years. Jeffrey had just turned sixteen, and Jermaine was seventeen. They were sent to special adolescent units of medium-security adult prisons.

Learning to Love Work

While Jermaine and Jeffrey were locked up, Lamar was flourishing. He never even thought about running away.

"Things were going well for me at Children's Village," he says. "I was busy and preoccupied with sports and getting praised for doing well. Plus I guess I wanted more from life than just material things. Jeffrey and Jermaine were selling drugs to buy the clothes, the shoes, the jewelry. That was nothing to me. I'd rather stay put in Children's Village and comply with all the regulations than be out on the street looking out for bullets."

"Although there's rules and regulations you have to follow, a lot of kids don't grasp that that's just life. One staff always used to tell me, 'Life ain't fair.' Growing up, it took me awhile to grasp that, but I was able to roll with it. A lot of kids at Children's Village, including my brothers, didn't get it. They always feel that if they do something, they should get something. It's just not the case."

Soon after he turned fourteen, Lamar was invited to apply to the village's Work Appreciation for Youth program. Children's Village had begun offering WAY in 1984 to help residents gain the attitudes and skills needed to become productive and self-sufficient adults. Participants are called "WAY Scholars" and make a five-year commitment to stay in school, work part-time, and save for future education. In return, Children's Village provides a "WAY counselor," basically a paid mentor, and matches each youth's savings dollar for dollar, up to a maximum of $500 a year. Research has found that WAY graduates have significantly better high school graduation rates than young people living below the poverty level nationally.

At its essence, WAY is a work-ethic and asset-building program embedded in a comprehensive independent living-skills building program. It provides sequenced work experiences, beginning with unpaid chores in a resident's cottage and progressing to paid jobs at Children's Village and then to paid jobs in the community.* "The first chore I remember

---

*By 2003, the on-campus work experiences had expanded to include jobs in a mobile computer lab, a greenhouse, a barbershop, a dog-grooming business, and a service-dog training program.

getting paid for was doing the dishes for the fifteen guys who lived in my cottage, plus the staff, and believe me, that was a lot of dishes," Lamar says with a laugh.

His next job was in the village's wood shop. He also worked as a groundskeeper and a pool cleaner. "All the jobs were fun," he says. "I think I got paid maybe $4.50 an hour. They really stressed savings, so I had to save some of that, but I could also spend it on the kinds of things that teenagers want."

Lamar's first off-site job was working after school in the kitchen in a local hospital. "It was probably the best job I ever had," he says. "There were great people there. Going to work was like going to a party."

But the WAY program wasn't only about work. Once a week, Lamar met with his counselor, who kept track of his academic performance and arranged tutoring, if necessary. Lamar had several different counselors during the time he was a WAY Scholar, each of whom contributed to his personal growth in a different way. "One guy named Steve was into architecture, and he was turning a silo into a house for himself," Lamar recalls. "He was really inspiring, and so for a while I wanted to do architecture. And then I had another guy, also named Steve, who liked the Yankees, and sometimes took me to a game. My final counselor, Carl Morton, was with me a long time. He was a great guy, very knowledgeable about a lot of things.

"All my scholarship counselors were pretty much alright. I never had a bad vibe from any one of them. We'd sit around and talk, and they'd ask me, 'How's school? What are you working on? What do you want to do for your future? How much are you saving?' They were really big on saving."

So was Lamar. He loved watching the balance in his savings account grow as a result of the match. "You put $1 into savings and get $2 back," he says. "Who wouldn't like that?"

But the most important thing that Lamar got from the WAY program was the feeling that somebody cared about him. "They really believed in me, which is one of the most important things anyone can do for a youngster," he says.

"A Normal Kid"

During eighth grade, Lamar moved into a freestanding group home on the edge of the Children's Village property. It's one of five group homes that Children's Village operates to help build independent living skills in older youth.

"I knew that the idea was to get me out of Children's Village and send me back home, but I didn't want to go back home," Lamar says. "I knew what would happen there. I wanted to stay where I was. Children's Village was perfectly fine with me. I was doing OK. You ask any kid growing up where I had grown up, 'Which would you prefer, your life or his?' and I think anyone would have chosen my life. Nobody likes to be hit."

In fact, the group home life suited Lamar even more than cottage life, which he had liked just fine. "They let us be more independent," he says. "The staff was there basically to make sure we didn't kill ourselves. We were pretty much in charge of ourselves. I don't want to sound like I'm bragging, but I was a leader at Children's Village. I was motivated."

Each year, Children's Village sends a few of its older, most academically motivated residents to local public high schools, and when it came time for ninth grade, Lamar enrolled at Ardsley High School. Ardsley is a small school in an affluent suburb, and 98 percent of its graduates go on to college. Another youth from the group home, Daryle Hamilton, enrolled there at the same time. Lamar and Daryle chose Ardsley mainly because they had become good friends with an Ardsley student, Alonzo Florence, whom they'd met at a community dance. Once Lamar and Daryle started at Ardsley, Lamar says, "the three of us became inseparable," much as Lamar and his brothers had once been.

Alonzo lived with an aunt and uncle in nearby Irvington, and they welcomed Daryle and Lamar into their home, exposing them to a different family dynamic and lifestyle than they either had known. "His aunt and uncle were really laid back and relaxed," Lamar says. "They had a big house with a pool, and we would end up there every weekend. They took us in like their own kids."

Since the rules at his group home were more relaxed than in the cottages, Lamar had no trouble participating fully in high school social life.

"I almost didn't feel like I was even part of Children's Village any more, because I was living in the community," he says. "It was like I was a normal kid."

In his eyes, the major difference between him and the other students at his school was that he couldn't drive. (Most youth in foster care cannot get licenses because of insurance issues.) But all his friends could, and they were always happy to take him where he needed to go. "I had so many friends," he says. "If you didn't know me, you was nobody. I was one of the cool kids. No one looked down on me. Everyone welcomed me into their homes."

Lamar had been enrolled at Ardsley too late to play football during his freshman year, but that winter, he played on Ardsley's basketball team. And after basketball season ended, he started weight training with the football team and played for the next three years. He had the size—6'-1", 294 pounds—and the motivation to be a good lineman, but his belated introduction to the game kept him from being a starter in tenth grade.

"I had a lot to learn when I first started," he says. "I really didn't get a chance to shine until my junior year. Then I played everything, defensive line, offensive line, special teams. Football is all about technique, and if you learn that at a young age, in your older years it's just about being reckless on the field. I'd be in the NFL if I had been exposed before tenth grade."

Lamar loved the discipline and team spirit of football. "Being able to take orders from someone, and to get yelled at and just stand there and suck it up, that builds character," he says. "You've got to do your part and be a team player, and acknowledge when you mess up. There are a lot of values you learn playing football, values that you carry throughout your life."

College coaches notice a high school player of Lamar's size and ability, and they came calling in the fall of his senior year. "Union, Monmouth, Georgetown, Albany, Pace, Iona—there were a lot of colleges that were interested in me," Lamar says. "Before they started recruiting me, I hadn't really thought I'd go to college. I figured I'd graduate from high school, get a job, and earn enough money to get an apartment. But these coaches got me thinking that I could actually go to college."

Lamar's WAY counselor, Carl Morton, has a background in financial aid, and he assured Lamar that by combining grants and loans for low-income students with a football scholarship, assistance from the city's Child Welfare Administration, and his savings, Lamar could afford almost any school. Morton took him to visit a few colleges, and Lamar settled on Pace, a private university in Westchester County, just a few miles from Children's Village. "If I needed something, I wanted to be close to Children's Village, since I didn't have any parents who were going to fly to where I was to get it to me," Lamar explains.

Lamar found out just how true that was on the day in June 1994 when he graduated from Ardsley High School.

"It was one of the most important days of my life, and nobody was there for me," he says, his voice cracking. "A lot of my friends asked me to be in pictures with their families, but there was no one who came there to take a picture of me. It made me feel as though my whole life was a fraud."

"It was a really hard day for me. I broke down in front of a lot of my friends."

"But the experience also toughened me up. It made me realize that I was really alone in this big world, and that I couldn't let that stop me. I had to keep going."

Jeffrey and Jermaine

While Lamar was making a name for himself on the high school football field, his older brothers were counting the days until they would be eligible for parole.

Jeffrey spent nearly a year at Greene Correctional Institution before being transferred in September 1992 into a work-release program at Edgecombe, a minimum-security institution in New York City. He was rearrested within six weeks, this time for armed robbery. He and a cousin and a friend held up a paint store in Brooklyn, and he and his cousin got caught.

His cousin agreed to a plea bargain and received a two- to six-year sentence. Jeffrey thought he could beat the charge by going to trial, but a jury found him guilty. He was sentenced to twelve and a half to twenty-five years in prison, the term he is currently serving. In December 1993, at the age of nineteen, he was sent to Coxsackie Correctional Institution, a maximum-security prison in upstate New York.

Jermaine was incarcerated at Cayuga Correctional Institution during Lamar's high school years. He was paroled in May 1994, just a few weeks before Lamar's graduation. But by then, the two of them had grown apart. Perhaps he didn't know about the ceremony, or maybe he thought he'd embarrass Lamar if he attended.

"I always felt like maybe he didn't like me too much because I never sent him stuff when he was in jail, or went to see him," Lamar says with regret. "But his prison was so far away, and I was still a kid. I needed help myself."

Help from Several Sources

Midway through the summer after he graduated, Lamar moved into a dorm at Pace's Briarcliff campus so that he could start summer practice with the football team. When it came time to register for classes, Carl Morton, Lamar's WAY counselor, was right by his side. "He stood in line with me and helped me figure out what to do," Lamar says. "He made sure my loan papers were in order, and when I needed books, he got the money from my account."

Despite lacking parental support, Lamar was better off financially than many of his classmates at Pace. Lamar not only had a partial football scholarship but also a federal Pell grant, available to all low-income college students. Since he had chosen to remain in foster care until he was twenty-one, New York City's child welfare agency was also contributing to his support. In addition, the balance in his WAY savings account had by this time grown to about $5,000, and the money was his to use for college-related expenses. Lamar therefore had to come up with just a few thousand dollars a year more to cover the $22,000 in college costs, and Morton helped him fill out the paperwork for a low-interest student loan. (He actually borrowed far more than he needed, and when the requests for repayment started after he graduated, he regretted it.)

Because of deficits in his academic preparation, Lamar was required to enroll in an academic support program called Challenge to Achievement at Pace (CAP). CAP is a one-year remedial program aimed at helping students with inadequate high school preparation. CAP students benefit from weekly meetings with an academic adviser, peer tutoring sessions, and a special weekly course, called University 101, which teaches college survival skills. To continue at Pace for a second year, CAP participants must achieve a C average, accumulate twenty-four credits, pass the University 101 course, and earn a minimum grade of C in their second-semester English class.

"My first semester, I did horrible," Lamar admits. "My life was football and partying and hanging out. I was as popular in college as I had been in high school, and if there was a party, I was there. After that, the coach put me on academic probation, and on top of going to the CAP program, I had to go to a special study program at the field house. A lot of people teased me about having to do these things, but they were really helpful. The second semester I really excelled. I got a 3.3 and I pretty much maintained it through college."

At the end of his freshman year, Lamar moved out of the dorm and into an apartment that Children's Village rents in White Plains for its independent living program. "I wanted to experience having my own place," Lamar recalls. "It was a fabulous place."

Carl Morton, Lamar's WAY counselor, dropped by periodically and took Lamar shopping for groceries. Children's Village paid the rent and some of his other living expenses, but Lamar was also working two jobs, a part-time day job at the big mall in White Plains and a $150-a-night job as a bouncer at a nightclub. He used some of his earnings to buy his first car—a 1992 Ford Escort. "It was kind of too small for me, but it was mine," Lamar says, laughing.

Jermaine came back into Lamar's life while he was living in White Plains. "Even though I wasn't supposed to let anyone live with me, I let him stay in my apartment and got him a job at the mall," Lamar recalls. "He was doing well, and then he met a girl, and she was bad for him." Lamar asked her to leave, and Jermaine left soon after as well.

A few months later, Jermaine begged Lamar to let him return. "He told me that he was sleeping on trains because he didn't have any other place to go," Lamar says. Lamar took him in and got him a seasonal job at the mall.

When the job ended, Jermaine left White Plains again. The brothers lost contact with each other for a year. Lamar later found out that during most of this time, Jermaine was in prison in New Jersey for selling drugs.

"Nothing Comes to You"

At the beginning of his junior year, Lamar moved back on campus. Although he had liked the sense of independence that he got from having his own apartment, he missed the camaraderie of dorm life. "When you're playing a sport, it's especially important to live in a dorm, so that you can hang out with the team," he says.

By this time, Lamar had declared a major: management information systems. He had taken mostly business courses during his sophomore year and in his junior year had begun taking computer-programming courses as well. "I didn't really know what I was going to end up doing with it," he says. "I just knew I wanted to make some money and have a family and be able to provide for them. The important thing was that I had a plan to be *something*. If you want something big, you gotta work towards it. Nothing comes to you."

He readily admits that playing football was still his main reason for staying in college. "To tell you the truth, I didn't really like school," Lamar acknowledges. "If it hadn't have been for football, I probably wouldn't have been there. I ended up being pretty good at it, but I didn't like it. I think the main value of school is that it disciplines you for the real world. School teaches you how to utilize your brain."

Pace's football team had won no games the year before Lamar enrolled. But starting in his sophomore year, the team had begun to win. Lamar was a major contributor to the team's success, and he was chosen as all-conference his senior year.

For a while, Lamar flirted with the idea of playing professional football in Germany. The former defense coordinator for Pace was working as a head coach there and asked him to play for him. But by then, Lamar had gotten involved in a serious relationship with a pretty graphic design major, Andrea McIntosh, who was a year behind him in school. "I didn't think she'd come with me, and I didn't want to leave her," he says. "I decided to stick around and stay in school and see where life would take me."

Lamar spent an extra semester at Pace to finish up some credits. In his last month of school, he began interviewing for jobs. It was November 1998, and with the expectation that the Y2K problem would cause massive computer failures thirteen months later, jobs in his field were plentiful. Lamar's third interview resulted in a job offer. The starting salary was $42,000, not bad for a young man from a family in which no one else had even graduated from high school.

"I Can't Do It"

Lamar's employer is a Fortune 500 company with $14 billion in annual revenues from travel operations, real estate, and financial services all over the world. He asked that its identity be withheld. Lamar liked being part of such a successful corporation, and he liked the challenges inherent in coding and programming as well. "I'm good at it," he says. "I'm known for understanding things fast. My job now requires me to think a lot and work out a lot of problems."

Lamar and Andrea had begun living together in an apartment in Ossining in the fall of 1998, and in May 1999, after she graduated from Pace, they moved into an apartment in Queens to be closer to his job on Long Island and hers in Manhattan.

When Jermaine got out of prison soon afterward, he tried to talk Lamar into letting him move in with him and Andrea. By now, Lamar's and Jermaine's lives were even more divergent than they had been a few years before. Lamar was making his way up the corporate ladder (he earned two sizable raises in his first year at work) and Jermaine was making his way on the street. With his prospects for a regular job hampered by a lack of skills and his prison record, Jermaine had returned to selling crack in the northern New Jersey suburbs. "He was making a killing," Lamar says. "He could get $50 for something he could get $5 for in Brooklyn."

Lamar and Jermaine didn't even look like brothers any more. Lamar wore Polo shirts and chinos, whereas Jermaine dressed like a gangster, with rings on every finger, multiple gold chains around his neck, and platinum caps on his front teeth.

Although Lamar had taken him in before, this time he refused. "I said, 'I can't do it,'" Lamar recalls with regret. "I tried to be there for him emotionally, but letting him move in with me again was something I couldn't do."

"It Didn't Really Sink In"

By the end of 2000, Lamar and Andrea began making plans to get married. They also decided to buy a house. They were making good salaries and felt that they were just throwing money away by paying rent. And, in Lamar's mind, owning a home represented stability and respectability. No one in his immediate family had ever owned a house.

Every weekend for months, they got in their 1994 Ford Explorer (the Eddie Bauer model) and went house hunting. At first, they looked at renovated houses in Queens. But they were dismayed to see how little house they could get for their money there, so they began looking in the far suburbs on Long Island, where they could get a lot more house for their money.

In February 2001, they signed a contract to build a 2,500-square-foot house on a half-acre lot in a new subdivision in Brookhaven, New York. With the upgrades they both wanted—ceramic tile in the foyer, central air conditioning, custom tiles in the master bath, and so on—the total price came to about $320,000. Based on their incomes, they were told they'd qualify for a low-interest, first-time-buyer mortgage.

But when the time came to meet with lenders, they got a real-life lesson in how credit works. Each had come out of college with about $32,000 in education debt, which neither had even begun to pay off, so their balances were growing. Also, the credit cards that they had begun using in college were carrying balances in the thousands, and several were seriously in arrears. The bottom line: Their credit ratings were bad.

"Carl Morton always told me not to mess up my credit, but I didn't really understand what credit was all about," Lamar says. "And I remember learning about compound interest my sophomore year in college, but it didn't really sink in. I didn't know that if I didn't pay this credit card today, it's going to have an effect on me having a home five or ten years later."

Before Lamar and Andrea could actually get a mortgage, they had to pay off their credit card debts, as well as $4,000 that Lamar still owed on an old car loan. They also had to begin paying on their college loans. Some serious belt-tightening was in order. They gave up their $825-a-month apartment and decided to camp out with relatives and friends while their house was being built. They were living with a friend in Brooklyn when they got word on August 1, 2001, that Jermaine was dead.

"He Wanted to Be a Don"

It turned out that Jermaine and an associate had driven to Brooklyn from New Jersey to pick up a stash of drugs. On the way home, the driver lost control of the car and hit a tree. The bodies were burned so badly that police couldn't tell who had been driving. Jermaine was twenty-eight years old.

Lamar took Jermaine's death hard. The two had grown closer during the previous two years, and despite their divergent lifestyles, they often got together on weekends. And whenever they did, Lamar tried to talk Jermaine out of selling drugs. At the very least, Lamar told Jermaine, he shouldn't be walking around with so much cash. "He was a flashy guy, always wanting to pull out a big wad of bills," Lamar says.

Lamar helped him open a bank account, his first ever, and tried to talk him into using some of his drug profits to buy a house or purchase stock. "I tried to talk him into putting that money in the right direction, using that money to create something for himself and get out of that game," Lamar says.

The two brothers last spoke two days before Jermaine's death, when they talked about starting a business together. "We agreed that he would save his money, and I would save my money, and we would pool it together and start a business. And once that got going, he would stop selling drugs," Lamar says.

Lamar believes that Jermaine had as much potential as he himself has to make it as a legitimate businessman. "Jermaine didn't need to do the drug thing," Lamar laments. "He was smart, money smart and street smart, and he could have made it in the business world if he'd had the chance.

"Jermaine's main problem was that he loved to surround himself with negative people. He surrounded himself with people he could control, people he could say 'do this, do that' to. He wanted to be a don. But he wasn't an evil person."

Nine Years and Counting

The view from the visiting room at Sing Sing Correctional Institution is dazzling. A wall of glass looks out over the Hudson River, which at this time of year, with the trees wearing their fall garb, seems right out of a painting by an artist from the nineteenth-century Hudson River school. The only thing marring the view is the barbed wire that tops the prison wall.

Two hours after his visitor arrives, Inmate No. 93A9580, Jeffrey Williams, is finally escorted to the visiting room. Fifty or sixty other inmates are already there, holding children on their laps, snuggling discreetly with their wives or girlfriends, or listening with half an ear as their mothers fill them in on neighborhood news. Some are enjoying lunch bought by their visitors from the vending machines that line a corner of the room. Others are posing with their loved ones against a mural with a South Pacific motif as a member of the prison's Jaycees Club takes Polaroid photographs for $2 each.

It's been a long time since Jeffrey Williams has had a visitor. His mother, drug free for the last few years, comes infrequently because she doesn't like the hourlong train ride from the city. And with the demands of his job and the construction of the new house, Lamar can no longer make it once a month, as he used to.

Jeffrey has been "inside the big house"—prisoner lingo for prison—since 1993. His first stop was Great Meadow, a maximum-security facility in Comstock, in upstate New York. After two months there, he was transferred to Coxsackie, another maximum-security prison, just about equally far from home. There he was assigned a job as a porter—basic maintenance work—

which earned him a "salary" of $6 every two weeks. He also worked, albeit halfheartedly, on his graduate equivalency diploma (GED).

Just nineteen years old when he arrived at Coxsackie and with absolutely no prospect of being released until he was almost thirty-one, Jeffrey was far from being a model prisoner for his first year or so. "I was always fighting, gambling, smoking weed, and beefing with the correctional officers," he admits. "I adopted the attitude of me against the world." As a result, he was frequently subjected to disciplinary actions, which usually resulted in him being "cell-locked" (confined by himself to a cell).

But as the realization set in that he was going to be there for a long time, Jeffrey began changing. "I got tired of getting cell-locked," he says. "I began to read, and to ask myself questions like, 'What the hell are you good at?' And then one day I found the answer to my question. I started noticing that whenever somebody had a problem, they came to me for help. It was like people noticed that I have some natural leadership ability, some mediation skills. It made me feel good being in a position to help."

After a year passed with no disciplinary actions, Jeffrey put in for a transfer to a facility where there would be more opportunities for self-improvement. (At the time, all Coxsackie offered was a GED program.) In 1995, he was transferred to Eastern Correctional Facility, another maximum-security facility in Naponich, New York, which put him somewhat closer to New York City and hence made it easier for his mother and brothers to visit. (Eastern is also known for its inmate education programs; it was the first of New York's seventy-one prisons to be accredited by the American Correctional Association.)

At Eastern, Jeffrey got involved with a group called Prisoners for AIDS Counseling and Education (PACE). In this voluntary program, prisoners lead workshops about AIDS and hepatitis prevention. "The guy who was running it was named Al Simon, and he mentored me," Jeffrey says. "At first, I volunteered for it mainly to get the certificate, but I turned out to be good at it."

Jeffrey then signed up for some black history classes "so that I could understand my past in order to recognize what lies ahead of me in my future." This interest, in turn, led him to an involvement with the

Resurrection-Consciencia Study Group that was started at Greenhaven Prison in the late 1980s by Eddie Ellis, a former Black Panther who was then serving twenty-five years in prison for a murder he denies committing. Under the aegis of the Harlem-based Community Justice Center, which Ellis, now a free man, founded, Resurrection-Consciencia study groups operate as crime-prevention programs within several New York prisons. The groups hold classes aimed at building self-esteem, promoting unity, and fostering cooperation among prisoners.

"We teach the brothers that we have alienated ourselves from society and need to take responsibility for actions, while recognizing that the system contributed to our downfall," Jeffrey explains. "The whole idea is to realize what you're up against so that you don't re-offend when you get out."

At Eastern, Jeffrey also taught a class on affirmative action and another called "Youth in Transition," aimed at helping young inmates make the transition to adulthood while they're imprisoned, just as he had. "A lot of us come in here with that youth mentality, which is what led us to negative behavior, along with the lack of integrity in our households," he explains. "We looked to the streets for meaning in our lives. We have to make a transition from that mind state. We have to understand our values and morals, or we're going to always do wrong. I try to get the young guys to visualize themselves in a leadership role after they get out."

And in his spare time, Jeffrey taught himself sign language and wrote poetry.

"Ready to . . . Do What's Right"

In June 2000, Jeffrey was moved again, this time to Sing Sing Correctional Institution, just a half-hour drive from Children's Village.

Since the 1890s, Sing Sing has been associated in the public mind with the electric chair. By 1963, when the chair was mothballed, more than 600 men and women had been put to death there, including Julius and Ethel Rosenberg, in 1953. Today, Sing Sing is New York's second largest prison, with about 2,300 inmates, almost all of them, like Jeffrey, from minority neighborhoods in New York City.

Although Jeffrey hadn't sought the move, there were clear advantages. Most inmates at Sing Sing are confined under maximum-security conditions, but about one-fourth of them, including Jeffrey, are housed in a medium-security section, which means a vastly better quality of life. Rather than living in a cell, as he had at Comstock, Eastern, and Coxsackie, Jeffrey has his own cubicle in a dormitory with seventy-six other inmates. Jeffrey can either eat prison food or cook food for himself in the dormitory's kitchen (assuming a visitor has brought him groceries or he has enough money in his prison account to buy some). He can take a shower any time he wants, watch virtually unlimited TV, make collect phone calls, and receive visitors nearly every day.

On a typical day, Jeffrey gets up at 7 A.M. and spends the morning working at two of his paid jobs—serving as clerk and co-chairman for the PACE program and chairman of the Sing Sing NAACP chapter. In the afternoons, he usually studies, hammering out papers on a portable typewriter that Lamar and Jermaine bought him a few years ago. And from 6 P.M. to 8:30 P.M. five nights a week, he attends college classes, and that counts as another job (altogether, he earns $10 a week).

This semester, he's taking four religion classes and a sociology class, part of a two-year certificate program in ministry and human services offered by the New York Theological Seminary. Because the state provides no funding for college courses, a nonprofit group called Hudson Link for Higher Education in Prison raises money to pay the teachers, and the inmates receive college credit at either Mercy College or the New York Theological Seminary.

Jeffrey is just as involved in the Sing Sing community as he was at Eastern. (If he were living in a New York City neighborhood, he'd be regarded as a community activist.) He started a chapter of the Resurrection-Consciencia Study Group and serves as its coordinator. He's taken courses in basic parenting, anger management, and alternatives to domestic violence. He's acted in *Reality in Motion* and *Slam,* two theatrical productions organized by Rehabilitation through the Arts, a project of Prison Communities International. He is also active in the Five Percent Nation of Gods and Earth, an offshoot of the Nation of Islam, which he joined while he was at Greene. And he's writing his autobiography.

"I'm doing pretty good," Jeffrey says, smiling as he pats himself on the shoulder theatrically. "I consider myself to be a model prisoner. I'm proud of myself."

Jeffrey will be eligible for parole on June 14, 2005. But being a model prisoner may not be reason enough for the New York State Parole Board to send him home. "It's not about a person doing good," Jeffrey says. "What I think is that they put a lot of names in a grab bag and pick them out randomly."

If the parole board turns him down, he might have to stay in prison until 2018, when he would be forty-four years old.

Lying on his cot late at night, Jeffrey thinks a lot about how he ended up where he has. Although he takes responsibility for his crimes, he traces them to his upbringing in what he calls "a household of nonintegrity."

"It was my mother's condition that made me who I am today, and who I will become tomorrow," he says. "I wonder if my mother was never on drugs, where would I be, and where would Lamar and Jermaine be? Would Jermaine still be living? Would I be successful? Would I be dead or in prison anyway? I continuously wonder."

Jeffrey has also given a lot of thought to why Lamar's life took a different turn than his and Jermaine's did. The difference, he thinks, is that Lamar allowed Children's Village to become his surrogate family, whereas he and Jermaine, who were older, rejected Children's Village and instead found a surrogate family on the streets. "We developed a surrogate family built around loyalty, realness, commitment and trust within our crews," he says.

With parole a possibility just a few years in the future, Jeffrey often dreams about what he's going to do when he gets out. "Feeding my visions is the only thing that keeps me sane behind these walls," he says. He's taken up boxing again, but he realizes that he's too old to become a professional boxer, which had once been his dream. Maybe he'll open a barbershop, or a social club, he says. Definitely, he'll start a family as soon as he can.

"I have been deprived of my childhood, my teens, and most of my early adulthood," he says. "I have not really enjoyed life to its fullest. But life isn't over for me. I have a whole life ahead of me, and I plan to enjoy it. I know that in time I will find love in a beautiful, intelligent woman."

"My morals and principles are in order now," he continues. "I'm a very different person than I was when I got locked up. I'm ready to go out in the world and do what's right."

"A Major Milestone"

It's a beautiful Sunday morning in November 2002. Lamar and Andrea, who married seven months ago on a beach in the Bahamas, are doing what they've been doing nearly every weekend since May 2002, when their builder finally broke ground—checking out the progress on their house. "We're still trying to save money, so this is our big entertainment every weekend," Lamar says. The house is supposed to be finished by Christmas.

"Well, let's see what they've done this week," Lamar says as he opens the front door. The electricity hasn't been turned on yet, so it's dark and cold inside. Even so, Andrea and Lamar are quick to notice the progress since their visit last weekend. The kitchen cabinets and the Formica countertops have been delivered, though not installed. The electrician has wired the outlets and light switches. And the walls have all been primed, though not painted with a finish coat.

Over the next hour, they escort a visitor from room to room, from the ceramic-tiled entrance foyer to the basement ("perfect for a kid's playroom," Lamar observes) to the master bathroom, complete with a double-sized Jacuzzi tub and a separate shower.

"And this is Andrea's closet," Lamar jokes as he opens the door into the fourth bedroom. "We're going to shelve the whole room so she has a place to store her shoes."

Lamar can hardly contain his excitement about being the almost-owner of a house like this, which reminds him of the home that the Brady Bunch lived in. "This is my pride and joy," he says. "I love this house. Once we move in, I think I will have achieved a major milestone in life."

"Life Hasn't Really Begun"

Later, over lunch, Lamar reflects on how far he's come and how far he wants to go. "Life hasn't really begun for Andrea and me yet," he says.

"The two of us have a lot of ambition. We know we've got a long way to go.

"Within a year, I see us as having our own business, and for the next few years, we'll be watching it grow. Then, when Jeffrey gets out, we'll make a place for him in it, and in our home, too, if he needs us. We want to provide something for him to get him going, so that he doesn't end up back in the environment he came from. I want him to come home and not get back into trouble."

"It's going to be tough. But he's come a long way. I'm proud of him. In prison, he was able to get his education and figure out where he was going in life, so he feels pretty confident that when he comes out, he's going to have a lot of opportunities."

"That's what counts, a positive attitude. I tell him, 'It's not going to be as easy as you think. The world is going to hold your record against you.' But by the time he gets out, I should have a network he can tap into. It's not too late for him. He knows that. I think he'll come out and get a nice job and forget about the fast life."

Lamar also feels a responsibility to serve as a positive role model for the fatherless children of several of his cousins, two of whom died in street violence and one who is serving a long prison sentence. "My aunt has a ton of grandkids who don't have fathers," he notes. "Two of her sons are dead, and one's in jail. When the house is finished, I want to have a weeklong camp at my house every summer. We'll call it Camp Williams. We'll set up the basement with sleeping bags, and do fun things during the days. That's an idea I got from Alonzo's aunt and uncle. They did that every summer for their nieces and nephews. It will show them another way of life, and hopefully send the message, 'Look, you can have this, too. You don't have to hang out on the streets or sell drugs.'"

"If I can save one of them, I'll be happy."

Succeeding in business is also a high priority for him. Five years from now, he hopes to be presiding over several small businesses and to be measuring his net worth in the millions. "You got to aim for something," he says.

And by the time he's fifty, Lamar hopes to be retired from business and devoting his life to a cause.

Lamar's major regret in life is that among the three brothers, he is the only one whom society would regard as a success. "That's what hurts me the most," he says. "The three of us had the same abilities. We were in the same basic position throughout our childhoods. But I was the only one who made the best of it.

"If they'd have gone along with the program, they'd be in the same position today as I am. In fact, we'd probably all be in business together. We could be neck in neck now in terms of success. We all wanted to be successful. But how they wanted to do it and how I wanted to do it was different."

"I don't fault either Jermaine or Jeffrey for what they did," he continues. "Growing up in the lifestyle we did, it was all about survival of the fittest. Everybody has to eat. If need be, I would have gone their route, too."

Postscript

In a ceremony at Sing Sing on June 4, 2003, Jeffrey Williams received a certificate in ministry and human services. The next day, he was transferred to a medium-security dorm at Woodbourne Correctional Facility. Budget cuts forced the closure of his medium-security unit at Sing Sing.

Jeffrey wasn't happy about the move, since Woodbourne is an hour farther from New York City, which makes visits from his relatives even more difficult. But the commissary is much better, "and that, my friend, is a big plus with me (smile)," he wrote in a letter in the fall of 2003.

Lamar is paying for Jeffrey to take correspondence courses in business management through Larchmont College in Atlanta. By his June 2005 parole date, he hopes to earn an associate's degree in business management.

Jeffrey has also enrolled in a HIV/AIDS peer educator apprenticeship program at Woodbourne. The program requires him to complete a minimum of 2,000 hours of peer counseling. "I already have over 2,000 hours in the fields of educating people about HIV/AIDS and other opportunistic infections," he wrote. "However, they weren't under the supervision of my staff adviser here, and she will not accredit me for all the hours because she did not witness my expertise in this field. I do not agree with her, but, hey, I have nothing else to do."

Lamar's life is proceeding much faster than planned. He and Andrea moved into their new house just in time to celebrate Christmas 2002. Within weeks, every room was furnished to perfection. As Lamar had promised Andrea, the fourth bedroom was set aside for her shoes.

And true to form, Lamar had gotten to know just about everyone in the subdivision. "He thinks he's the mayor of the neighborhood," his wife jokes.

In fact, life in the suburbs was everything Lamar had hoped it would be. "It's beautiful, and it's very quiet and peaceful," Lamar said. On nice weekends, the couple barbecued on their patio. On football weekends, Lamar was glued to the big-screen TV in the living room.

In November 2003, a college friend made Lamar an offer he couldn't refuse—to start a business together in Georgia. The proposal couldn't have come at a better time.

Earlier in the year, Lamar's company had moved its headquarters to northern New Jersey, transforming his leisurely ten-mile commute into a stressful ninety miles. Although his company allowed him to work at home three days a week, it often took Lamar three hours to drive home on the other two days. "I couldn't see myself driving that far for the next ten years while I was trying to build a family," he says.

Lamar's friend proposed that they start a chain of restaurants, which had been Lamar's dream for years. "With my job situation and the opportunity he was offering, I had to push up my timetable," he says. "It's a nice, up-and-coming area, twenty-five minutes west of Atlanta. The houses are beautiful. I figured, 'Why not align myself with someone who's on the same track as me?'"

In January, Lamar and Andrea broke ground on a new five-bedroom, 4,000-square foot house in Villa Rica, an outer suburb of Atlanta that occupies a ridgeline in the Appalachian foothills. They sold their house on Long Island for a $150,000 profit.

And on April 21, Totsy's Seafood, the first of a planned twenty-site chain of restaurants, held its grand opening celebration in Villa Rica. Lamar and his partner plan to open four more sites by the same time next year, and after launching twenty sites themselves, they hope to sell franchises. Andrea, who has started a graphic design business, designed the restaurant's logo, graphics, and Web site.

If Jeffrey is paroled, as expected, in June 2005, Lamar plans to set him up with a garden apartment nearby and a job in one of the restaurants. "He'll be all set," Lamar says. "With the business courses he's taking, I expect him to be able to move into management."

Although his life today seems a million light-years from his childhood, Lamar hasn't forgotten where he came from. "My bad family is basically my backbone," he says. "It's what drives me. I had the childhood that was dealt to me, and I don't complain about it. I've always believed that it's important to remember where you came from so you know where you want to be going."

Lamar Williams and his wife, Andrea

Lamar Williams

"I KNOW THAT I'M NOT ALONE"
Patty Mueller, Boston, Massachusetts

Patty Mueller has been making the transition to adulthood in the way that most other young people do: by going to college. Patty, twenty-two, gushes with enthusiasm as she describes living in a college dorm as "the perfect transition" between living in a foster home and living on her own. "College gives you an idea of what the real world is like without throwing you to the wolves," she says. "You feel like you're making your own decisions, but there are people who are monitoring what you're doing so you don't fall flat on your face."

For many children who grow up in foster care, attending college is not an option. Children in foster care are half as likely as other children to be enrolled in college preparatory classes in high school, and frequent moves and schools changes make it hard to compile the academic record necessary for admission to many four-year schools. Finding the money is another common roadblock. And even when they achieve suitable academic records and pull together ample financial aid packages, many flounder in college because they lack emotional and moral support, not to mention a place to spend school holidays, when most college dorms close. Only 20 percent of foster youth who graduate from high school go on to college, compared with 60 percent of all high school graduates.[1]

Patty is one of the lucky ones. Although she lived in seven different homes and attended five different schools during her high school years,

her private foster care agency, Casey Family Services, provided her with
tutors to help her make up missing credits. The agency is also providing
ongoing financial assistance through college. In addition, Patty's longtime caseworker still serves as an ongoing source of emotional support,
meeting with her monthly to help her stay on track.

On her own initiative, Patty has also developed a strong support system to help see her through college. Unable to rely on a parent for moral
support or advice, Patty gets those things from other adults with whom
she's built supportive relationships, including her first foster parents and
her boyfriend's mother. She calls them her "constructed family."

"I have an incredible amount of financial security and emotional security because I have people out there to back me up," she says. "I know
that I'm not alone in the world."

"She Stopped Coming Home"

Any way you look at it, Patty Mueller had a rocky start in life. She arrived
three months early, weighing only two pounds, so from the start her survival was in question.

But Patty, a fighter even then, survived. And considering the many
medical problems that can afflict preemies, she was relatively un-
scathed. Her biggest residual problem was amblyopia, commonly known
as "lazy eye."

After spending a few months in the hospital, Patty went home to her
parents' apartment in a public housing complex in the Irish American
neighborhood of Boston known as Southie. Patty's mother, a sixth-grade
dropout, was only seventeen. Her father, who suffered from paranoid
schizophrenia, was in his fifties. The couple already had an eighteen-
month-old daughter, Michelle.

Her mother's start in life was not much more promising than Patty's.
She was one of a dozen children born to an alcoholic mother, and they
all grew up in foster care. When Patty's mother was in sixth grade, she
ran away from an abusive foster parent, and her formal schooling came
to a temporary halt. She fended for herself before hooking up with

Patty's father when she was fourteen. He turned out to be physically and emotionally abusive, and Patty's mother left him when Patty was eighteen months old and Michelle was three.

Even so, Patty's earliest childhood memories are largely happy ones. "My mother loved to play with me," she recalls. "One of my favorite games was 'restaurant.' My mother would dress up as a waitress, and we'd spend the morning making menus and coloring them in. And then when lunchtime came, she'd serve me like we were at a restaurant."

For a couple of years, Patty attended a Catholic preschool. On weekends, she remembers her mother sometimes taking her and Michelle to the Children's Museum or the Boston Museum of Science. And at Christmas, Patty's mom would dress up the girls in dresses that she had hand-smocked and take them to watch *The Nutcracker.* "Up until I had my first communion at age seven, my mother was pretty functional," Patty says. "That's not to say she didn't spank us, but we had food and clothes and got to go to the park."

Then, almost overnight, things started to change: Instead of taking Patty to a museum, her mom would take her to a bar, Patty recalls, "and I'd sit under her table drinking Shirley Temples and coloring in my coloring books while she got trashed."

Patty believes that her mother began using hard drugs the year that Patty entered second grade and Michelle, fourth. "That's when she just stopped coming home," Patty says.

Since there was no one else around to make sure that the girls were fed, bathed, and clothed, let alone nurtured, Michelle became the mommy in the household. She did the laundry, tried to keep the apartment neat, and sent Patty off to school while she stayed home and watched for their mother's return. Patty hated school, but she knew that by going, she would at least get lunch. Even so, she missed eighty days of school that year.

Obtaining enough food was a constant problem, Patty says. Nearly every afternoon, the girls would walk over to the neighborhood Boys and Girls Club and stuff themselves with free snacks. If they got hungry later, Patty would ask a neighbor for a cup of milk and some eggs, and Michelle would make them an omelette. Sometimes, Patty would steal a package of Twinkies or a box of macaroni and cheese from the store across the street.

The girls had been in foster care for a few months after their mother left their father, so the family had an open case with the state Department of Social Services. But their caseworker's visits were infrequent, Patty says, and were usually announced in advance. "My mother would find out the caseworker was going to come by, and she'd come home and clean up the apartment and be the perfect mother for the day," Patty says. "She'd prepare us for the visit, and tell us what we were supposed to say. And when the caseworker arrived, Michelle and my mom and I would be baking cookies together in the kitchen, just like a happy family. I remember wondering why she couldn't make a surprise visit and see how we really lived."

At one point during the year, an aunt who was alarmed by conditions in the apartment took the girls home with her for four months. When their mother promised to give up drugs, the girls returned home. But within a few weeks, she was using again, Patty says.

Finally, two months into Patty's year in third grade, child-abuse investigators made a surprise visit to the home. "The apartment was in really bad shape," Patty says. "There was no working shower, and the bathtub was clogged up with puke. The refrigerator wasn't working, and all the food in it was bad. There were maggots in the sink, and dirty clothes everywhere. They told my mom, 'The girls need to be taken now.'"

Patty recalls feeling relieved. "I was thinking, 'OK, that means we'll get food.'"

"Like a Vacation"

The Department of Social Services placed the girls with an aunt for the weekend while the department looked for a longer-term placement. On a Monday morning in October 1989, Patty remembers her aunt taking her and Michelle to a meeting in an office building. Their mother was there, as well as people who seemed to be lawyers or caseworkers. So was JoAnn Villiard, a licensed foster parent for a private agency, Boston Children's Services.[2] Villiard and her husband had been recruited to provide a temporary home for the girls while their mother attended a detoxification program.

"Everybody talked about what was going to happen," Patty says. "My mother was really upset. But I was excited because I was told we were going to live in the country. I thought, 'Wow, this is going to be fun. It'll be like a vacation. My mom will get it together in a couple of weeks, and we'll go home.'"

JoAnn Villiard and her husband, Richard, had been foster parents for fifteen years. They had raised five children of their own and had adopted two children who had come to them for foster care. The family lived in a big Cape Cod–style house on a large rural lot outside Pembroke, Massachusetts, a South Shore community of 17,000 people. Then in their forties, the couple specialized in providing temporary foster care. The Moffett girls were to stay with them for six months at the most.

Patty remembers the first dinner at the Villiards' home as though it were yesterday. "My foster mom has this theory that on the first night a new child is with them, they need to go to some trouble and provide a real dinner," Patty says. "She made spaghetti and meatballs, because most kids will eat that. The family also had a rule that you have to clean your plate. Well, I couldn't eat that much food in one sitting, because I hadn't had real food for so long. So I just sat there and cried and cried. In the end, they had to give me Jell-O."

Patty's mother completed the rehabilitation program. "But the second she got out, she got trashed," Patty says. The planned six-month stay with the Villiards turned into nine months, and then a year. All told, Patty ended up staying more than four years. Today, when Patty refers to her mom and dad, it's the Villiards she's talking about.

"A Very Normal Childhood"

Patty adjusted surprisingly well to the prospect of a longer stay with the Villiards. They provided the kind of supportive family life that she had previously known only through storybooks.

"I loved it there," she says. "The house was always clean, and we had nice, big meals every night. There was an acre of woods that we could play in, a basketball court, and a swimming pool. I had friends in the neighborhood. And there was always a lot going on. They have fifteen grandchildren, and some of them were always around. I felt like I had a family. It was a very normal childhood."

The Villiards saw to it that Patty got to do all of the things that most kids in middle-class America get to do—play on a softball team and take lessons in tennis, swimming, dance, gymnastics, and piano. On school holidays, the whole family would pile into an RV and go camping. And on Sundays, the family attended the local Congregational Church together. "I loved it," Patty recalls. "I was in the choir, and I was an acolyte and got to light the candles. There was a special service for children, and lots of activities during the week."

While Patty quickly became part of the Villiard household, Michelle had a hard time adjusting. "My sister had always been in control of our household, and now she wasn't," Patty observes. "Michelle resented the Villiards, because she still wanted to be the one to take care of me. But they told her, 'We want you to be a kid, too. You can look out for your sister, but you don't have to take care of her.' No adult had ever told her what to do before, and she had trouble with that."

Because reunification with their mother was the court's long-term goal for the girls, one Tuesday a month Mrs. Villiard would drive them fifty miles to Boston for a supervised meeting with her. On the other Tuesdays, she would drive them into the city for therapy.

Patty liked the visits with her mother because she usually brought presents or special food. But she hated the therapy sessions. "They were very worried about me, because I wouldn't tell people how I was feeling, and I wasn't doing well in school," she says. "I remember once overhearing one of their testers tell someone else, 'She doesn't show emotion. Maybe she can't love.' It made me feel like I was going to grow up and be a psychopath."

"We Want a Real Family"

About two and a half years after the girls moved in with the Villiards, their mother entered another residential drug-treatment program. This one allowed the children of patients who made it past a probationary period to come and live with them. Boston Children's Services began allowing the girls to spend weekends with their mother, with the goal of letting them live with her when the school year ended. "The deal was that we would live with her in the program for nine months, and at the end she would get a Section 8 voucher for an apartment," Patty remembers. "We were very excited about being able to live with her again."

But about two weeks before the scheduled move, the girls' mother got kicked out of the program for breaking rules. "I was really mad at my mother," Patty says. "It really bothered me that we didn't matter enough to her to try harder. My mom wanted to blame it on everybody else but her."

The next week, a meeting was called to reevaluate the reunification goal for the girls. "There were like fifteen adults in the room, I guess anybody who'd ever had anything to do with our case," Patty says. A social worker asked the girls to express their feelings about their future. They addressed their comments to their mother, telling her that they were tired of waiting for her to get her life together.

"We lived in a really nice community," Patty says. "We had started seeing how other people were living, and we thought, 'We deserve this.'"

"We told her, 'Look what you're doing to our lives. Look how many times you've made us excited about going back and then disappointed us. You've had so many chances to do what you need to do to get us back. We can't do this any more.'"

"We told her, 'We want a real family.'"

The court changed the permanency goal for the girls from reunification with their mother to long-term foster care.

The Sisters Are Separated

In the fall of 1992, Patty entered sixth grade. A lackluster student previously, she blossomed that year.

"It was my favorite year in school ever, and my experience that year is why I want to be a teacher," Patty says. "I had the best teacher, Mr. Anti. He's the kind of teacher I want to be. He made learning fun, and he had respect for us. We did all sorts of group learning projects, plus he in-dividualized math and spelling, which was good for me."

Meanwhile, Boston Children's Services, which specialized in short-term foster care, had turned the girls' cases over to Casey Family Ser-vices,[3] a private agency that specializes in long-term foster care. Casey, a fixture elsewhere in New England, had just opened an office in Massa-chusetts. Although the girls didn't realize it at the time, the transfer of their case to a different private agency meant that they would probably have to move to a different foster home. The Villiards lived too far from Casey's office in Lowell, Massachusetts, to make supervision feasible. Besides that, the Villiards wanted to return to their original mission of providing short-term foster care.

Patty and Michelle began meeting regularly with Ginny O'Connell, the social worker for Casey Family Services who took over their case. Af-ter spending a few months getting to know the girls, O'Connell asked each of them a sensitive question: If they couldn't stay with the Villiards any longer, what kind of home would they want?

"Michelle and I sat down with Ginny, and she said, 'Tell me what you want from a family,'" Patty recalls. "We each wrote down what we wanted so we wouldn't be able to influence each other. It turned out that we wanted different things."

"Michelle wrote that she wanted to have her own family in a nice community, and she didn't want me to live with her. She wanted to be an only child, and she didn't want to have any animals around. I wrote that I wanted to live with people in the country who had other kids and ani-mals. And I wanted Michelle to live with me."

O'Connell had already talked with the girls' former caseworkers, their therapists, and the Villiards in an effort to figure out what kind of foster home would best meet their needs. Everyone had suggested that the sisters be separated, and the fact that the girls had stated preferences for different types of families, along with Michelle's desire to live apart from Patty, added weight to their views.

Although foster care workers usually try to keep siblings together, that becomes less of an imperative if the relationship between the siblings is deteriorating, as Patty and Michelle's apparently was. "You think long and hard before you make the decision to take siblings and pull them apart," O'Connell explains. "Everybody who knew them felt they were no longer good together. They saw a pattern developing that they didn't like."

Because Casey Family Services had just started operating in Massachusetts, it had few foster families lined up, so the girls continued to stay with the Villiards while O'Connell searched for families that would be right for each of them. She found a match for Michelle first. During the summer before she started ninth grade, Michelle went to live with a couple in Newburyport, Massachusetts, two hours from Pembroke.

Patty, who was emotionally dependent on Michelle, was initially devastated by the separation. Michelle had been her mainstay through years of neglect by her mother, and living apart was unimaginable. But on a subconscious level, she knew that their relationship had grown destructive, she says. And in retrospect, she agrees with the decision to separate them. "We both know it was good for us in the long run," she says. "Once Michelle got over wanting to take care of me, we became enemies. I think it was too hard for her to switch roles. She and I were constantly fighting. I think that in some ways, maybe unconsciously, she knew that she needed to get away from me to be a kid."

"And now, I realize that separating us wasn't only for Michelle's benefit. I think they were thinking about me, too, because as long as Michelle was around, I let her speak for me."

Once Michelle left, the dynamic in the Villiard household changed. "There was incredibly less tension," Patty recalls. "My [foster] mom and I started spending a lot of time together, because she thought I needed that. Sometimes she'd wake me up early and ask me to go out to breakfast before school, and every afternoon, she'd work with me on my piano lessons. She taught my Sunday School class, and she chaperoned a lot of my school field trips. We got very close in ways we hadn't when Michelle was there."

JoAnn Villiard says Patty turned into a different child without Michelle around.

"When she came to us, Patty was a very needy little girl," she says. "She didn't feel good about herself and felt as though no one liked her.

To a great extent, I think her sister had encouraged that, because it made Patty more dependent on her."

A New Home for Patty

Seven months after Michelle moved away, O'Connell found a set of foster parents who seemed perfect for Patty. The Smiths[4] lived in a rural community not too different from Pembroke, but closer to the community in which Michelle was living, which would make visits between the sisters easier to arrange. Both foster parents were musicians and were eager to support Patty's desire to continue with piano and voice lessons. They had previously been foster parents to two other children, both of whom they had adopted. Although those children were now grown and living elsewhere, the couple frequently hosted exchange students. A seventeen-year-old boy from the Ukraine would be Patty's de facto brother.

Patty spent five weekends with the couple before she agreed to move in. "Whenever I visited, they seemed to be very supportive of the things I wanted for myself," Patty recalls. "They said they would support my relationships with my sister and with the Villiards. The junior high school I would be going to had a renowned music department, and I was going to get music lessons and voice lessons, too. Plus I knew if I agreed to be a Casey kid, then Casey would send me to camp and help me go to college. It sounded great."

Patty moved in with the Smiths in February 1994, midway through seventh grade. Moving out of the Villiards' home was in many ways even more traumatizing than being removed from her mother's custody. The first night in the new home, she cried all night long. "The very first night is the worst night you spend in a new home, because all you want is to be in your previous home," she says.

But even after a few weeks there, Patty wasn't happy. She missed the Villiards terribly and talked about them constantly. She said the Smiths seemed jealous of her relationship with the Villiards and told her that they thought she would adjust to the move more easily if she didn't call or see them for a while.

"I didn't unpack my bags for five weeks," Patty recalls. "I was the saddest I've ever been in my life."

The Smiths also weren't as supportive as Patty had hoped concerning her desire to see her sister regularly. Since Patty and Michelle lived about fifteen miles apart, they needed their foster parents to transport them, and Patty felt that the Smiths didn't do their fair share. To add to Patty's misery, she didn't get along with the exchange student.

But what bothered Patty the most was that the Smiths didn't seem to accept her as she was. They seemed to want to play the role of Henry Higgins, with Patty playing Eliza Doolittle. "I was a tomboy, and they wanted me to wear nice clothing," Patty says. "I played music for fun, and they wanted me to take it more seriously." When she got bad grades, they insisted that her IQ be tested to determine whether she was retarded. "I scored at the post-college level in everything with the exception of economics," Patty says triumphantly.

There were good times with the Smiths, to be sure—frequent outings to Boston to attend the symphony or the opera; weekend visits to Cape Cod; a two-week summer vacation in Williamsburg, Virginia, three weeks in Marco Island, Florida. "Culture-wise, it was an incredible place to live," Patty says.

And it was largely because of the Smiths' encouragement that Patty made great progress musically, she acknowledges. "They supported me in the Young Americans, a touring musical group, which takes a huge time commitment and costs lots of money," she says. "And they encouraged me to play the clarinet. I was in chamber music, and the select chorus, and the drama club, and I made the district choir, too. I had so many musical activities when I lived there, and they paid for a lot of it on their own."

But all in all, it was not a good match. O'Connell, Patty's caseworker, remembers being summoned to the home many times to mediate disagreements between Patty and the parents. "Patty has a very strong personality, and she's extremely opinionated," O'Connell says. "They wanted her to be more like them, and she didn't want to be like them. We did a lot of work together to try to make it work out."

Another Transition

At the Smiths' urging, Casey Family Services agreed to pay for Patty to attend an expensive month-long summer music camp in Maine during the summer between her eighth- and ninth-grade years. Just before she left, she learned that the Smiths didn't want her to return home after camp. They thought that attending camp would make a good transition between their home and a new foster home.

Patty was upset because she had just started to think that things might be working out at the Smiths. In addition, she had no way of knowing whether she would like the next home any better.

Even though she was worried about where she would live when camp ended, she threw herself into the daily regimen—playing clarinet in a jazz chamber group, composing a piano piece in honor of her sister, taking voice lessons, and even winning the role of Tzietel in the camp's production of *Fiddler on the Roof.*

The reality of her estrangement from her foster parents set in when she learned that they weren't coming to watch the performance, as the other performers' parents were. "I really worked my butt off to do well at the camp, and I wanted someone there to watch me perform," she said.

However, Patty's previous foster parents, the Villiards, came, which mitigated her disappointment. "I was so excited when I saw them," she says.

In her mind, they still epitomized everything that foster parents should be.

"The Worst Possible Place"

When camp ended, Ginny O'Connell had not yet found Patty a new foster home, so she returned temporarily to the Smiths', where she had to stay in a guest room in the basement because the couple had given a foreign visitor her old room.

As weeks passed with no new placement on the horizon and a new school year about to start, O'Connell decided that it was important to keep Patty in the same school system, even if it meant placing her with a foster mother who didn't seem quite right for her. O'Connell placed her in the home of Sally Jenkins,[5] a specialized foster parent who had several years' experience caring for children for another agency. Jenkins had sometimes provided weekend care for Patty while she was living with the Smiths (the foster care system calls it "respite care").

Patty hadn't minded staying with Jenkins on occasional weekends, since she loved playing with the animals that Jenkins kept at her farm. But she wasn't crazy about living there for the long term. The Smiths' household may not have been right for her, but in her mind, this one was clearly wrong. "The house was really disgusting," Patty says. "It was cluttered, and dank and depressing. She let baby goats walk around inside."

O'Connell admits that the home was not a good match for Patty. "I didn't think it was the right placement, but it was the only one we had at the time," she said. "The main good that came of it was that she was able to stay in the same school."

Patty didn't feel as though she had anything in common with the home's other long-term residents, a brain-damaged adult woman and a developmentally disabled teenage girl. As Patty remembers it, she "ended up taking care of both of them." And she felt threatened by some of the teenagers whom Jenkins took in as emergency placements for forty-five days at a time. "They were mainly kids from Lynn who were involved with gangs and used to doing all sorts of bad stuff," Patty says. "They drank and stole from me, and threatened to beat me up. Then their behavior started rubbing off on me, and I started doing bad things, like skipping school." That semester, she received straight Fs on her school report card.

All in all, Patty says, "It was the worst possible place they could have put me."

One cold night in February 1996, six months after Patty had moved in, Patty and Jenkins fought. Jenkins called the emergency number for Casey Family Services and demanded that Patty be removed from her home.

"Moving Was So Hard"

Diane and Ken Sterling,[6] Patty's next set of foster parents, had a reputation for doing well with tough kids. Like Sally Jenkins, they were licensed as specialized foster parents, which meant they had special training in how to cope with the needs of children with emotional or medical problems. They lived eight miles from Patty's high school and agreed to drive her back and forth until another foster home in the school district could be found for her.

When Patty arrived at their home in the middle of the night, the couple was already caring temporarily for two other children, both developmentally disabled. They also had two little boys of their own, and Diane was pregnant with a daughter.

Again, Patty felt from the start that it was the wrong place for her. "These people were used to working with very troubled teenagers," she said. "I was sad, but I wasn't troubled. Their home was very, very structured. Living with them was like living in a kiddie jail. They had alarms on all the windows. I had to ask permission to go to the bathroom or get a drink of water. They'd pat me down after leaving a store."

"But the biggest problem was losing my freedom. Personal freedom was very important to me. I had grown up in a rural community and was used to being able to roam around outdoors. But they wouldn't let me go anywhere after school. And if I was home, but out of their sight, they'd shout, 'Patty, where are you? We need to see you.'"

"It's not that they were bad people. That was just the way they ran their house."

Although she wasn't happy with the placement, Patty decided to try to make it work so she wouldn't have to move again. "Moving was so hard for me," she explains. Also, she began to like Diane Sterling a lot, and she adored the couple's little boys. After a lifetime of being the little sister, she relished the role of being a big sister to boys who didn't seem to care that she was in foster care.

Although Patty had hoped to stay in her old high school, Diane Sterling didn't want to keep driving her there, so Patty transferred to the high school in the Sterlings' community.

Changing schools in the middle of a school year is hard on anyone, but for someone in Patty's position, it's even harder. For one thing, she brought a dismal record with her from her previous school, which meant that she was put in classes for slow learners, which she felt stigmatized her. In addition, the Sterlings' rules made it hard for her to develop a social life. "I was allowed to walk to school and back, and that was it," she says. "When you're fifteen years old, you want a little more freedom than that."

A few months into her stay, Patty began taking what she calls "freedom walks," which usually involved skipping school. Patty's "freedom walks" only made the Sterlings tighten their rules.

One day in the spring of 1996, Patty called Ginny O'Connell in desperation, demanding to be moved. It was one of many such calls that Patty had made to O'Connell that spring, and O'Connell tried to calm her down. "She told me, 'You can't keep moving every time something goes wrong,'" Patty recalls. "The whole idea of long-term foster care is staying in one home. You need to tell them how you feel and work out your problems.'"

That sounded too difficult to Patty. "I thought, 'I can't live this way,'" she recalls. She decided to do something that would force O'Connell to find her a different foster home. She stole a box of Exacta blades from a hardware store, went back to her room, and began cutting herself. "I thought I'd only do it a little, and that way Ginny would get the point and remove me, and Diane and Ken would get in trouble for being too strict," she said.

But Patty cut a little too deeply, and she nicked a vein. "After I did it, I freaked out," she said. "I had all this blood all over me. I crawled out my window and ran down the street and into the woods. I hid in the woods. I thought I was going to die, and I didn't want to die. I just wanted to make a point."

Patty finally left the woods to find a pay phone. She called the Casey after-hours number and reached the social worker who was on call. "I told her that I was sorry for leaving the house, and that I was going to go back," Patty says. "The bleeding had stopped, and I was really sorry I'd done it. I thought I could hide it."

Then she walked home and tried to sneak up to her room. Mrs. Sterling called the police.

"The Longest Night"

The police took Patty to an emergency room, where a doctor stitched up her wound and gave her intravenous fluids. She spent the night at North

Shore Emergency Services, a crisis-screening center. "It was the longest night of my life," Patty says. "I was really scared about what was going to happen. I knew I was causing a lot of trouble for people who cared about me—my sister, the Villiards, and Ginny."

The next morning, O'Connell met with a social worker for the state Department of Social Services, which had legal custody of Patty, although Casey managed her case. Because Patty had a self-inflicted injury in her recent history, the state worker wanted to have her committed to a psychiatric hospital. "I didn't actually try to kill myself, but to everyone else, it seemed that way," Patty said. O'Connell thought that Patty wasn't suicidal and that a less restrictive environment would be more appropriate. In the end, the social workers compromised and sent Patty to a Community Intervention Program—an inpatient diagnostic program where her mental health status could be evaluated. The center agreed to admit her for forty-five days.

Patty was initially worried about going there but ended up really liking it. "It was structured, but it was fun," she said. "I really liked being around the other kids who were there. And they kept us really busy. We played mini golf, and went bowling and to the movies, and I didn't have to go to school. I was one of the most functional, so the staff really liked me."

Although Patty depicts her stay there as one fun outing after another, O'Connell recalls it being a period of intense emotional upset for her. "She had a lot of new memories of past abuse," O'Connell says. "She was really dealing with a lot."

At the end of the forty-five-day assessment period, the staff recommended that Patty be transferred into a residential treatment program, where she could get more therapy than in a foster home. "I didn't disagree," O'Connell says. "She hadn't been doing well in school, and things hadn't been going well in the foster home."

"I Decided to Change"

Because Patty was no longer in a Casey foster home, O'Connell had no formal role in her life anymore. It was up to state workers, who had only met Patty recently, to decide where she lived. "I had no say whatsoever about where she would go," O'Connell says. "I tried to influence the state worker's decision so that Patty would at least be placed close to her sister or the Villiards, and the answer was, 'She'll go where there's an opening.'"

The only residential program that had an opening was not on O'Connell's list of places likely to be good for Patty. As Patty describes it, "It was a group home filled with kids with extreme anger management problems. I got beat up in this home all the time, once in a group therapy session."

Patty was the only resident permitted to attend the local public high school, which became the third high school she attended in two years. But she found herself stigmatized because of where she lived. And because she had done so poorly in school the previous year, she was repeating ninth grade, which was humiliating. (Children in foster care are twice as likely to have to repeat a grade than children in intact families.)

That fall, she developed an ulcer. "Every time I ate something, I'd end up on the floor crying with pain," she says. And in November, she had to have surgery to correct her amblyopia because it was impairing her sight. The recovery was more difficult than expected, and because of that, in addition to the problems she had had adjusting to the local high school, Patty began receiving her schooling at the group home.

Meanwhile, even though O'Connell was no longer Patty's caseworker, she was working behind the scenes to get her transferred to a different group home. "Patty didn't have a strong advocate in the Department of Social Services because her case had changed offices so many times," O'Connell says. "I thought it was important to stay involved. I finally got an audience with the area director of the Department of Social Services. I told him how this kid was being scapegoated at this place, and that she'd actually been hurt by another resident because of something she'd said in group therapy. He finally told me, 'If you can find her another place, we'll pay for it.'"

O'Connell's task wasn't easy. "At the time, Patty was very off-putting," she says. Patty dressed like an urban gang member, talked disrespectfully to most adults, and was on the verge of flunking ninth grade for the second time. In other words, she wasn't likely to strike an intake worker at a group home as a good prospect.

However, the director of The New England Home for Little Wanderers in Waltham decided to take a chance on her. The home had been founded in 1865 to care for children orphaned by the Civil War but in the twentieth century had switched to providing services to abused and neglected children. In March 1997, Patty moved in. She liked it from the start.

"The people who ran this group home were really on top of things," she says. "They had lots of great activities for us, and they did a lot to prepare us for independent living. We did our own laundry, and cooked dinner once a week, and made our own doctor's appointments. I loved living at Waltham house. It was like a constant party. Plus they let me get a job at McDonald's, and let me visit the Sterlings on weekends." (By this time, Mrs. Sterling had given birth to a little girl, and Patty was in heaven whenever she was around her.)

Moving to The Little Wanderers Home had meant enrolling in a new high school, her fourth in two years. But this time, Patty loved the school. Although she was still in danger of failing ninth grade, the principal of Waltham High School cut her a deal.

"He told me that if I earned mostly As in the final quarter of the school year, he would let me go on to tenth grade," she says. So she did. "There was no way my pride was going to let me do ninth grade a third time," she says indignantly. "I wasn't a dumb kid."

Besides being her best academic period since sixth grade, this was also the year in which Patty came into her own socially. With her wandering eye corrected, she no longer needed to wear the thick lenses that had been prescribed to tame it, and she stopped being embarrassed by her appearance. Without glasses, she looked like a young Cybill Shepherd. "Before, I had been a real ugly duckling, and now people started to tell me I was pretty," she says.

To her amazement, she also began making friends. "I think it's because I decided to change," she says.

"I Had Grown Up Overnight"

As Patty blossomed, it became clear to her caseworkers that she no longer needed the highly structured—and expensive—environment of a group home. Both the state caseworker and O'Connell thought that she was ready to live with a foster family again. Casey Family Services took over primary responsibility for Patty once again, and the Sterlings agreed to take her back into their home.

But Patty agonized over whether she should return there or try a new family. "I really loved the kids and the mom," Patty says. "While I was living at the Waltham Home, I spent a lot of weekends with them, and the mom and I became almost like sisters. But the dad was really strict, so I told Ginny the only way I was going to move back was if the Sterlings signed a contract with me, and they agreed. So we all signed a nice little contract that said there were basically no rules if I did my chores and kept up my grades. Plus I'd have my own room, and there wouldn't be an alarm on my windows."

"I didn't need all that structure and supervision any more. I had grown up overnight. I was very responsible."

Because Patty was now more motivated academically and doing well in school, Casey Family Services agreed to pay her tuition at a private school. In November 1997, she enrolled in tenth grade at St. Mary's High School, a Catholic school in Lynn, about a half hour by train from the Sterlings' home. St. Mary's was to be her fifth and final high school.

An Extended Honeymoon

St. Mary's was about as different from Patty's previous high schools as could be. Founded in 1881 by the Sisters of Notre Dame de Namur, it is a serious college preparatory school with an annual tuition, in 1997, of about $8,000. If any other students were in foster care, Patty didn't know it.

The first week there, she called O'Connell every day to say she hated it. "She'd call me and say things like, 'This is the stupidest school,'" O'Connell recalls. "'Why did you send me here?' I'd remind her that she picked it, and that I had gone to a lot of trouble to get her in and to get Casey to pay for it. I told her to give it some time."

O'Connell also called Vice Principal Carl DiMaiti and asked him to try to ease the way for Patty. He called Patty into his office, and the two of them hit it off. "He is the single nicest man I've ever met," Patty says of DiMaiti. "I loved him, and he loved me."

And then Patty met a boy, which made any complaints she had about St. Mary's irrelevant. Like Patty, he was an outsider, not because he was in foster care but because he wasn't a jock. Tall and good-looking, he spent his free time watching classic movies instead of driving around looking for parties. Within weeks of meeting, he and Patty were virtually inseparable. "He's so charismatic," Patty says. "His face lights up when he talks."

Meanwhile, at home with the Sterlings, things were going well, too. "I helped out a lot with the kids," Patty says. The Sterlings were also living up to their end of the bargain with Patty. "I had a lot of freedom," Patty says. "They realized that I needed to be treated like I was human and given some credit for making good decisions."

Patty got through her sophomore year and most of her junior year with no major problems. It was the longest period of stability in her life since she'd lived with the Villiards.

"The Worst Decision . . . in My Life"

In the spring of her junior year, however, Patty's home life began to deteriorate. The Sterlings were having marital problems, and there was a lot of tension in the household. Patty wanted to move, but O'Connell didn't have another foster family to offer her.

An argument at the Sterlings in March 1999 forced the issue. Patty and another youth who lived there had come home one evening and found themselves locked out. "The rule of the house was that foster kids don't get keys, which meant we couldn't get in if we came home when no one was there," Patty explains. "Well, it was dark and cold, and we didn't want to wait outside, so Mark broke a window so we could get in. When the dad got home, he hit the roof."

Patty called the emergency number for Casey Family Services and said she needed to be moved immediately. The social worker on call told her that O'Connell was on vacation and that Patty would have to wait for her to return to request a move. Patty didn't listen to her.

"I made the worst decision I ever made in my life," Patty says. "I moved back in with my mother."

Yet Another Move

Patty's relationship with her mother had run hot and cold throughout her years in foster care. In her early teens, she had looked forward to their monthly visits largely because she also got to see her sister. Later, when she and Michelle became old enough to arrange to see each other independently, the scheduled visits became less important, and Patty sometimes skipped them.

At the time of the altercation at the Sterlings' house, Patty and her mother were getting along. Her mother was living in the Jamaica Plain neighborhood of Boston with a man who had a good job, didn't use drugs, treated her well, and liked Patty. Patty persuaded herself that she and her mother could live together amicably. After all, Patty would be home only a few hours a day, because it would take two hours each way, by subway and train, to get back and forth to school. And on weekends, she could stay with an aunt or with her boyfriend's family.

Almost from the start, however, Patty and her mother did not get along. "She was still a drug addict," Patty says. "She would steal the grocery money and sneak out in the middle of the night and do drugs. She'd come home drunk or doped up, and I would have to pick her up off the floor, and drag her to bed. She disgusted me. We fought every day."

When O'Connell returned from vacation, she suggested that Patty move into a supervised independent living program with several other youth in their late teens. "I went and looked at it and decided I couldn't live there," Patty says. "It was in a bad neighborhood, and it was too crazy a program. They expected you to work full-time and go to school full-time and spend a lot of time with their therapist."

Then O'Connell found a prospective foster home in Groveland, Massachusetts, almost thirty miles from Patty's school. Patty said no to this option, too. "I would have loved living there, but I would have had to take a Greyhound bus to school," Patty says.

A third alternative was for Patty to move back in with the Villiards, who were willing to take her. But they lived forty miles from Patty's school, so she would have had to transfer to a sixth high school. And it would have been almost impossible for her to continue to see her boyfriend.

In Patty's mind, she had no alternative but to stay with her mother.

Senior Year

Because of her chaotic home life, Patty's senior year was even more stressful than for most teens. Just before school started, Patty's mother told her she would have to pay rent if she wanted to continue living with her. Outraged, Patty moved in with her boyfriend's family. She stayed there for three months and then decided that her presence was creating tension between family members and jeopardizing her relationship with her boyfriend.

She moved back in with her mother, and to satisfy her mother's demand that she pay room and board, she took a part-time job in a movie theater. The situation at home was no better than before. "She was doing drugs again," Patty said. "She'd disappear for weeks at a time. I decided I just had to suck it up. Her boyfriend wanted to kick her out, but he didn't, because he wanted me to be able to finish high school."

To add to her stress, attending five different high schools had left her short of the credits she needed to graduate. As a result, she had to take two extra math courses in addition to a heavy senior load, which included an Advanced Placement class in English. O'Connell arranged for outside tutors, at Casey's expense. "There was a very real question about whether she was going to pass her senior year," O'Connell says, "and a lot of the problem was the stress of living with her mother."

The college admission process was yet another source of stress. Without a parent who could help her with it, Patty had to rely more than most students on the two guidance counselors at St. Mary's. O'Connell tried to play a parental role, taking Patty to an informational session about financial aid options and filling out the federal financial aid form for her.

"A lot of foster kids have great foster parents that they can rely on," O'Connell notes. "After she left the Villiards, Patty really didn't have that. And with all the times Patty had to move, she didn't have anyone else who could be her anchor. I felt that this was a kid who could benefit from a stable relationship. If I didn't take her to the financial aid meeting, how was she going to get there? If I didn't take her to her sister's graduation, who was going to do it?

"These are important rituals in a child's life. There was no one else to make sure she got to experience them, so I decided to be the one."

Fortunately, Patty already had a career goal: to become a teacher. And she knew that she had to go to school in Massachusetts to qualify for the $6,000 annual grant that Massachusetts was planning to begin offering to all foster care alumni who attended in-state schools. Then she drew up a list of about eight Massachusetts schools that offered teaching training programs.

She was particularly attracted to Emmanuel College, a small girls' school in Boston that had been founded by the Sisters of Notre Dame de Namur, the same religious order that founded her high school. She'd been going there on field trips since she started at St. Mary's and knew that she'd feel comfortable there. Also, she could live in a dorm, which meant she could get away from her mother.

Patty was so busy her senior year that most of her memories of it are foggy. "I barely made it through the year," she recalls. "I had to take all those extra courses to make sure I'd have enough credits to graduate. Plus, I was working nearly full-time. I had to save up for college, since I didn't know if I was going to get a scholarship."

In addition to her sister and mother, the audience at her graduation on June 1, 2000, contained the people who are most important in her life, her "constructed family": the Villiards, her boyfriend's family, and Ginny O'Connell.

"Graduating from high school was the biggest thing I'll ever do," Patty says. "Even if I go on to get a Ph.D., my high school diploma will still be my biggest accomplishment."

On to College

Following the stress of her senior year, the summer afterward was relatively carefree. Patty continued to live with her mother and her mother's boyfriend and work at the movie theater. She spent weekends either with the Villiards or with her boyfriend's family. "I spent as much time elsewhere as I could," she recalls. She could hardly wait to go off to college, although the prospect also terrified her.

Late in August 2000, Patty moved into a dormitory at Emmanuel College. Emmanuel had offered Patty a generous financial aid package, including a scholarship. Combined with a scholarship from Casey and the expected grant of $6,000 from the state, it meant she would need to borrow only $1,500. (At the last minute, the state grant failed to materialize, so Casey kicked in more money and borrowed an additional $3,000.)

Most children who grow up in foster care are totally on their own when it comes to patching together the financial resources to pay for college. Only a dozen or so states waive the tuition for emancipated youth who attend state schools or local community colleges. And there's not enough other help available for the costs of room and board, books, and health insurance, let alone incidentals like toiletries, ink cartridges for computers, transportation, and entertainment. Patty was fortunate that Casey Family Services is committed to making sure that the children to whom it provides foster care aren't disadvantaged when they go off to college. Besides paying for her room and board, books, and health insurance, Casey gave Patty a generous monthly allowance for personal expenses.

Patty knows that she couldn't have attended a four-year college without the agency's continuing support and is grateful for it. "Casey is treating me better than lots of parents treat their kids when they go off to college," she says. "They've really given me a sense of financial and emotional security."

In return for the support from Casey, Patty is expected to take her education seriously. She must work part-time and save money for the future. During both of the summers since she began college, she's worked between thirty and forty hours a week, one summer at a children's learning store and the next at a day-care center.

"Casey helps me, but they also make it clear that I have some responsibilities, too," she notes. "If I don't do what I've agreed to do, they'll stop supporting me."

On the Fast Track

Although transitions had often unnerved her in the past, Patty adjusted quickly to both dorm life and the academic rigors of college. She joined the school choir and the History Club, and was selected to serve on the Program Council, which oversees student activities.

Because she had scored a 700 on her verbal SAT and also performed well on her Advanced Placement test in English literature, Emmanuel gave her credit for two college-level English classes. She piled up additional credits by taking five classes rather than the customary four during several semesters and by attending summer school between her sophomore and junior years. As a result, she's planning to finish all the course work for her bachelor's degree in three and a half years instead of four and then enroll immediately in a master's program.

Why the rush? "I want to spend what would be my fourth year in college in a graduate program," she explains. "That way, I'll be able to get a bachelor's degree and a master's degree in five years. As much as I love the idea of teaching, I hate school. I want to get out in the real world."

Patty's goal is to teach sixth grade. Sometimes she even daydreams about teaching in the elementary school that she attended during her first four years in foster care. To that end, she's already collecting supplies for the classroom she hopes to preside over. "I've spent a lot of my own money going to yard sales and buying materials for a classroom," she says. "I have a closet full of six hundred children's books that I either read when I was little or heard were good."

"More Than a Foster Child"

Many people who grow up in foster care never get over it. Forever after, they blame every setback in their lives on the fact that they grew up in foster care. Patty had bad experiences in foster care, to be sure. But rather than dwell on them, she prefers to remember the positive experiences that foster care made possible.

"If I had been left with my mom, I'd probably have starved to death," she says. "And if we'd have been allowed to go back, by now I'd be pregnant, or in jail, or dead. That's what's happened to just about all of the kids we grew up with."

"Living in seven different homes during high school, yes, that was hard. Yes, it meant I had to go to five different schools. Yes, crap happened. But there are other foster kids who move every forty-five days, who get stuck with a really horrible foster family and get abused, who don't have anyone helping them go to college."

"Having to move so many times meant that I learned a lot about other people. I got to pick and choose what I wanted from each family I was exposed to. I've been able to take the things I like and discard the things I don't like. And all the people I've met, even those I didn't like, have made me a better person. I don't feel like I've had a bad life."

A key to Patty's success is surely the depth of the relationships she's forged with people whom she's met along her path to adulthood, especially her first foster parents, JoAnn and Richard Villiard. More than seven years after she moved out of their home, she still calls them Mom and Dad. She spends weekends with them every chance she gets. It's because of the Villiards, she says, that she has "very, very fond memories of being a little girl."

"They're going to be the grandparents to my children," she adds.

Another key to her success has been the continuing support of Ginny O'Connell, her Casey Family Services caseworker for all but a few months since she was twelve years old. "I don't even remember the names of the caseworkers we had before Ginny," Patty says. "Every time my mother moved, we got a new worker, and my mother moved a lot."

"Ginny was different. Once I started moving around, she was the only consistent influence in my life. I saw her all the time. She came to my recitals, my concerts, my birthday parties, and all my visits with my mom and my sister. She made it a point to get to know my therapist very well, and a teacher that I really liked a lot in junior high. And then when I got involved with my boyfriend, she spent a lot of time getting to know him."

"She's really had a hand in raising me. After my sister, she's the next person I call whenever I'm excited about something in my life. She really cares about me. She's more interested in my life than my birth mother is."

Even now, O'Connell treats Patty to lunch or dinner once or twice a month. "And we'll spend an evening together gabbing," Patty says. "I love to talk, and she's a good listener. I know it's her job to check in on me, but she makes me feel like she really cares. She makes me feel like I've been more than a foster child to her. I'm also her friend."

At any given time, O'Connell has eight or ten other Pattys in her case-load. She says she tries to give them all the attention they need, even if it means giving up her weekend to drive them to sleep-away camp. "Casey is a small agency, and when kids come into the program, we tell them that we're going to be there for them, whatever happens," she says. "We strive to provide the continuity in their lives that they haven't had before."

Postscript

Patty's job in the summer of 2003 confirmed her career choice. She worked with fourth graders as a special ed teacher at the Italian Home for Children, a residential and day treatment center for emotionally disturbed children. "It was so much more rewarding than working with normal kids, but it was also so much harder," she said. "I had only ten kids in my classroom, and it felt like forty. They had a lot of problems, but I loved them, and I was heartbroken when I had to leave."

For her final semester as an undergraduate at Emmanuel, she moved into an on-campus apartment with two other seniors. Through the fall of 2003, she was interning as a student teacher in a fourth-grade classroom in Dorchester. "When they asked me what age of children I wanted, I said, 'Anything but fourth grade,' because there are so many classroom management problems with that age," she said. "So they gave me fourth grade. I wasn't happy about it at first, but now but I love my kids. I think these kids will be perfect the second half of this year."

Patty finished her undergraduate casework in December 2003 and began a four-semester master's program at Simmons College in January 2004. "I think I should try to be the best teacher I can be," she said. "Part of that is getting the know-how you need to be good. You get a lot of theory in undergraduate courses, and more on the art of teaching in grad school. I think it's important." Besides working on her master's degree, she is working full time as a nanny. She hopes to line up a full-time job as a teacher in the fall of 2004.

Because Emmanuel doesn't offer a midyear commencement, Patty received her degree on May 8, 2004, with the class with which she entered college. In the audience her mother and sister and a few aunts or two, along with her "constructed family"—her boyfriend and his mother and sister; her former caseworker, Ginny O'Connell; and her first foster parents, Mom and Dad Villiard. Without their support during her transition from foster care, Patty says she doesn't know what would have happened to her.

JoAnn Villiard says that Patty gives other people too much credit for her success. "It's her own inner strength," Villiard says. "Some people have this inner thing that can pull them up and out of a bad situation. Others will just give in to it."

"Yes, she's had a lot of support from the outside, but it wouldn't have gotten her to where she is today if she didn't want to do it herself."

Alfonso Torres

"ALL MY LIFE, I HAD PRAYED FOR A FAMILY"

Alfonso Torres, Pembroke Pines, Florida

Two weeks before his eighteenth birthday, Alfonso Torres was locked up in the Miami-Dade Regional Juvenile Detention Center, sick with worry about where he would live once he got out.

Alfonso, separated from his parents since he was ten, knew that his right to foster care would end on Christmas Eve 2002, the day he turned eighteen. He was getting out of juvenile hall a week later and had nowhere to go. "I called my social worker and asked, 'What's going to happen when I turn eighteen?'" Alfonso recalls. "And he said, 'I don't know.'"

Alfonso felt more depressed than at any other point in his life. "I was thinking, 'How can I stay away from crime if I don't have any place to live?' I was more than depressed. I was scared."

And then something happened that even now, months later, Alfonso regards as a miracle. A woman came looking for him. Years before, she told him, she had adopted his two younger brothers—siblings he didn't even remember he had. They wanted to meet him, and she wanted to help him, she said.

It was a fairy-tale beginning to his life as an adult.

But as every child knows, not all fairy tales have happy endings.

"A Very Sociable Child"

Alfonso was born on Christmas Eve 1984. His twin sister, Angel, died at birth of complications from prenatal exposure to cocaine. Alfonso spent part of his first year in a children's shelter while the Florida Department of Children and Families (DCF) looked into whether his parents were fit to care for him.

Alfonso's father was a twenty-two-year-old landscaper, who, by his own admission, was a second-generation wife beater. Alfonso's mother was a twenty-three-year-old college dropout from Massachusetts who had met his father while vacationing in Florida with her parents. She told a caseworker that she had started shooting heroin right after high school and then moved on to cocaine.

Alfonso was her third child. She had allowed the father of the first, born when she was seventeen, to take him to Italy to raise. And she had placed the second for adoption because she and Alfonso's father had been separated when he was born.

An investigation by the Florida DCF concluded that the chief threat to Alfonso's well-being was his mother's drug use, so after the parents agreed to separate, his father was allowed to take him home.

The court record contains no information about Alfonso's life over the next few years. But sometime during that period, the parents got back together again, because Alfonso remembers living with both of them. In September 1988, his mother gave birth to another drug-affected son, who was placed in state custody. And in September 1989, she gave birth to another one, who also went into foster care. The birth of that child triggered an investigation into Alfonso's circumstances, and he was placed in foster care in October 1989 because of neglect.

This time, Alfonso stayed in foster care for almost two years. Court records suggest that he had a difficult time. The foster home in which he was placed was not a good fit, his *guardian ad litem* (GAL) reported to the court in May 1990. "Alfonso is currently placed in a foster home with parents that speak Spanish as their primary language," the GAL reported, whereas Alfonso spoke only English. "Alfonso is behind in his education, and shows learning difficulties. At five and a half years of age, he does not yet know his colors, the alphabet, or numbers. He is at home all day with his foster mother, who speaks only Spanish; his activities (including educational, physical, and social) are thereby extremely limited. He has little or no exposure to English-speaking children or adults."

"Alfonso wishes desperately to be returned to his natural parents. He also wants very much to go to school. He is a very sociable child and wants to be with other children his age."

To try to regain custody, both parents agreed to attend parenting classes and marriage counseling, maintain a stable home address and employment, visit weekly with Alfonso, and refrain from drug use. Alfonso's mother failed to achieve all but one of the goals, and although pregnant again with her seventh child, was testing positive for drugs. Alfonso's father, however, met most of his goals, and in August 1991, a judge gave Alfonso back to him.

At the GAL's request, the judge barred Alfonso's mother from all but supervised visits. "The mother has failed to remain drug-free," the GAL told the court. "This, combined with the mother's turbulent marital relationship with the father, suggests that the child should not be exposed to the potential violence that cohabitation of the parents or the mother's visits to the home might cause."

There's no indication in the court record that his father's potential for violence against Alfonso was a concern.

"All Well"

For a while, Alfonso and his father lived with relatives in Homestead, a poor community southwest of Miami. A state social worker visited periodically. Her final memorandum to the court, in December 1991, reported "all well" and recommended that the court terminate the agency's jurisdiction.

Soon afterward, father and son moved into a home with the father's new girlfriend and her two children, twins who were about the same age as Alfonso. Alfonso didn't get along with them and remembers often being blamed for problems that they caused.

After his stepmother gave birth to his father's child, the stress level in the household grew, and Alfonso says he became the scapegoat for everything that went wrong. "If I was five minutes late from school, my stepmother was telling my dad, and he'd beat me," Alfonso says in a matter-of-fact way. "If he beat me bad enough, I'd run away. And when he'd catch me, he'd beat me again."

"It went on for a year, or a year and a half. It would be an everyday thing. Sometimes it would just come out of nowhere. He would come up behind me, and boom."

From Alfonso's description, the abuse bordered on torture. "Sometimes he made me hold a twenty-five pound weight over my head and jog in place, and if I didn't jog fast enough, he'd hit me," Alfonso recalls. "I also remember him strapping me naked to a post and beating me with a fishing pole." The beatings left Alfonso with a broken front tooth and scars on his buttocks and a foot.

Every now and then, Alfonso's teachers, and even sometimes the Homestead police, would question him about his bruises. "I would never admit that he beat me," Alfonso says. "Even when the police picked me up, I'd say I hurt myself. I loved the hell out of my dad and didn't want to be taken away. My real mother left us, which hurt him so bad, and I think my dad beat me so much because I reminded him of her. He brought me to this world, so no matter what, I love him, even if he did beat me."

Finally, however, after a particularly bad beating in September 1995, Alfonso, then ten, called the police himself. This time, he was placed in foster care. He would never return home again.

Praying for a Family

Initially, Alfonso stayed at Miami Bridge, an emergency shelter in Miami. Then his social worker found a home for him with a Trinidadian couple that was already caring for about a dozen other children.

Alfonso had a hard time settling in because he missed his father and stepmother so much. In the beginning, he called them often. "As soon as they picked up the phone, I'd cry," he remembers. "I'd cry so much that my heart hurt. I would beg them to come and visit, and they never would. I remember one time I talked to my parents on the phone, and they told me that they loved me and missed me and wanted me home. I was all happy and told my social worker about it, and she said, 'Well that's funny, because they signed papers saying they don't want you.' Every night, I prayed to have my family back."

In retrospect, Alfonso says, the Trinidadian couple provided a good home. But as he entered adolescence, he began hanging out with the older, streetwise boys who lived in the home. His role model was an older child named Jerry. "He taught me how to steal cars and smoke marijuana," Alfonso says.

The first time that Alfonso got caught shoplifting, his foster parents warned him that he'd have to move out if he ever did something like that again. When he got taken into custody again five months later, they made good on their threat. "I called them from jail, and the dad said, 'I gave you a second chance, and you didn't listen. I can't take you back no more,'" Alfonso recalls.

"It hurt me really bad. I had been starting to gain trust in people again. I had started to think of them as my family. And they treated me like their own son. But I don't blame them. It was my fault."

Over the next two years, Alfonso moved from one foster home to another—more than a dozen in all. As a result, he has no mementos from childhood, not even a single school photograph. "I never had enough money to buy the school pictures," he says.

Moving so often deprived him of the opportunity to fully engage in school and community life. Because he never attended a regular high school, he never got to play high school sports, which he regrets. And it left him with only a single childhood friend, a youth he met at Miami Bridge and still sees occasionally.

Alfonso readily accepts part of the blame for his frequent moves. Soon after settling into a new home, he says, he'd get caught committing a crime and would be locked up in the Miami-Dade Regional Detention Center for three weeks. (For most offenses, Florida law permits youths to be detained for a maximum of twenty-one days before adjudication.) When he was released from detention, the foster family would usually refuse to take him back, so he'd have to live at Miami Bridge, the emergency shelter, while his state social worker looked for another foster home. Within a month or two of moving in with the next family, the cycle would repeat itself.

Since 1998, Florida law has permitted judges to appoint citizen review panels to advise them on particular cases. Five volunteer citizens sit on each review panel, and before a judicial hearing, they review the case history and make recommendations. Alfonso's case first came before a citizen review panel in March 1999. After reviewing his file, the panel expressed concern that "this child has had no stability in his life, especially in foster care placements." It recommended that the judge order DCF to "pursue a more structured stable placement," such as a therapeutic foster home, where he could get more help with his behavior problems, and to enroll him in Outward Bound. The judge issued those orders, but by the next review in September 1999, neither had been accomplished, and Alfonso was back in detention.

By his midteens, Alfonso had stopped praying to get his own family back. Instead, he says, each time he changed foster families, "I prayed that I could stay there for good."

"Beware of Alligators"

In November 2000, Alfonso, then fifteen, was caught stealing a car for the fifth time, and the juvenile justice system came down hard on him. Police had arrested Alfonso at least fifteen times previously, with the charges ranging from trespassing to resisting arrest to vehicle theft, but he had usually been placed on probation or moved from a foster home to a group home for delinquents, which didn't seem much different to him than the foster homes in which he had lived. This time, a judge committed him to a Level 8 state juvenile facility—the level just below maximum security—for an indeterminate period.

Alfonso spent six months in detention waiting for an opening in a Level 8 program. In May 2001, the Florida Department of Juvenile Services sent him to a boot camp-like facility for serious or chronic male offenders—the Everglades Youth Development Center, which is operated for the state by Ramsay Youth Services, a privately owned company, just outside Florida City, Florida.

Alfonso spent fourteen months there, during what should have been his sophomore year of high school. "It's a place I don't recommend anyone to go to, swear to God," he says of Everglades. "It's out in the middle of nowhere, down a long dirt road, and there's a little sign when you first get there that says, 'Beware of Alligators.' Sometimes, we'd even see cougars in the parking lot. There are these fences twelve feet high, with three or four feet of razor wire on top. And man, oh man, is it humid."

Alfonso, who is proud of never having committed a violent crime, says he was thrown in with youths who had committed violent felonies. "There were kids in there for kidnapping, and even one or two for murder," he says. "They were all around me."

A typical weekday began at 5:30 A.M. and ended at 8 P.M., with the hours in between devoted to schoolwork, quasi-military training, and instruction in construction skills. In his spare time, Alfonso drew and wrote poetry.

Every day, the young men also participated in group therapy sessions. "There would be eight or nine of us in the group, and the counselor would go around asking each of us, 'What's your name? How old are you? What kind of crime did you commit?'" he explains. "Then after that she'd go back around and ask why you did it. I'd tell her that I felt I was forced to because I was in the system. In my whole life, I had nothing to look back at and feel good about. The only thing I ever accomplished was to steal some cars and make a lot of money."

Because he never carried a weapon and never confronted his victims personally, Alfonso told himself that his crimes were victimless. "I never was the type of person who would hurt someone physically," he says. "I would never snatch a chain from around someone's neck or take a purse from a lady or break into someone's house while they were there. I never did assault and battery or home invasion. Grand theft auto, yes."

He says he committed crimes partly for the thrill, partly out of need, and partly out of anger at the foster care system. "They were my legal guardians and I wasn't getting anything from them or the people they were putting me with—no allowance, no clothes, and hardly any food," he said. "I thought, 'I can't stand this any more. I'll get my own money.' And I would."

Although Alfonso felt he was simply biding time at Everglades, his academic records indicate that for the first time in his schooling, he was earning As and Bs. "I got good grades at Everglades because I was forced to go to school," he says. "I'm real smart when I get down to it."

And Alfonso grudgingly acknowledges that his enforced removal from the streets was probably a good thing. "While I was there, I had a friend who got hit by a car when she was trying to steal a car, and she died," he says. "She was only like fourteen or fifteen. And I had another friend who would rob people's houses while they were in them. Who knows? If I hadn't have been sent away, I might have progressed to more serious crimes or even died."

All in all, however, he describes his stay at Everglades as a period of extreme loneliness. No one visited him besides caseworkers from DCF, a different one each month. "And I didn't talk to anyone on the phone except my one friend," he says. "They weren't supposed to let me call a friend, but some of the staff felt sorry for me because I didn't have any family to call."

"Five or Six Women . . . I called Mama"

When Alfonso completed the program at Everglades in July 2002, he was placed on probation and sent to a group home in Homestead. He attended classes at Dade Marine Institute, an aftercare program for delinquent youth.

Within a week, he was taken into custody again, this time for burglary, and he spent three weeks at the detention center. When he was released, he couldn't get back into the group home, so he was sent back to Miami Bridge, the emergency shelter.

Because Alfonso had already spent so much time there, Miami Bridge was the closest thing to home that he'd had since he was ten. "To me, it was a pretty good place," he said. "It never got my hopes down. It was like my family. I cared for them, and they cared for me. There were five or six women in there I called Mama."

But within three weeks of returning to Miami Bridge, Alfonso was in trouble again, this time for kicking a police car. He spent three weeks in detention before the charges were dropped.

While he was in detention, Miami-Dade County's Citizen Review Panel convened for its final review of his case. One of the saddest entries in his file is a social worker's comment in response to a question about the significant relationships in Alfonso's life: "There are no known significant relationships in Alfonso's life," the caseworker wrote.

At the review, the panel urged DCF to find Alfonso a more suitable home than an emergency shelter for his final months in foster care. The panel also expressed concern over Alfonso's lack of preparation for independent living. A representative of DCF countered that Alfonso didn't want its assistance with preparation for independent living, and furthermore, his delinquency record made him ineligible for the agency's independent living program. (At the time, department policy required that a youth be free of arrests for six months to qualify for independent living services.)

By the time Alfonso got out of detention, DCF still hadn't found him a foster home, so he was sent back to Miami Bridge.

This time, more than a month passed without incident. "Then a girl and me stole a car," he admits. Alfonso was taken back to the detention center again. It was December 9, 2002, two weeks before his eighteenth birthday and the end of his eligibility for foster care.

"Oh, Man, I Was Scared"

Through his teens, Alfonso had spent just about as much time at the detention center as at Miami Bridge, so it, too, felt like home. He had never really minded being sent there—until this time.

"Oh, man, I was scared," he said. "I was about to turn eighteen, and I didn't know where I was going after I left there. I knew I didn't have anyone to depend on. Nobody cared about what was going to happen to me. I was afraid I'd end up in prison, where I might get raped."

In a previous stay at the detention center, Alfonso had become close to a volunteer named Eddie Williams, who came twice weekly to counsel youths and read the Bible with them. "As soon as I met Alfonso I could see that he stood out," says Williams, who has been volunteering at the detention center since 1995. "He had a winning personality. And he was respectful and soft-spoken."

Williams met with Alfonso and told him he was disappointed to see him back in detention. "I sat down with him and said to him, 'You have all the signs of a kid who has got it together,'" Williams recalls. "'You're decent. You're kind. You're smart. I don't understand. Why are you back here?'"

For the first time in their relationship, Alfonso told Williams his life story, or what he knew of it anyway. The death of his twin at birth. His mother's drug abuse. The beatings by his father. His odyssey through foster care. And finally, his fears about his future. "He said to me, 'Mr. Williams, when I leave here, I have no place to go,'" Williams recalls. "'I'm afraid.'"

During their next few visits together, Williams tried to strengthen Alfonso's self-confidence and his faith in God. "I told him I was proud of how he was studying the Word and seeking to apply it," Williams remembers. "I told him he was a good kid, an extraordinary human being. He'd been kicked around and beat up pretty good, but I told him I knew he was going to come out OK."

Alfonso listened, but Williams' words didn't allay his fears. "The pastor was telling me, 'Don't fear anything. Put God first, and don't have any doubt, because God is not a worrying person,'" Alfonso recalls. "And I was like, 'There can't be a God if I'm going through all this.'"

A System in Flux

In the years leading up to emancipation of youth from foster care, the agency that holds legal custody is supposed to help them gain the skills to make it on their own.

A model foster care system begins training these young people in independent living skills soon after they enter adolescence, providing instruction on money management, homemaking, personal hygiene, nutrition, and family planning, and, in the best of cases, giving them opportunities to practice what they've learned. A General Accounting Office (GAO) study of independent living programs in 1999 found evidence of improved outcomes for young people who received independent living services like these.[1] But in Florida in 2002, more than half of teens in foster care were receiving no training in independent living skills before being discharged.[2] Alfonso was among the unlucky majority.

One of the problems was that while Alfonso was moving through his teens, he was sometimes in the custody of the Department of Children and Families and sometimes in the custody of the Department of Juvenile Justice. It was easy for his caseworker at one agency to assume that his caseworker at the other was preparing him for life on his own. This is a problem for many older teens in foster care. In the parlance of social service workers, they are "dual jurisdiction," "cross over," or "overlap kids"— on the one hand, foster children, and on the other, juvenile offenders.[3]

Another complicating factor for Alfonso was that in the months leading up to his eighteenth birthday, Florida's approach to transition services was in flux. Less than two months before Alfonso's birthday, Governor Jeb Bush signed the Road to Independence Act, a wholesale revision of the state's independent living program.

State officials portray the Road to Independence Act as a huge improvement over the state's old approach to transition. The 2002 law mandates that transition services be provided beginning at age thirteen (three years earlier than they were offered before). It also provides generous stipends for living expenses, plus Medicaid coverage, for emancipated youth who are in school and maintaining GPAs of at least 2.0. And to help avert homelessness for those who aren't either eligible for or interested in education assistance, the law for the first time authorizes aftercare services for youth age eighteen to twenty-one, including cash assistance of up to $1,000.[4] State officials argue that the law will improve outcomes for the 4,200 or so Florida youth age thirteen through seventeen who are heading toward emancipation at any given time, and a nearly equal number of youth age eighteen through twenty-two who have aged out of care.

However, critics of the new law derisively call it the "Road to Homelessness Act." They are especially concerned about the impact on former foster youth with mental health disorders or learning disabilities and those who, like Alfonso, haven't yet finished high school before they turn eighteen. They predict that for these young people, the law will actually increase homelessness and incarceration. Florida's Children First, an advocacy organization of children's rights attorneys, is trying to persuade the legislature to amend the law to permit children with disabilities to receive foster care subsidies until age twenty-three, as they could elect to before the law changed.[5]

Although prohibited by law from commenting on a specific case, a state official said that the Road to Independence Act provided more options for someone with Alfonso's background and capabilities than Florida's previous law did. "Under the old law, unless he went to school, there was no program established and no financial support past eighteen," she said. "Based upon the availability of funds, we might have provided money to pay a light bill, or maybe a referral to an employment program, but it was at our discretion. And we certainly didn't have money to use to help him avoid homelessness, as we do now."

Regardless of whether Alfonso would have been better off under the old law or the new law, there's little doubt that in the months before and after the new law took effect, many older teens in foster care were confused about what their options were. Some workers were still applying the old rules, and others the new. Florida newspapers were full of stories about the confusion. The information Alfonso remembers getting was clearly based on the old law. "One of my workers told me that before I could get into independent living, I had to have six months of maintaining a job or progressing in school with a C average, and no arrests," he recalls. "And then after that sixth month passed, I would be eligible for some money to help me. But she expected me to find a job, and a place to stay, on my own."

"People . . . Never Follow Up"

On December 21, 2002, with three days remaining until the end of his eligibility for foster care, a DCF caseworker, Paul Christian,[6] came to the detention center to visit Alfonso. He was relatively new to Alfonso's case; Alfonso says they had only talked once before.

"I asked him, 'What about getting into independent living?'" Alfonso says. "And he told me, 'It's too late for that.'"

But there was another possibility, Christian added. He told Alfonso that a woman who had adopted his two younger brothers wanted to help him. She even seemed willing to let Alfonso live with her, the caseworker said.

At first, Alfonso didn't understand what Christian was saying. "He kept talking about some lady who had adopted my brothers, when I didn't even know I had any brothers, except my half-brother," Alfonso recalls. "I said, 'Hey, man, stop playing with me.'"

When the caseworker told him he was serious, Alfonso lapsed into denial. "I wanted to believe it, but I couldn't," he said. "I kept thinking to myself, 'It's not true, it's not true. My sister died at birth. I'm an only child.'" Alfonso simply couldn't let himself hope. "All my life, I'd been getting my hopes up and then being disappointed," he said. "People keep promising me things and never follow up."

The woman was Marilyn Dillon of Pembroke Pines, Florida, a fifty-four-year-old paralegal and divorced mother of an adult daughter and two adopted sons. She had known of Alfonso's existence since 1988 when she glimpsed him as a three-year-old during the court proceeding in which she became the foster mother to his five-month-old brother, Sam. A year later, she saw Alfonso again when she became a foster mother to another brother, Michael, then four months old.

Years later, as Dillon's boys were approaching their teens, she began wondering about Alfonso's whereabouts. She decided to look for him in case her boys wanted to meet him some day. A friend with state connections found out the name of his caseworker, and Dillon called her.

"She said, 'I'm really not supposed to talk to you, but yes, he's one of my cases,'" Dillon recalls. "Then she asked me, 'Are you interested in taking him, too? You should know that he's been in and out of trouble.'"

"I said, 'No, I just want to try to keep track of him so that if the kids want to meet when they're older they can.' I also told her that maybe it would be good for him to know he has brothers, maybe it would change his life. I was thinking that maybe one reason this boy has been troubled was because he had no idea what happened to his siblings."

The caseworker promised to think about the situation and call Dillon back. "And then she never did," Dillon says. "I called again and couldn't get her, and then I have to admit I just let it drop. I was pretty busy with my boys."

A year or so later, Dillon tried again. Once again, her inquiries led nowhere.

And then, in November 2002, Dillon happened to watch a television show about the problems that many youth face when they age out of foster care. The program upset her greatly. She remembers thinking, "'Alfonso's going to be eighteen soon. He might come out and have a terrible life. Maybe I can help. At the very least, since I'm a paralegal, I can make sure that he has due process and that he gets into a program for youth who are leaving foster care. And I can also help him to psychologically connect with his family.' So I started calling again."

Alfonso's old worker told her she no longer had his case and gave her Paul Christian's name. "When I finally got him, he said that he didn't know anything about Alfonso, that he had just gotten the case," Dillon says. "But apparently, because of my call, the next day he went to see Alfonso."

"We Want to Help You"

After telling Alfonso about Dillon, Christian called her to report that Alfonso doubted that he was the person she thought he was. She decided to go to the detention center to meet him. However, because she wasn't a relative, she wasn't allowed to see him. Instead, she dashed off a letter, enclosed a picture of herself and his brothers, and gave it to Christian to deliver to him.

"Alfonso," the letter began. "So sorry I did not get to talk to you today. I want to see you very, very much. I am the lady who adopted your two brothers when they were babies. We want to help you get a better future. Please make your best effort to put the past behind you and look to the future with hope. We care about you. And God loves you very much."

Alfonso stared at the picture for hours, searching for a resemblance between himself and the two boys who were said to be his brothers. "I thought, 'This is crazy, man,'" he recalls. "I really didn't know what else to think. Everybody else who was in jail with me had pictures of their families on the wall beside their beds, but I didn't want to put the picture on my wall because I was afraid they weren't my real brothers."

Over the next week, Eddie Williams, the detention center volunteer, tried to help Alfonso process the news that he had brothers and that a woman he had never even met wanted to help him. "He pulls bad thoughts out of my brain and puts the right thoughts into it," Alfonso says of Williams. "He told me, 'Even though she's not your real mother, she's accepting you. You're going to a family now.'

"And so I started thinking, 'Well, maybe it is true,' which would make me happy, because it would mean that I had a family. All my life, I had prayed for a family. But then I'd get afraid that if they really were my real brothers, they wouldn't accept me because I was in jail."

Dillon had not actually told anyone that she was willing to take Alfonso home with her, but both Williams and Christian suggested to Alfonso that she was. For that reason, over the next few days Alfonso started to think that he was going to live with Dillon and his brothers after he was released from detention.

"This lady sounded like an angel from heaven," he said. "She had taken it into her heart to adopt my two brothers, and then somehow find me in time and offer to take care of me. I thought, 'Well I'm going to give it a try.' I knew it was my only chance to break from the streets."

"This Is Meant by God"

On December 30, Dillon received a message on her cell phone from an attorney for DCF. "She said, 'There's a hearing today, and he probably is going to be released, and he has nowhere to go,'" Dillon recalls. "'I'm going to suggest that he be kept on another night until you get here and can pick him up.'"

Dillon had planned only to arrange a meeting between her boys and Alfonso and then help Alfonso access Florida's transition benefits. But after the call from the attorney, she felt she had no option other than to take him home for a few days. "When I saw that he was just going to be thrown out on the streets with no help, and not even an ID card, I thought, 'I've got to do something. He is the brother, and, after all, I looked for him,'" she recalls.

"I was a little worried about taking him home, because of all the trouble he'd been in. Other people told me, 'Don't let him in your house. Just give him $100, or pay the first month's rent.' But I didn't think it was right to find him and let him go like that on New Year's Eve. I kept thinking about what my boys would think if they knew I had let their brother go from jail to a shelter."

In midafternoon on New Year's Eve, Dillon went to the detention center. Alfonso was summoned. "She was in the waiting room when they brought me out," he recalls. "I had to sign some papers, and then I walked over to her. I was going to give her a handshake, but then I said to myself, 'No, man, this is meant by God,' and I gave her a hug and called her 'Mom.' Everyone is afraid of rejection, of being abandoned, so I knew I was taking a chance. But it was a good feeling, man. She was my savior. I owed her."

On the drive home, Alfonso peppered her with questions. "I was asking her questions to see if she really had the right person," Alfonso admits. "I still didn't believe that I had two brothers. But she knew my parents' names, and when I was separated from them, and where I had lived, so I started realizing it really was me she was looking for. She had the right Alfonso."

When they arrived at Dillon's house in Pembroke Pines, a suburb of Fort Lauderdale, Alfonso met his brothers for the first time. "I just flipped," Alfonso says. "I could see a resemblance, especially in Sam. He looks like me, and he dresses like me, and he's got the same personality. It was cool."

Dillon remembers thinking that she'd done the right thing. "They all hugged, and for the rest of the evening, they couldn't take their eyes off of each other," she said. "It was amazing to me how they felt like brothers right away."

"Don't Make Me Go"

The next few days were like a party without end. Friends and neighbors came to meet the "long-lost brother." Alfonso pored over childhood photographs of his brothers, as if to find a place for himself in their lives. And the conversations lasted late into the nights. "Every night was like a sleepover," Dillon said.

Since Alfonso had lived for four years with the parents from whom Mike and Sam had been taken as infants, they questioned Alfonso about what they were like. Alfonso's recollections of their mother were vague, more impressions than actual memories. But he was able to clarify their ethnic heritage: Their mother was white, he told them, and their father was Puerto Rican.

Meanwhile, with the winter school holiday—and Dillon's time off from work—almost over, Dillon decided that Alfonso needed to move on. Her friends' warnings kept coming back to her. "My boys have led a very sheltered life," she confided. "I was worried about what he might expose them to."

A few days into the new year, Dillon sat down with Alfonso and broached the subject of his future. "Where are you going to go next?" she asked him.

Alfonso seemed perplexed by the question. His caseworker had told him that he could live with her, he told her.

Dillon told Alfonso that she didn't have enough space to let him live there for the long term. Her adult daughter and her husband and six-year-old son were living in her home, making the three-bedroom house seem smaller than it actually was. (Alfonso was sleeping on a mattress on the family room floor.) "I never told your social worker that I was planning to keep you," she explained to Alfonso. "You can stay here for a few days, but we have to come up with another plan."

Dillon suggested that they check out Covenant House, a 104-bed shelter in a converted motel just a block from Fort Lauderdale's famed beach. Covenant House is a national faith-based organization that helps homeless and runaway youth. Dillon had heard about it from the director of Miami Bridge.

Alfonso didn't want to look at it, but he agreed to just to please Dillon. Dillon drove him there and sat in on an orientation session. She came away impressed by the array of services that Covenant House offered—counseling, case management, drug treatment, GED preparation, job-search and transportation assistance, and even subsidized apartments for older teens. And she had learned that many of the residents had, like Alfonso, recently aged out of foster care. It seemed to her like a place where Alfonso could get more help than she could provide.

Alfonso told her that Covenant House seemed too much like foster care and that he'd rather stay with her. "I've lived in shelters for the last few years," he told her. "I don't want to live in a shelter again. Don't make me go. I want to be with my brothers." Sam and Mike also begged their mother to let him stay.

Dillon let the subject drop for a few days, and then brought it up again. This time, she told Alfonso that he had to move into Covenant House the following day.

"I was upset, because I thought someone else was letting me down," Alfonso says. "But she told me, 'No matter where you are, we're going to be there for you.'"

"It Hurts"

Alfonso moved into Covenant House on January 6. Every day for the next week, he called Dillon, each time pleading to be allowed to return to their home. "Now that I've found my brothers, I want to be with them," he told Dillon. "I'm tired of talking to them over the phone, because it hurts. I want to see them and be with them."

"You've got to give Covenant House a chance," Dillon urged. "Give it a month."

Alfonso didn't want to give Covenant House a chance. "I knew they were trying to help me there, but I didn't want to be there," he acknowledges. "I felt like I'd finally found a family, but I was still separated from them. It made me sad."

After eight days of pleading, Alfonso wore down Dillon's resolve. By this time, Dillon's daughter and her family had moved out, freeing a bedroom, and Dillon had lost her excuse. In addition, her boys were pressuring her to let Alfonso move back in. "I decided to let him come back and see how it worked out," she says. "I just couldn't be mean to him like everybody else in his life."

Dillon did set some ground rules for his return. Alfonso would have to take on some household chores and agree to a curfew. He would have to attend night school to prepare for the GED test. He would have to get a part-time job. He couldn't have friends over while she wasn't home. And he would have to apply for any transition benefits that the DCF offered.

"And I told him that if he ever committed a crime while he was living with me, he would never see his brothers again," Dillon added.

"It's Going Well"

Back in Dillon's home, Alfonso moved into the bedroom that Dillon's daughter had vacated, happily sharing it with his youngest brother, Sam, who is fourteen. Alfonso threw himself into the role of big brother.

"I really want to help Mike and Sam, because I don't want them to go through what I did," he said. "I don't want them to follow my path. And I want them to look at me and think, 'I can depend on him.' I want them to know that I'll always be in their lives."

The three brothers seemed to get along really well. They traded clothes and CDs, and often went to a neighborhood park to shoot some baskets or just hang out together. Despite the age difference, Sam and Mike's friends became Alfonso's friends. Evenings were filled with roughhousing and good-natured bantering. "He's a really nice boy to have around," Dillon said of Alfonso in early February. "And it's been really great for the boys to get to know each other."

But as days passed without Alfonso making any apparent progress toward two of the goals she and he had jointly set—to enroll in GED preparation classes and find a job—Dillon began getting impatient. She nagged and prodded, and still nothing happened. Finally, she realized that Alfonso didn't really know how to do what he needed to do to get on with his life.

For one thing, he had been discharged from foster care without any identification, a necessity for enrolling in school and applying for jobs. She took him to obtain a copy of his birth certificate and found out for him how he could use that to apply for a Florida ID and a Social Security card.

Dillon also identified the nearest GED preparation class—at a school about six miles from her house—and helped him enroll. A placement test showed that he read at the eleventh-grade level and understood math at the tenth-grade level, but his grasp of language was at the level of a fourth grader. Even so, the GED prep teacher assured her that if Alfonso spent twenty hours a week in preparation classes, he would probably be able to pass the GED test in four months. As an incentive to finish quickly, Dillon promised to take him on a family vacation if he received his GED by June, and her daughter promised to throw a "graduation" party for him.

Dillon also badgered DCF to find out what transition benefits Alfonso might qualify for. She learned about the new payment of up to $1,000 that Florida was offering youths to avert homelessness and helped him apply for it. He opted to take it in four monthly installments of $250 each, and to pay her $150 a month for room and board.

And finally, Dillon made an appointment for Alfonso to talk with an attorney about how he could qualify for the state's premier transition benefit—the Road to Independence Scholarship—which would provide him with $892 a month as long as he was working on his GED or attending college (and doing well). Based on his academic background, Alfonso wasn't a prime candidate for higher education. But since becoming a full-time student was the only way to receive further assistance from the state, Dillon thought he should try.

"At times, it's tough," Dillon said, a month into Alfonso's stay with her. "I would like him to be a little more aggressive in his job search. I see hesitation about taking low-level jobs. All four of us were talking about what he would make as a stock boy at a grocery store. To the other kids, it sounded like a lot of money. But to him, it was nothing, because he had gotten easy money in the past, stealing cars."

Alfonso agreed that there had been some difficult moments adjusting to life in a family. "At first, it was hard to adjust to living with a family again," he admitted. "I wasn't raised knowing about house skills. And I was really worried about what they thought of me, since Mom's first impression of me was when I was in jail.

"But as time has gone by, it's going well. She says she's proud of me. And I still think of her as my savior."

Stumbling Blocks

It is early March 2003, just over two months after Alfonso came to live in Dillon's home. He's been attending the GED preparation class for five weeks now—sort of. Sometimes he goes, and sometimes he doesn't. He has to bicycle six miles each way to get to class. And "it's independent study, which means you've got to teach yourself," he says. "It's kind of hard to stay focused when you have no one to help you. It's pretty boring."

Although he says he's spent a lot of time looking for a job, he's had no success. "I've put in thirty or forty applications, and so far I had one interview with Wal-Mart and another one with a pizza place," he laments. "They were like, 'What do you do?' I was like, 'What do you mean?' And they said, 'Do you still attend school?' And I told them, 'I go to night school.' And then they said, 'Well, we'll give you a call,' but they never did."

Fortunately, Alfonso doesn't have to disclose his juvenile record when he applies for work. But his lack of previous experience is surely a strike against him. Most eighteen-year-olds who are applying for jobs have worked part-time jobs during high school; Alfonso couldn't, because he was usually locked up or living in a shelter. "I've never had a legitimate job," he admits. "When they ask about experience, I don't have anything to tell them about."

His appearance may also give prospective employers pause. He's applying for jobs in a middle-class suburb of Broward County, but with his mustache and goatee and his penchant for hip-hop clothes, he looks like a streetwise kid from Miami. When he went job hunting yesterday, he wore a tight black muscle shirt, a couple of neck chains, and baggy black jeans. And he had a friend in tow—a heavily made-up fifteen-year-old girl who was dressed like a "gangsta girlfriend" and clearly skipping school.

Today, Alfonso is taking a break from his job search to meet with his attorney, Bernard P. Perlmutter, director of the Children and Youth Law Clinic at the University of Miami, and to sign his application for a Road to Independence Scholarship.

Perlmutter believes passionately in the rights of children in foster care to assistance in their transition to adulthood, and since the Road to Independence Act became law in October 2002, he has been one of its harshest critics. He and his colleagues are already representing about a dozen recently emancipated youth who are seeking state help.

"So, am I going to get this Road to Independence Scholarship?" Alfonso asks Perlmutter as he settles into a chair in his office, which is piled high with case files.

"To be honest, after rereading the law several times, I'm more confused than ever, and I'm a lawyer," Perlmutter says. "I can't understand what the intent was except to make it as confusing and difficult as possible to stand on your own feet as you transition to adulthood. I think there are some good things to the legislation, but they mainly help kids who are thirteen and still in the system."

Even so, Perlmutter tells Alfonso that he's going to do his best to help him qualify for what he calls "the Cadillac program"—the $892 monthly stipends for full-time, high-achieving students. Based on the experience of his other clients, he warns, the stipend will be tough to get. Applicants who are still in school must show a 2.0 GPA for the two semesters preceding their eighteenth birthdays. And those who, like Alfonso, are enrolled in GED preparation programs must have someone certify that they are "making satisfactory progress."

"Once you complete the GED, which I'm confident you'll do, then you'll have the option to enroll in a college program or a vocational program that suits your own needs," Perlmutter says. "In theory, you should be able to sign up for community college and attend tuition-free. The

Road to Independence Scholarship would be over and above any tuition benefits available to you."

But Perlmutter goes on to warn Alfonso that even if he qualifies for the Road to Independence Scholarship, the program is not an entitlement. That means that "if DCF runs out of money in the middle of the year, the scholarship will stop, and you'll be out of luck," he explains. The Florida legislature probably hasn't appropriated enough money to meet the demand, he warns. "The money will be spent by the middle of the budget year, thereby leaving deserving young people like you without a safety net," he predicts. (DCF officials admit to being worried about how little money they have. "I don't really think it's going to go that far," June Noel, assistant director of family safety programs for DCF, told a reporter for the *Tallahassee Democrat* in February 2003. "It's just a drop in the bucket.")[7]

On his application for the scholarship, Alfonso has indicated that he plans to obtain his GED and then "enroll in a post-secondary institution to obtain a degree in architecture." He's always liked to draw, he tells Perlmutter, which is why he thinks architecture might be a good career. "Art, that's me," he says. "I love to draw."

After reviewing Alfonso's application, Perlmutter pronounces it ready to submit, except for two things. He needs DCF to certify that Alfonso had been in foster care, and the agency says it can't find his records. Also, Alfonso needs to decide how he wants the scholarship money distributed, if he qualifies. "Basically, you've got three options," Perlmutter explains. "You can have all the money sent to someone like Marilyn [Dillon], who agrees to spend it wisely in your behalf. Or you can have it split between you and her. Or you can get all the money and spend it wisely in your own behalf."

Hearing the last option, Alfonso pulls out a piece of paper that he's been carrying in his wallet for a few weeks. It's an ad for a 1994 Nissan Maxima with a sale price of $3,980. "I've been doing a lot of research on cars," Alfonso says. "I think if I got a car it would solve many of my problems. So I'd like to have all the scholarship money sent to me so I can use it to buy a car."

Perlmutter guides him gently in a different direction. Noting that Alfonso doesn't have a bank account, he says, "My recommendation would be for the money to be paid to Marilyn. You and she can work out how much of this stipend you'll use for housing, and how much you can set aside for a car and insurance. You're really, really fortunate to have someone like her watching out for your interests. It's very unusual. But don't let me force you. I want you to make the choice."

Alfonso agrees, though reluctantly, to go along with Perlmutter's recommendation. The meeting ends with a handshake. "I'm just glad I've got someone like you who's helping me," Alfonso tells him.

"Trying Hard"

Back at Dillon's house, Alfonso ruminates about the challenges ahead of him.

Perlmutter's comments about the Road to Independence Scholarship have left him thinking that the scholarship may not be coming his way anytime soon, if at all. And even if he does get it, he realizes that it will be hard to hang on to, given his spotty preparation for higher education and the requirement for good grades.

The preparation work for the GED test is proving to be more tedious than he expected, he admits. It seems unlikely that he'll earn his GED by June.

And his job search has been completely discouraging. Without a job, he has little pocket money, and he also has very little to occupy his time. He's been spending his days hanging out with younger teens who are playing hooky from school. (Although Dillon doesn't know it yet, Alfonso has been letting them hang out at her house while she's at work. With their cigarette butts littering her patio, it's just a matter of time until she figures it out.)

Recently, too, there have been some flare-ups in the household that have driven home the tenuousness of his presence there. Dillon calls him from work several times a day, which makes him feel like she's checking up on him. "Mom asks me a lot about what I'm doing with my time," he says. "Am I going to school? Looking for jobs? Putting forward effort to help the family, keep up the house, be a good role model to my brothers?"

Based upon past experience, Alfonso can't help but worry about getting thrown out. He had to worry about that every time he moved into a new foster home, so it's second nature. However, until he turned eighteen, he knew that he could always count on the state to find him another place to stay. "If I have to leave here, where do I go?" he asks. "I feel like this is where I need to be, so I'm trying hard not to make mistakes."

Alfonso can't quite figure out just what kind of relationship he's supposed to have with Marilyn Dillon. He makes a point of calling her "Mom" and would like to think of her as a mother figure, but he senses that she doesn't think of herself that way. "I don't feel that Mom trusts me all the way," he says. "But I can't blame her. It's not like she brought home an eleven-year-old. I'm an ex-con."

On the other hand, he says, he's not such a bad person. As though to persuade himself of his self-worth, he starts listing his strengths.

Many young people come out of foster care bitter and full of anger, but he's trusting and open, he notes. "I have good people skills, when I should be like Eeyore, in *Winnie the Pooh*, given what I've been through," he says. "I have a good sense of humor, which is pretty amazing.

"In a lot of ways, I'm better off than some other eighteen-year-olds. There are some who can't read and write. At least I can do that. And I understand what I came through, but I don't let it bring me down, not no more.

"Plus I have my faith in God. After all that I've been through, no one else could have got me through except God. I know that he has plans for me. He's going to help me be what I want to be. Now that I've got my basic needs met, I'm ready to move forward."

For the moment anyway, he sounds convinced.

"You're on Probation"

Alfonso's stay at Dillon's house came to an end on April 6, 2003, just over three months after he'd arrived.

Both Alfonso and Dillon trace the beginning of the end to his arrest on March 9 for giving a false age to a police officer who questioned him about vandalism in a neighborhood park. He spent a night in jail, and later pleaded no contest to the charge.

The arrest crystallized Dillon's concerns about Alfonso's influence on her sons, who had been with him at the park. When Alfonso came home from jail, Dillon confronted him about his poor attendance at the GED prep class, evidence that he was entertaining while she was at work, and her suspicion that he was regularly sneaking out of the house in the middle of the night. She gave him an ultimatum: admit what he'd done and agree to abide by her rules in the future, or leave.

Alfonso admitted to the infractions and begged for another chance. She told him that he could stay for now, but that she would reevaluate her decision weekly. "As far as I'm concerned, you're on probation," she told him.

Privately, Alfonso complained that Dillon was too hard on him. He hadn't understood that he wasn't supposed to entertain his friends when she wasn't home, he claimed. And why was skipping a few sessions of GED prep class such a big deal? He complained of feeling like a scape-goat for any problem in the Dillon household.

"She brought me here, and I'm trying to let her know I'm thankful, but it's hard," he said. "She thinks I'm a bad influence on my brothers because I've done some bad things in the past. She thinks it's because of me that they're doing bad in school. She says it's my fault they stay up late. She says it's my fault that they don't pray before they go to bed at night. She thinks I'm the devil and leading them to hell.

"I'm so frustrated, man. I'm getting tired of it. I'm starting not to care about anything. Yeah, I do make mistakes, but so do my brothers, and she doesn't want to kick them out of the house. Maybe I'll just have to go back to a life of crime."

Shortly before dawn on April 6, Dillon got up to let her cat out and noticed that none of the boys were in bed. It was the final straw. She went looking for them. And when she found them, she told Alfonso: "I don't want you in my house anymore."

Later that day, Dillon gave Alfonso $50 and offered to drive him to Covenant House. He refused her offer. Instead, he asked the parents of a sixteen-year-old girl who had befriended him if he could stay there. The couple agreed to let him live with them until he obtained a GED.

Theresa Salazar's mother operated an emergency foster home while she was growing up, and as a result, Salazar said, she had "something inside of my heart" for youth like Alfonso. "My husband and I are trying to do the best we can do for the kid," she said. "The priority is his GED. I can monitor him and make sure he gets back and forth to his schooling, and my husband's willing to help him get a job. It'll work out as long as he stays in line."

In retrospect, Dillon says she's glad she tried to help "because he can't say nobody tried. But I wish I had never allowed him into my home. I never really intended to, but I didn't know how to say no. I should have made him stay at Covenant House while we got to know him. I hope he can realize his mistakes one of these days and be truthful with himself so that he can succeed at something other than just surviving."

She can't help but wonder how different his life might have been had she taken him into her home years before. "After going without love for so long, I think it might be too late for him to trust and take advice from others," she said.

Alfonso feels a mixture of sadness and anger about how his stay in Dillon's home ended. "I was depressed at first," he says. "I was planning to stay there forever, and live happily every after. And then boom, she threw me out.

"I made mistakes, and for them I said I was sorry. But the mistakes I made weren't really serious. It wasn't like I stabbed someone. I was skipping school or coming home late. I'm coming from foster care. I have no experience with real family life, and Marilyn didn't really take that into account.

"But she tried to help me, and I appreciate that. I owe her the world for giving me a place to stay when I got out of foster care."

The hardest thing about being forced to leave, Alfonso said, was realizing that Dillon "didn't think of me as family."

"When we were arguing, I asked her, 'Since I've been here in your home, have you ever looked upon me as a son?' And she didn't answer.

That hurts me the most, that I know now that she didn't look at me as a son. Yet I'm Sam and Michael's brother, and she looks at them as sons, even though they're not her real sons. Even with all that's happened to me in my life, I hardly ever cry. But that day that she said that, I was crying."

"I'm sorry it ended the way it did, but I kind of got over it. I learn from my mistakes. This has made me stronger. I'm better prepared for life. I realize that nothing's free. Everything you get you have to really work hard for.

"So, I'm moving on. The family I'm living with is kind. Their kids are all doing good. Just being around them, you can tell that they're a happy family.

"They think I'm a good kid. They set goals for me, and I plan to achieve them. They want me to get my life straight, and that's what I want, too."

Postscript

As she'd promised, Theresa Salazar drove Alfonso to his GED preparation course every day, and by June, his scores on the practice tests indicated that he was likely to pass the real thing. Salazar found him a place to take the test in August so that he could enter Broward County Community College later in the month.

In April 2003, and again in June, Alfonso was arrested for shoplifting. He told the Salazars that he was innocent and was being harassed by the Pembroke Pines police, but pleaded no contest to the April and June charges. (He initially sought a jury trial on the May charge, but eventually agreed to a plea.) The couple stuck by him, even lending him money for his court costs and fines.

In late June, almost seven months after he had aged out of care, the Department of Children and Families approved his application for a Road to Independence Scholarship. DCF also gave him a $1,000 check for start-up costs—the first and last month's rent—a voucher for $139 in food stamps, a new set of bedroom furniture, and some pots and pans.

Theresa Salazar helped him rent a bedroom in a shared condominium unit close to the community college. In early July, Alfonso moved in. With his rent at $450 a month, including utilities, that left him almost the same amount for his other expenses.

Salazar ran an ad in a local newspaper soliciting donations of household items for him, and between the donations and her own family's castoffs, she equipped him with a TV and VCR, a bicycle, various kitchen appliances, a vacuum, a fan, a phone, and some lights. She also filled out and filed his application for a Pell grant, the federally financed educational grant for low-income students.

In an interview soon after he moved into the condo, Alfonso sounded upbeat. "I have my own place for the first time in my life," he said. But he admitted to being bored and frustrated by his inability to find a job. And he suggested that he was finding it hard to resist the temptation to commit crimes. "I've been living my life doing this," he said. "I know what to do and when to do it. It's all I know how to do."

However, he said he knew he couldn't continue in his old ways if he wanted to move forward in life. "Now I've slowed down, and I'm coming to a stop," he said. "I have no excuse for continuing, because I have someone helping me. I'm not going to mess up. It's all on me."

On August 2, he was arrested again on suspicion of breaking into a car. He spent three days in jail before being released on his own recognizance on a reduced charge of trespassing. (He claims he was falsely accused.) A week later, he was arrested on ten counts ranging from petty theft to felony burglary. Alfonso's roommate was upset about the arrests and threatened to evict him, backing off only after Perlmutter intervened.

The nearly back-to-back arrests clearly unnerved Alfonso, who started worrying about where he could live if he got thrown out. "I'm worried that I'm repeating myself," he said. "I remember when I was living with Marilyn, I thought it was all going to work out, and then the next thing you know, boom, my whole world fell apart."

Classes started at Broward County Community College on August 23. Although just the week before he had talked excitedly about the courses he planned to take, he failed to enroll. The main reason was that

he had missed the appointment for his GED test, a condition for enroll-
ment. He'd also failed to follow through on the Pell grant application that
Salazar had filed for him. And though he'd put $105 aside from his sec-
ond Road to Independence Scholarship check to pay the tuition, he
claims he lost the money. He seemed oblivious to the likelihood that failing to attend school would jeopardize his Road to Independence Scholarship. Instead, he was worrying about a new problem: He owed his
roommate $200 because he'd accepted dozens of collect calls from a
friend, without realizing how expensive they would be. As a result, his
roommate had canceled their phone service and was again threatening
to evict him.

On the job front, there wasn't even a hint of promise. "They keep
telling me they can't hire me because I don't have any experience," he
said. "It's discouraging. But the good thing is I don't give up. I keep going
back and making them see my face again so they'll give me a job."

With no job to go to or classes to attend, Alfonso was spending his
days playing video games and shooting baskets with neighborhood kids,
most of them younger teens. He said he had run out of money for food
and was getting groceries from a local food pantry.

"I'm a Changed Man"

On the morning of September 14, a neighbor called Pembroke Pines
police to report a disturbance in Alfonso's condo. When police arrived,
Alfonso's roommate told them that the two had argued because Alfonso
had let three friends spend the night. Alfonso went for a walk to cool
off, and while he was gone, police searched his room. When he returned, he was arrested and charged with eleven crimes, ranging from
possession of stolen property to burglary. The police seized all of his belongings, except his furniture and clothing, as evidence. His arrest made
the Fort Lauderdale and Miami papers.

Alfonso spent six weeks in a Broward County jail before the charges
were dismissed because the police hadn't obtained a warrant for the
search. He was penniless when he was released on October 27 and set

out to walk the twenty miles to his home, finally hitching a ride on a bus. When he arrived at the condo, he found that the lock had been changed.

Alfonso was philosophical about his time in jail. "I look at it as payment for the crimes I got away with," he says. And the time was well spent, he says. He studied for the GED and listened to the advice the older inmates gave him.

"Jail is a lot different than juvenile, and I don't want to go back," he said in November. "You have to watch your back all the time. The people who were in there were facing big time, like thirty years, and they spilled their hearts out to me. They told me that if they had a chance to do things differently, they would. They were people like me, and I could see myself in their shoes a few years from now if I didn't change.

"I'm a changed man. I know I've said that before, but this time I am. I'm tired of living that life. I was being greedy, and not appreciating what I had. I was thinking that no one loved me, so why shouldn't I do what I knew how to do."

"But now I've seen what can happen, and I'm going to stop. There's only one person who can help me, and that's God. I don't know what's going to happen with me, but I know I'm going to make it. I know God's going to help me pull through."

About three weeks after his release, Alfonso was arrested on outstanding warrants. He spent about a month in jail before the charges were dropped. He got out on December 23, 2003, the day before his nineteenth birthday.

Over the next six weeks, he stayed with friends, and friends of friends. Because he had missed two appointments to take the GED test and never enrolled in college, DCF cancelled his Road to Independence Scholarship. He was checking in periodically with Theresa Salazar, who reported that he was depressed and spending his days hanging out with younger youth. He told Salazar that he felt he had no future in Broward County because of police harassment.

On February 3, 2004, he was arrested for providing a false ID to police, petty theft, and resisting a merchant. He spent three weeks in jail before someone he met there bailed him out.

He was out for only a day before being arrested again, this time for felony burglary, trespassing, and petty theft. Unable to post $1,000 bond, he spent eight weeks in jail before pleading no contest in return for a 120-day sentence, with credit for forty-two days of time served. He was released on May 24, 2004.

Theresa Salazar still holds out hope that Alfonso will decide to go straight and perhaps enlist in the military or sign up for Job Corps.

Marilyn Dillon is less optimistic. "I think it's too late for him to learn to trust people and take advice," she says.

Because he spent his teen years in group homes and juvenile detention facilities, Alfonso Torres says he never learned "house skills," including cooking and cleaning. Above, he listens to music in a room he rented briefly. Right, he plays in a pickup basketball game.

Raquel Tolston

"I NEVER WANT TO SLEEP ON THE STREET"

Raquel Tolston, San Francisco, California

Most people think of home as the place where they receive uncondi-tional love. By that definition, twenty-year-old Raquel Tolston has never had a real home.

For most of her childhood, home was the place where her mother beat her whenever she was in a bad mood. From an early age, Raquel pretty much took care of herself.

By Christmas 1993, when Raquel was twelve, the relationship be-tween her and her mother had deteriorated so much that child-protection officials placed her in foster care. Raquel's mother refused to do what she needed to get her back, so home for Raquel became a succession of foster placements—an emergency shelter for a few days, a succession of foster homes for a few months, a series of group homes for a few years.

When Raquel turned eighteen and became too old for foster care, she moved on to another institutional setting—a Job Corps dormitory in rural Utah.

And for the last sixteen months, Raquel has been truly homeless, bouncing from one shelter to another, with brief stays in a motel or a boarding house whenever she's had enough cash to pay her own way.

Most recently, she's been staying at the Lark-Inn Shelter for Youth, located in San Francisco, an emergency shelter for homeless youth between eighteen and twenty-three. The Lark-Inn provides not only shelter but an impressive array of educational, psychological, vocational, and housing assistance services. If Raquel does everything she's supposed to, she has a shot at winning a coveted place in one of the three transitional housing programs for homeless youth in San Francisco. It's her best prospect for achieving housing stability since leaving foster care two and a half years ago.

Because of the demand for beds, the Lark-Inn limits stays to four months. Raquel has just two more weeks to accomplish the goals she and her Lark-Inn caseworker have set—progress on her GED, a job, and enough savings to pay her first month's rent.

"I'm an inch away from being out on the street," Raquel says. "That's my biggest fear. I never want to sleep on the street. That's why I'm trying not to mess up."

Discharged to Homelessness

Drop by any homeless shelter in America and you'll meet people like Raquel who have spent parts of their childhoods in foster care. A 1996 study by the National Alliance for the Homeless concluded that a minimum of 9 percent of the adult homeless population had spent time in the foster care system, with reports in some cities running as high as 45 percent.[1]

The forces that drive young people from foster care into homelessness are the same as those that drive older people there: a shortage of affordable housing, insufficient personal income, chronic health problems, lack of family support, and personal crises of one sort or another.

But there are additional forces at work, too. Because of frequent moves while in the state's custody, many youth in foster care are unable to develop the support networks that could help them through a personal crisis. Others have come to view rootlessness and group living as a normal way of life. And the foster care system itself is partly to blame for failing to prepare some for independence. In 1994, the National Association of Social Workers reported that one in five homeless youth who sought emergency shelter had come *directly* out of foster care—"discharged to homelessness," in agency parlance. Almost four in ten of all homeless youth seeking shelter reported having been in foster care in the previous year.[2]

Because of its colorful street life, generous social services, and mild climate, San Francisco attracts more homeless youth and young adults than most other cities. And a higher percentage are youth who have aged out of—or run away from—foster care.

Larkin Street Youth Services has been providing services to homeless youth and young adults since 1984. Seventy percent of the people who seek help from Larkin Street have spent time in foster care or juvenile detention. Most of the rest have spent parts of their childhoods in informal placements with relatives or the parents of friends. "We provide the safety net for a lot of programs that fail, including foster care and juvenile probation and the mental health system," says Anne B. Stanton, Larkin Street's executive director until October 2003.

Some of the youth who turn up at Larkin Street haven't received any training in independent living skills because they ran away from the system before they formally aged out. "We see a lot of kids who blew out of the system at fifteen or sixteen by running away," Stanton says. "At sixteen, they may still think it's cool to be living on the street. But at eighteen or nineteen, they're tired. They don't want to do it any more. Fortunately, there's usually been huge maturational growth by then. They're more ready to do what they need to do."

In the early 1990s, as the agency's outreach workers were circulating through the city's toughest neighborhoods, they began seeing more older teens and young adults sleeping in doorways on makeshift cardboard pads. At the time, there was no place for them to seek refuge besides the city's adult shelters, which can be dangerous, says Stanton.

"We saw that we needed to be offering a continuum of services so they could make successful transitions to adulthood, and that that continuum needed to include shelter," Stanton says. The result was the establishment in April 2000 of the Lark-Inn for Youth, San Francisco's first emergency shelter for young adults.

Lark-Inn offers each homeless youth not only a bed and three meals a day but also job-readiness training, wage-paying employment, GED preparation, computer classes, case management, life-skills training, and health care. "From day one, they're asked, 'What do you want to work on?'" says Sam Cobbs, the agency's deputy director for over-age services. "We work with them on a blueprint, and we hold them accountable to achieving what they say they want."

In fact, youth who request only a bed are limited to a twenty-night stay at Lark-Inn. To stay longer, youth have to be working on an "independence plan." Of all the youth who spend more than sixty nights at the Lark-Inn, 80 percent move on to stable housing. Raquel is determined to be in that group.

"Just Me and My Mom"

Raquel is an engaging, though emotionally needy, young woman. Her hunger for connection is palpable. Her puppy-like quality causes some people, particularly peers, to keep their distance, perhaps out of fear that she will become dependent upon them. Although her education has been spotty, she's smart and incredibly resourceful. For instance, through research on the Internet she found herself a free voicemail and e-mail service.

Born prematurely in June 1981, Raquel was told by her mother, who was twenty-seven when she was born, that she was the product of an affair with a married shipyard worker fifteen years her elder. "My dad was cheating on his wife, and that's how I came into this great picture called the world," Raquel once told a caseworker, making light of her father's failure to acknowledge her, which pains her beyond measure.

Through her childhood, the man she believes to be her father paid the rent and came around once a week or so. But he insisted that Raquel's existence be kept from his wife and other children. (Inexplicably, he told a brother, who was a good uncle to Raquel for a while.) No doting grandparents ever came calling; indeed, Raquel has no idea whether her mother even told her relatives in Louisiana or Illinois of her birth. "As for grandparents, I don't know if I even have any," she says. "It was always just me and my mom."

Raquel first came to the attention of Alameda County's child-protection system when she was a week short of her fourth birthday. Court records indicate that her thirty-year-old mother, crying and distraught, called a county-run parental stress hot line. Raquel would not eat her breakfast, her mother told the operator, and she was on the verge of losing control and hurting her.

Two hours later, an emergency response worker knocked on the door of the family's one-room apartment in Emeryville, a suburb of Oakland. By then, Raquel's mother had calmed down. But she told the investigator she was "going crazy" being with Raquel in the tiny apartment day after day and was hitting and yelling at her constantly, the investigator reported to the Alameda County Juvenile Court.

She also said that Raquel's conception had been an accident and that she had thought about either aborting her or giving her up for adoption. Now, nearly four years later, she wanted to "get rid of her," she said.

The investigator characterized Raquel's mother as "lonely, depressed, angry, isolated and in need of nurturing. The mother loves the minor. However, at this time she seems too emotionally upset and needy herself to tolerate any resistance to her by the minor or any more deprivation as she perceives it. The mother is very involved in her own thoughts . . . and perceives the minor as someone who is inhibiting her economically."

The investigator proposed putting Raquel in respite care for three days, but her mother refused, saying it wouldn't solve anything. The investigator concluded that Raquel was at risk of harm if she were left in the home, so she summoned a police officer to take Raquel to an emergency foster home. Raquel still remembers being led away. "The policeman held my hand and walked me across the street," Raquel says. "I thought I was just going for a ride, and it would be fun. I remember looking back and seeing my mother standing there crying. I didn't know why."

Raquel spent about six months in foster care. She remembers liking her foster family. "And they really liked me," she says. "They wanted to adopt me. They were sad when I left."

Home Cooking and a Black Eye

Raquel has only a few other memories of her childhood. She remembers watching her mother fry chicken and sauté collard greens, something she, too, likes to do when she has access to a kitchen. She remembers riding on the bottom of a grocery cart while her mother shopped and sneaking her favorite snacks into the cart. She remembers the second time child-abuse authorities took her into custody—when she was five or six and her mother hit her with a broom, blackening her eye. And she remembers that her final months with her mother, when she was twelve and a half and in the seventh grade, were a time of loneliness punctuated by conflict.

"Often, my mom wouldn't come home at night, and I'd have to take care of myself," Raquel says. "She'd be gone like every other night. It seemed like she didn't care about me at all. And when she was home, she used to hit me a lot because she was mad at my dad because he wouldn't come and see her."

Not surprisingly, Raquel rebelled. As she moved into puberty, she experimented with sex, ignored homework assignments, skipped classes, and earned abysmal grades. "I started running with the wrong crowd," Raquel admits. "I ran away a lot." Raquel's court records mention "a lengthy history of 601-type behavior," referring to the section of the judicial code that deals with incorrigibility, truancy, and running away.

Just before Christmas 1993, police detained Raquel for fighting. They couldn't reach her mother, so they took her to an emergency shelter in the Oakland hills. Police finally reached Raquel's mother two days later, and she told them she didn't want Raquel to return home. Raquel spent Christmas in an emergency foster home in Fremont. When police took Raquel to her mother's home to pick up clothes, "There were words," Raquel recalls. "She was sitting in the living room shouting out all this stuff, like the fact that my dad wasn't really my dad. I told her I was glad I was being taken away because I was tired of her hitting on me."

Three days after Christmas, authorities petitioned the court to make Raquel a dependent of the Alameda County Social Services Agency. Before a hearing could be held, Raquel ran away from the foster home, a pattern that was to repeat itself several times over the next few months.

The hearing was finally held in March 1994, and the county formally assumed legal custody.

"There are no reasonable means to protect the child's physical or emotional health without removing the minor from the parent's physical custody," the judge held. He ordered that reunification services be offered to Raquel and her mother, including counseling and supervised visits.

"It's Still No Excuse"

Although it doesn't fully explain her actions, Raquel's mother clearly had a rough childhood.

According to a social history submitted to the court, Raquel's mother was born on a sofa in her maternal grandfather's home in Monroe, Louisiana, in December 1954. Her unmarried mother had already given birth to four children by several different men, and she wasn't sure who the father of her fifth child was. "I don't know who to call Daddy," Raquel's mother told the social worker who compiled her social history.

Raquel's mother lived with her grandfather and his second wife until she was nine. She had mixed memories of her childhood, mostly of hard work. By today's standards, she would have been considered a battered child. She once needed twenty-eight stitches because she ran into a mirror while trying to escape a beating.

Her most vivid childhood memory was of an incident in which her step-grandmother threw boiling water on her husband because he had stayed out all night. After that, the couple separated, and Raquel's mother was sent to live with her mother in northern Illinois. "The explanation given to her was that her natural mother wanted her for the purpose of income through welfare monies," the social history says.

By this time, her mother had three new children; a ninth was still to be born. Her mother treated her like "a Cinderella," Raquel's mother said, forcing her to clean up after everyone else. "I never got a chance to be a kid," she told the social worker. "I always had too much work to do."

Although she was not beaten regularly, Raquel's mother told of one occasion on which her mother placed her head between her knees and beat her with a strap while two older brothers kept her from getting away.

When Raquel's mother was thirteen, her mother's boyfriend and his brother made sexual advances. She told her mother, who didn't believe her. She resolved to leave home as soon as she could. Four years later, she found a job as a live-in housekeeper and baby-sitter and broke off contact with her family. Over the next two years, she obtained her GED. Although court records make no mention of it, Raquel believes she gave birth to a daughter, whom she turned over to the father's family to raise.

In 1980, Raquel's mother moved to the San Francisco area and found work as a housekeeper. Through what she characterized as a casual relationship, she became pregnant with Raquel. "I didn't want to get pregnant," she told the social worker. "I had all I could do to take care of myself. I didn't have money for an abortion."

Raquel's mother received spotty prenatal care, and Raquel was born a month early, weighing less than five pounds. Raquel's mother talked to someone at the hospital about relinquishing Raquel for adoption, but she didn't follow through. Instead, she went on welfare and began raising Raquel on her own. She apparently told no one in her family about the baby.

Raquel has only recently learned the details of her mother's life and her own early life from court files. In her mind, they help explain why her mother turned her back on a twelve-year-old girl.

"She didn't have much money," Raquel noted sympathetically after she finished reading her mother's social history. "She didn't have a job. And she had a child by a married man. I can understand why she felt overwhelmed."

Still, knowing the facts doesn't make her experiences any less painful. "It's still no excuse for what she did," Raquel says. "I'd never have a child and treat her like that."

"Very Poor Judgment"

After Raquel ran away from foster care a fourth time, authorities decided that she needed more structure than a foster home could provide. In March 1994, they placed her in a group home for eighteen girls in Oakland. Raquel's placement there cost the county $3,642 a month, almost five times the cost of family-based foster care. But the placement held.

Raquel didn't run away. "It was one of my longest placements, seven or eight months," Raquel remembers.

Meanwhile, social workers kept trying to interest Raquel's mother in various reunification services, all of which she turned down.

In September 1994, Raquel's mother was declared to be in "non-compliance" with the court-ordered reunification plan. She had made no attempt to contact Raquel in seven months. She was reported to be unemployed, several months behind in her rent, and seeking state disability benefits for unspecified medical problems. The whereabouts of Raquel's father were listed as unknown.

By this time, Raquel was experiencing problems both at her group home and at school. "The minor gives the impression of being tough and sophisticated, but is really fairly needy and vulnerable," a social worker stated in a report. "What is most alarming about Raquel and what the staff is most concerned about is that Raquel has very poor judgment and . . . puts herself in dangerous situations by responding to adult men either at school or on the street."

At school, teachers reported that she was "unable to function appropriately in class, with a low tolerance for frustration around tasks, constant fighting with peers and not following instructions." They recommended that she be evaluated for special education.

Raquel's placement in the group home was supposed to be temporary, since the home was licensed only for emergency placements. But given her history of running away, Raquel was hard to place elsewhere.

Raquel's caseworker finally found a promising foster family in Pittsburg, a nice Alameda County suburb. "The family is a very experienced family with teenagers," her caseworker reported to the court. "It is hoped that once Raquel is placed in an environment that can set limits, where the minor experiences consistency yet is given positive reinforcement, where there is good role-modeling and the minor is in therapy, that Raquel will settle down and the behaviors that we see now will diminish." But after a trial visit over a weekend, Raquel never heard from the prospective foster family again.

Through all these months, Raquel continued to hold out hope that her mother would let her come home. In December 1994, Raquel called her to wish her a happy fortieth birthday. Her mother hung up on her. Soon after, Raquel was suspended from school for being disruptive and disrespectful. Then she ran away from the group home.

Around this time, Raquel's social worker reported that she was suffering from severe depression and exhibiting a "great need for acceptance and affection." With the prospective foster family out of the picture, Raquel was instead moved to a six-bed long-term group home in Fremont, which cost $3,539 a month.

Moving yet again was disruptive both socially and academically, but Raquel says that the new home was the right place for her at the time. "It was a good place," she says. "I settled down and went to school."

Foster Care Limbo

Over the next five years, county social workers dutifully reported on Raquel's status to the juvenile court every six months, as required by law. And Raquel settled into the limbo called "long-term foster care."

For nearly a year, Raquel attended a continuation school, which serves students who are socially and educationally challenged. Then she was mainstreamed at a regular high school. Moving from the more supportive, flexible environment of an alternative school to a large urban high school proved to be too much for her. Her teachers described her as being "disruptive and defiant"; she was suspended numerous times. In November 1995, her GPA was .50, indicating grades of Ds and Fs.

A court report dated March 1996 suggested a glimmer of progress as she was approaching her sixteenth birthday. "Raquel's progress is described by [her] group home as being slow, but steady," the court was told. "For the most part, she is described as a child who is appreciative and proud of her accomplishments. She is learning to be more responsible and assertive, and less intrusive and aggressive."

But in the fall of 1996, Raquel was forced to repeat the ninth grade. To avoid being stigmatized, she switched high schools. It turned out to be a good move. As part of a work-study program at the new school, she spent nearly every afternoon working at a day-care center, which she loved. "It made me look forward to going to school," she says.

"Every day, I'd go over there at 1:15, and I'd spend the whole afternoon playing with them. I used to have a baby in each arm, and a two-year-old hanging on each leg. They'd call me Miss Raquel. Sometimes I'd get on the little bitty tricycles with a kid on my back, and ride him around the room."

Raquel continued to hope that she would eventually move home. In December 1996, she again called her mother to wish her a happy birthday. As before, her mother refused to talk to her. The next report to the court indicated that Raquel was "having difficulty with aggressive behavior and not working the program."

By May 1997, Raquel had begun receiving special education in English, math, science, and reading and was doing better in school, with grades of mostly Cs. "Raquel appears to have settled down," a report to the court said. "However, she can be physically and verbally aggressive at times. Raquel is trying to work on her impulsive behavior. She has unresolved issues concerning her family. She feels rejected and abandoned by them. She is seen by [a therapist] on a weekly basis."

That summer, for reasons not explained in her files, Raquel had to move out of the group home where she'd lived for more than two years. "I don't know why," Raquel says. "My worker just moved me, no explanation given."

"The Minor Is AWOL"

Raquel's next placement was a group home in South San Francisco, a community clear across San Francisco Bay, in a different county and, of course, a different school district. (All told, Raquel attended seven schools in her six years in foster care.) Alameda County paid the home $4,375 a month—$52,500 a year—for her to stay there.

Raquel entered the tenth grade at South San Francisco High School and tried to live the life of a typical high school student. She wanted to be on the swim team, but her grades weren't good enough, so she served as the team's manager instead.

Reports to the court during her junior year in high school describe a teenager who seems to have finally found some focus for her life. "The minor's grades have improved tremendously this school year," the court was told in December 1998. "Although the minor is classified as special education, the minor reads well (twelfth-grade level) and is an avid reader. The minor's behavior has improved 100 percent in the classroom, with no negative reports from the school."

"The minor takes advantage of therapy by expressing her feelings well. The group home reports that the minor's behavior has improved drastically, and she has begun to take responsibility for her actions. The minor's depression has decreased and reportedly her self-esteem has increased. The minor, however, continues to have low self-esteem."

Seven months later, in July 1999, the foster agency's report to the court was equally positive. "The minor continues to attend twice monthly therapy," the social worker wrote. "The minor has occasional outbursts, but mostly presents herself as being calm and cooperative with adults. The minor engages in passive-aggressive behaviors to get her needs met, rather than being direct. Her self-esteem is generally positive, but she can be derailed by environmental stressors, particularly related to interaction with peers."

"The minor generally has done well at the program and made improvements in many aspects of her functioning. It appears that the minor's current placement is appropriate and she can remain there through emancipation. It is not known at this time the degree to which Raquel is ready for independence."

Almost as a postscript, the worker added that her report was based on secondhand information, since she was new to the case and had not yet met Raquel. In addition, she noted, Raquel had run away from the group home right after school ended. "As of June 18, 1999, the minor is AWOL," she wrote.

"My Last Resort"

Raquel's immediate reason for running away was that she was afraid that the group home's manager was going to turn her in to the police for a theft she hadn't committed.

But Raquel had other reasons for running, too. She had just turned eighteen and no longer wanted to be treated like a child. She was fed up with the rules and strictures and lack of privacy that were part and parcel of group-home living. In short, she was tired of being in foster care.

However, she was not the least bit prepared to function on her own. She had completed nine sessions of an independent living-skills course. But she hadn't acquired what is needed to be truly independent—a high school diploma, a nest egg, self-confidence, and a network of supportive friends and relatives.

On the run yet again from the foster care system, she made her way to Fresno, about three hours south of San Francisco, and spent the summer with the family of a friend. When she wore out her welcome there, she went back to San Francisco, where she sought out a social worker at the public hospital. The social worker found her a bed in an emergency shelter and reported her whereabouts to Alameda County, where she was still a ward of the Social Services Agency.

A few months past eighteen, Raquel was already at the end of her eligibility for foster care. Alameda County won't keep an eighteen-year-old in foster care unless the young person is still enrolled in high school and likely to graduate before turning nineteen. Raquel didn't have enough credits to guarantee her graduation before she turned nineteen. (Six states allow young people to stay in foster care until they're twenty-one, as long as they're enrolled in school.)

With few other options, Raquel decided to enroll in the Job Corps. "The Job Corps was my last resort," she says.

Seven Months in Utah

The Job Corps was established in 1964 as part of President Lyndon B. Johnson's War on Poverty. Modeled on the depression-era Civilian Conservation Corps, the Job Corps was meant to provide job training in a structured residential setting to disadvantaged youth sixteen to twenty-four years old. Since its inception, more than 2 million young adults—70,000 a year in recent years—have participated. Even today, seven presidential administrations later, it is still the federal government's largest single effort to move youth from poverty to employment.

Raquel was assigned to the Job Corps site in Clearfield, Utah, a small city north of Salt Lake City, near the base of the Wasatch Mountains. She arrived on February 8, 2000, with $18 in her wallet.

The Job Corps was both better and worse than Raquel hoped. "I liked getting away from the drama in California and starting over somewhere else," she says. Also, she had her first experience with cold weather. "I really loved the snow," she says. But, she continues, "It wasn't everything that I thought it would be."

For one thing, there were three times as many males as females, a total departure from the atmosphere of the all-girl group homes in which she had lived for six years. For another, many of the 1,300 other students were a lot like her—poor minorities who had dropped out of high school. Some had been steered to the Job Corps by their probation officers, others by foster care caseworkers. Many came from chaotic backgrounds and were fighting drug dependencies.

Raquel enrolled in the School-to-Career program, with a concentration in health occupations, which she soon found didn't interest her. (Child development courses, which would have interested her, weren't offered at this site.) She found it hard to make progress on her GED. There were just as many rules as in the group homes in which she'd lived since she was twelve. And although drug use was forbidden, Raquel says it was rampant. "I almost started selling drugs to make a little money," Raquel says. "But I knew that if I started selling it, I would start using it, and it would lead to other things."

After nearly eight months in Utah, Raquel had had enough. Although a youth can stay in the Job Corps for two years, the average length of stay is about the same as Raquel's. On September 29, 2000, Raquel boarded a plane back to Oakland.

On Her Own

Raquel had $700 in her purse when she landed in Oakland, her savings from her Job Corps stipend, along with a "readjustment allowance."

Never having lived on her own, she thought of it as a fortune. She rented a room in a residential hotel in downtown Oakland and looked for a job.

The money ran out in a week. Raquel called a caseworker at Alameda County's Social Services Agency, which had always bailed her out of tough situations in the past. She learned that the Alameda County Juvenile Court had held her emancipation hearing while she was in Utah. She was eligible for limited independent living services—a bus pass, access during business hours to computers and telephones, a list of apartment complexes in Oakland, and participation in various work-shops, such as résumé writing, job hunting, and tax preparation. In addi-tion, she could receive Medicaid coverage until she was twenty-one. But the agency didn't have the resources to satisfy Raquel's pressing need: a roof over her head.

Over the course of her six years in foster care, the government had spent more than $225,000 just to feed and shelter her, not counting the cost of counseling or health care or caseworkers' time. Now, three months past her nineteenth birthday, the best her caseworker could offer was a referral to one of the private agencies that try to catch the unfortunates who fall through government safety nets. The caseworker referred Raquel to Covenant House, a national faith-based organization that helps home-less and runaway youth.

A Covenant House employee arranged for Raquel to stay at the YMCA in Berkeley, which rents rooms by the week, and drove her there and paid her rent for two weeks. Raquel thought that two weeks would give her enough time to find a job, after which she would be able to pay the rent herself.

Although she applied for dozens of jobs, she never got called back. "With no high school diploma, and not much job experience, I couldn't get anything," she says ruefully. In the middle of October 2000, less than three weeks after leaving the Job Corps, she moved into a forty-bed shel-ter for homeless women run by the Berkeley Emergency Food and Hous-ing Project.

"That was the weirdest experience I've ever had," Raquel recalls. "I was the only teenager, and it was really intimidating. Just about everybody else who was there was either mentally ill or a drug addict. But most of them were really nice to me. They treated me like a daughter. For a while, it was as though I had a lot of moms."

The shelter is open only from 7:00 P.M. to 7:30 A.M. For the other eleven and a half hours, residents must go somewhere else. A few have jobs, but many panhandle on Telegraph Avenue, lounge on park benches, or roam the nearby University of California campus.

Raquel rode the bus. "I didn't have any other place to be," Raquel says. "I'd go from Berkeley to San Leandro, which burned up a lot of time."

Finally, a Job and a Home

A few weeks into her stay at the Berkeley shelter, Raquel found a job as a $7.70-per-hour photo clerk at a drugstore. For the first time that fall, she felt she was making progress. She saved most of her pay so she could rent a place for herself.

Because it's meant to provide only temporary shelter, the Berkeley Emergency Food and Housing Project limits a person's stay to ninety days. In January 2001, as Raquel's deadline for moving out approached, she realized she wasn't going to have enough money saved for her own apartment. She called every housing hot line she could find. (More than a year later, she can still rattle off many of the hot line numbers.)

Someone at the Homeless Youth Cooperative told her about Our House, a group home in Oakland for homeless youth operated by the East Oakland Community Project. After an interview and a trial stay over a weekend, Raquel was admitted on a ninety-day probationary basis. "It was really cool," she says. "It was just me and two guys, plus a staff member, in a three-bedroom, two-bath apartment. I had my own room. It was really huge and nice."

Financed largely with federal anti-homelessness funds, Our House charges residents $150 a month for rent and permits them to stay for up to two years. They're expected to work and save a substantial portion of their earnings. The house is staffed around the clock, so there's always an older adult to consult for advice.

When Raquel moved into Our House, she received a onetime $1,000 stipend from the Alameda County ILS Auxiliary. Every youth who ages out of foster care in Alameda County can apply for such a grant.

The supportive environment at Our House should have been ideal for Raquel. But she didn't do well there. She broke rules, sometimes staying out all night and then lying about her whereabouts. And she lost her job at the drugstore because of absenteeism. At the end of her probationary period, Our House asked Raquel to leave.

"She is an intelligent, beautiful girl, but she's self-destructive," Linda Fuentes, the manager of Our House, says about Raquel. "Whenever something good happens to her, she does something to make it fall apart. I told her when she left that she needs to find out why she's sabotaging her life."

Back to the Shelter

In April 2001, Raquel returned in defeat to the homeless shelter in Berkeley. She had only a week of eligibility left.

She still had part of the stipend from the ILS Auxiliary, so she decided to rent a room at the Berkeley YMCA for as long as her money held out. "At the Y, I had my own room, a TV, a little refrigerator, a nice warm bed," she says. "I had a regular closet where I could hang my clothes up. It was really nice."

She kept looking for a job, without success. "People would just look at me funny when I handed in my application," she says. "When I'd get an interview, they'd ask me, 'Why do you have so many gaps in your work history?' It's a hard question to answer without going into your whole history. If I'd tell them it's because I've been homeless, they'd just get quiet, and then they'd say, 'OK, we'll call you if we need you,' and they never did."

Late in the summer of 2001, she heard about the Lark-Inn, across the bay in San Francisco. She began calling daily to ask if there was a bed open. "I only had like $50 left when they told me there was a bed," she says.

In early September, a worker from Covenant House gave her a ride across the Bay Bridge to San Francisco. She carried all her belongings in two plastic garbage bags.

"You Got to Live by the Rules"

The Lark-Inn Shelter for Youth occupies a former nightclub on Ellis Street, just a block down a steep hill from busy Van Ness Avenue, one of San Francisco's main thoroughfares. Down a few steps from the lobby is a combination dining and recreation room, where residents eat three meals a day. Beyond that, a warren-like collection of windowless, concrete block–walled bedrooms can house up to forty young adults. There's even a kennel for the stray animals that homeless youth often adopt as companions.

When Raquel first moved in, she rebelled against the shelter's rules. "It was a lot like a group home, except we were all adults," she says. "There have to be rules, I know, but some of the Lark-Inn's are ridiculous. Like you can't wear sleeveless shirts. They'll have a cow, even though it's not like I'm showing anything. And there's a 9:45 P.M. curfew, which I really don't like. Plus there's no privacy. You can't have visitors, and there's no place to go and talk with your friends."

On the plus side, the other residents were Raquel's age, unlike the residents of the homeless shelter in Berkeley, and they were a lot like her in other ways, too. "There were actually people I could relate to," she says. "As I got to know the people here, I found a lot had actually been in the same situation I was in. They'd been in foster care, too. I thought that was really cool."

During the first twenty days of her stay, Raquel did everything she could to test the staff's patience, as she had every time she'd moved to some new place in the past. Instead of signing up for Hire-Up, the day-labor program, she hung out at the drop-in center operated by San Francisco's Independent Living Services unit. She missed appointments and broke rules. "Like I would go with a friend to her boyfriend's house, and we'd spend the night, which meant we'd get a write-up," Raquel admits. "Eventually I got so many write-ups that I almost got kicked out. I was horrible. I just didn't care."

"Then I realized that it was the only youth shelter in the Bay Area and it was my last option. I did a whole 180. I began to realize that instead of looking at the Lark-Inn negatively, I should look at it positively.

When you live in these programs, you got to live by the rules. Life sucks, but you got to do it. I went to Hire-Up. I went to Job Readiness. I started on my GED. My caseworker was so happy with me."

Ruth Nuñez, Raquel's caseworker, said she always knew that Raquel would come around. "At first, she was hard to engage and get motivated," she says. "If I had rated her on a scale of one to ten when she started, she would have been a one. She was very young, and she had basically failed out of a lot of programs. We set up various jobs for her, and she failed a couple of times.

"But we provide a safety net here, so we just tried other things. She didn't believe she could do it. But we kept after her, like a protective parent would. It took a while, but she suddenly realized that if she didn't do this stuff, she wasn't going to get into transitional housing. She's made tremendous progress. Right now, I'd rate her an 8.5."

Nuñez says Raquel's behavior was typical of youths who have been in foster care. "While they were in care, they got away with a lot of stuff, either because they didn't have enough supervision or they needed things their caseworkers couldn't provide," she says. "They knew that if they didn't want to go to school, nobody could make them, and if they got kicked out of one placement, the county would have to find them another. The ramifications of their actions didn't really sink in, because while they were underage, they were protected. Their caseworkers tended to hold their hands too much."

"At Lark-Inn, we treat them like adults and give them adult consequences. We tell them, 'This is what's going to happen if you don't do X, Y, or Z. You're not going to eat. You're not going to be able to go to the movies. You're not going to have a place to sleep.'"

"We hold hands a little bit, but we tend to be more firm."

An Avenue to Independence

It is the week before Christmas 2001, just about eight years to the day after Raquel went into long-term foster care. The December holidays are a notoriously difficult time of year for children without families, which may account for Raquel's gloomy mood.

Besides everything else, she's got a big deadline looming. There are just a few weeks left until she reaches the four-month maximum stay permitted at the Lark-Inn. Lately, she's been doing better at following the house rules, and she's completed both a computer course and a job-readiness course, as required of her. But she's still got some goals to meet, including making progress on her GED and finding a job.

Her lack of progress on those two fronts isn't entirely her fault. The state recently decided to change the GED test, which has set her timetable back a few months. And with the local economy in a downward spiral, jobs are hard to get. Raquel has put in applications all over town, but she's only gotten one call back, from a day-care center. She had a promising interview there, but the operator doesn't expect to have an opening for a few months.

To add to her gloom, last night she lost her wallet while riding a city bus home from the Christmas party at the San Francisco Independent Living unit. In it were several gift certificates that she'd received at the party, her bus pass, and her Lark-Inn ID.

But today, Sam Cobbs, the agency's associate director, has some good news for her. A bed has become available at Avenues to Independence (ATI), the transitional housing program that Larkin Street Youth Services operates. Even though Raquel hasn't yet met all of her goals, she's close enough that the agency is willing to let her move in. "What we saw with Raquel in the last few months is that internal motivation that it takes to succeed at ATI," Cobbs says.

Larkin Street Youth Services opened Avenues to Independence in 1996 in a former nursing home in San Francisco's Haight district, once the domain of the city's hippie culture and even today a haven for alternative lifestyles. ATI is one of only three transitional housing programs for older teens and young adults in San Francisco.

ATI provides private or semiprivate rooms, food, and an array of services, including case management and training in independent-living skills. The atmosphere is a cross between a private apartment complex and a college dorm, though with many more rules. Residents can live there for up to eighteen months. They must work full-time and pay 30 percent of their income—or a minimum of $100 a month—as "rent." The money is actually put into escrow, and when residents move out, they receive the money they have paid for "rent" to help with the expenses of renting an apartment. Many residents leave with nest eggs of more than $5,000.

Ninety percent of the young adults who have lived at ATI since 1996 have moved on to independent housing. "The thing about ATI is that it really is 'avenues to independence,'" Cobbs says. "There isn't a whole lot of structure, like at the Lark-Inn, where you have the 9:45 P.M. curfew, and staff wake you up to go to work, and your case manager kind of rides you to get you into shape. At Avenues, you really have to be self-motivated. We give them freedom but make sure that someone is in a position to handle that type of freedom."

"I'm Glad You're Here"

With her belongings stashed in two plastic garbage bags, just as they were when she arrived nearly four months ago, Raquel stands in the lobby of the Lark-Inn waiting for a ride to ATI, a few miles away. It's surprisingly balmy for late December, and Raquel is wearing the young adult equivalent of "Sunday best"—orange shorts, a navy blue T-shirt, an orange bead necklace, an orange baseball cap, and orange-and-white Nikes with orange shoelaces. (Not surprisingly, orange is her favorite color.) She wants to make a good impression when she moves into ATI.

Although she's trying not to show it, Raquel is giddy with excitement. After all, she's one of the Lark-Inn's success stories. She's moving on. As residents and staff members come and go, they give her a hug or a high five and wish her luck.

"I'm sorry to see you go," a staff member named Liz tells her. "You're one of my favorites."

"I'm not gonna cry," Raquel says as she hugs her. "I'm not."

On the fifteen-minute ride to ATI, Raquel is chatty, pointing out the interesting ethnic restaurants that line Haight Street, the convenience stores, and the frequent bus stops. "I wasn't sure I wanted to be in The Haight," she says, "but it looks OK."

At ATI, Raquel arrives just as another former resident of the Lark-Inn is returning from a shopping trip. He and Raquel greet each other warmly. "I didn't know you were moving over here," says Shawn. "I'm excited for you, Raquel. It's really great. You'll like it."

A tall young resident named Mark answers the door. "Welcome to ATI," he tells Raquel. "You just moved out of the Lark-Inn, eh?"

"Yeah. I just had my interview a few days ago, and I was accepted, and the next thing I knew I was moving in," she says. "I'm kind of excited."

"Well, come on in, and I'll show you around," Mark says. "It's a lot better than the Lark-Inn. You can get food from the kitchen any time you want, and even walk around the halls with it. And you can even have visitors in your room."

Just then, Gina, the staff member on duty, walks up to greet Raquel. She knows Raquel well, having previously worked at the Lark-Inn, and gives her a big hug. "I see you met our unofficial greeter," she tells Raquel, referring to Mark. "Don't listen to him. He'll get you in trouble. He's on restriction right now himself for staying out until 2:30 A.M." Mark winks and gives Raquel a thumbs-up sign.

Gina shows Raquel to her room, which she'll share with another former Lark-Inn resident. Although her roommate has gone away for the holidays, she's decorated the door with wrapping paper, ribbons, and Christmas lights. In addition, lights twinkle above her bed. The effect is magical.

Unlike the linoleum-floored sleeping areas at the Lark-Inn, the floor of Raquel's new room is carpeted. The walls are smooth, not cement block. Three people share a bathroom, instead of twenty. And best of all, there's a window that looks out over the neighborhood and lets in natural light, in contrast to the Lark-Inn's windowless dorm.

A gift bag filled with toiletries awaits Raquel on her bed. She goes through it with all the excitement of a child emptying a Christmas stocking. She's most impressed by a clothbound journal in which she can record her transition to independence.

Gina spends thirty minutes briefing Raquel on the house rules—no loud music, no visitors past midnight, no visitors of the opposite sex in her room at any time. "The counselor on duty has the discretion to make your visitors leave if they're making too much noise," Gina warns.

"I'll make them leave before the counselor does," says Raquel, eager to please.

"And there are no wake-up calls here," Gina continues. "You'll have to get your own alarm clock."

"I've already got one," Raquel says.

"And when you go out, you have to tell someone you're leaving," Gina says. "You can walk around here all day not saying a word to anyone, but you've got to tell someone when you leave.

"You'll find this is a lot different from Lark-Inn. Lark-Inn is very strict, with lots of rules. Here, we have rules, too, but we want you to figure things out yourself, and deal with problems like an adult. We're not going to do everything for you. You need to do things for yourself. If you mess up, you're going to have to deal with Sam. He can time you out for a week and send you back to Lark-Inn. You don't want to go back to Lark-Inn.

"I'm glad you're here, sweetie," Gina concludes, giving Raquel another hug. "I'm proud of you. You deserve to be here. How do you feel?"

"Good," Raquel says, beaming. "Good. Good. Good. Good. Good."

"I'm Making It"

Later, relaxing on her bed, Raquel reflects on the challenges that lie ahead of her.

With no family to depend upon, she knows she has to look for emotional support elsewhere. At the moment, she has a support system she can count on, though they're mostly people who are being paid to help her—the caseworkers at Larkin Street and at San Francisco Independent Living Services, the city-county agency charged with providing transition services to youth who have aged out of foster care.

But Raquel has also been trying hard to forge relationships with foster care veterans like herself, particularly the savvy young people who work for the California Youth Connection (CYC), a statewide organization that tries to empower youth in care to advocate for systems change. Because they've been through many of the same experiences she has, they understand better than most people why it's been so difficult for her to make her own way.

Her housing seems assured for eighteen months, as long as she gets a job and completes her GED, both achievable goals. She knows that she must work hard to succeed at Avenues to Independence. But she believes that ATI will provide the balance between freedom and supervision that she needs so that she can learn how to live on her own. She hopes that she will mature enough over the next year and a half—and will save enough money—to be able to make it on her own. "Right now, I need more structure than I'd have in my own place, because I know how I am," she says. "If I don't have someone on me 24/7, I will mess up. I don't take what I have now for granted."

Although many young people in her position would be inclined to blame the foster care system for sending them into the world unprepared, Raquel blames only herself. "I should have stayed in the Job Corps," she says. "If I hadn't have left Job Corps, I would have learned a trade there. But I figured I'd be able to make it if I came back here and got a job. I thought I'd meet with a job counselor and get a job the next week. But it didn't work out that way."

With her basic needs met, Raquel wants to turn her attention to some other unfinished business: her feelings about her birth family. Years of therapy have done little to erase the pain of having been rejected by both parents. She longs to know her family and is planning to try to track down her mother's relatives in Louisiana, and, she hopes, the older sister she's heard rumors about.

And despite having been rebuffed repeatedly over the years, Raquel still wants to make peace with her mother. "I haven't seen my mother in eight years," she says, "but I still miss her. I miss talking to her."

She also wants to find out why her father didn't step forward and take her into his home instead of allowing her to spend her teenage years in foster care. She's very angry with him. Even so, she yearns for a relationship with him, on her terms.

"If my parents do want to come back into my life, I want to be able to say, 'Hey, I went through rough times. I haven't been able to depend on Mom and Dad all the time, like some kids do. I've had to depend on myself.'"

"'But I'm still alive. I don't have any kids. I'm not a failure. I've made it this far without you. I'm making it on my own.'"

Postscript

Raquel lasted at ATI for just over eight months. She was asked to move out because she failed to get a full-time job, as required. She went back to the Lark-Inn for two and a half months, and then moved in with a boyfriend.

When they broke up in November 2002, Raquel moved into Ark House, a transitional living program in San Francisco's Castro district that serves homeless lesbian, gay, bisexual, transgender, and questioning youth who are age eighteen to twenty-five. Her contract with the organization that runs the house permitted her to stay through November 2003. Between February 2002 and September 2003, Raquel held four different jobs, most of them part-time. Each job ended abruptly, and there were sometimes long periods of unemployment in-between.

She says she lost the first job, as a part-time restaurant cashier, because ATI required her to miss several shifts to attend house meetings. After being unemployed for a few months, she got work as a $9-per-hour phone interviewer.

But she quit that job after just a few months when she was offered the part-time job of her dreams: as a $15-an-hour youth liaison for the California Youth Connection (CYC.) CYC had played an important role in her life in the years since she aged out of foster care, and she was proud to be working for the organization. "Things are on a roll," she said in May 2003, nine months into the job. "I'm happier than I could ever imagine being."

A few weeks later, however, she was fired. She says it was because a mandatory team-building trip for Ark House forced her to miss a training workshop for CYC. "Basically, I had to choose between my job and my housing, and I chose my housing, because I wouldn't have had anywhere else to live," she said.

In July 2003, Raquel got a part-time job as a $12-per-hour relief worker on the weekend graveyard shift at Restoration House, a residence for people with AIDS. Two months later, she quit because she was upset with a supervisor for complaining about her work performance to her case manager at Ark House. "When you have a problem in the real world, your supervisor doesn't call your parents. I needed to keep things separate between my work and my home," she says.

On September 26, 2003, the Ark House administrators asked Raquel to move out, two months early. "I'm happy to leave," she said then. "I don't feel like I have the support there to help me progress."

Raquel would have liked to move to her own place. "I'm tired of living in a cubicle and bouncing from program to program," she said. But she didn't feel as though she could swing it financially.

Instead, she moved into Guerrero House, a twenty-bed transitional living program affiliated with Catholic Charities. She's now lived at all three of San Francisco's transitional living programs for homeless youth and young adults.

As of late April 2004, Raquel had been unemployed for eight months. Between September 2003 and January 2004, Guerrero House provided her with room, board and case management services at no cost. "They're not quick to kick you out when you don't have a job," she says. "They put you on a plan where you're doing job search. They actually provide a lot of support here instead of just dictating things."

But by January, her caseworker at Guerrero House was pressing her either to work or to go to school, so Raquel enrolled in a child-care course at San Francisco City College. If she sticks with it, she says it could lead to a certificate that qualifies her for a child-care job.

Guerrero House also required that she apply for general assistance, a county-financed welfare program for single adults, so she could contribute to her upkeep. Since January, she's been receiving a check for $410 a month. Guerrero House charges her $120 a month, half of which it places in a savings account that she will be able to take with her when she leaves the program.

In March, she began volunteering thirty hours a week at an after-school program at an elementary school, which she hopes will improve her chances of getting a paid internship in January 2005.

Perhaps the most exciting development in Raquel's life is that she's connected with several relatives whose existence she discovered only in

2001 when she read her case file. She's had several telephone conversations with relatives in Louisiana, though they have since cut off contact. She's also developed a close relationship with her maternal step-grandmother, who lived in nearby Oakland until early 2004, when she moved back to Mississippi. She's even attempted to reconnect with her father, though he rebuffed her. She's now trying to locate her half sister, Ursula, who, she believes, lives in Illinois.

As for her mother, Raquel says, "I have her phone number, but I don't feel like the time is right. I'm going to wait."

Raquel turned twenty-two in December 2003, which means she's now too old for most of the assistance authorized by the Chafee Act.

Raquel says she regrets that she wasn't mature enough to take better advantage of the help she was offered in the years since aging out of foster care.

"When I was at Our House in Oakland, I just didn't listen," she says. "I didn't take full advantage of Lark-Inn or ATI either. I wish I had opened my eyes and ears to the people who were trying to help me succeed. I know there were opportunities that I missed out on."

Raquel Tolston earns spending money by braiding hair.

Casey-Jack Kitos

"IF I'D BEEN TOUGHER"

Casey-Jack Kitos, Lawrence, Kansas

By the second month of his senior year in high school, Casey-Jack Kitos thought he had his future figured out.

Right after graduation in June 2002, he would enter basic training for the U.S. Army Reserves. He would complete his skills training in the fall of 2002, and by January 2003 he'd be free to attend college full-time, with the army paying most of the cost.

One of the factors in his decision to enlist was a burst of patriotism following the terrorist attack on the United States on September 11, 2001. Another was his lifelong rivalry with his older brother, who had joined the army immediately after aging out of foster care two years earlier. But the main attraction was money. Having been in foster care since he was fourteen, Casey-Jack didn't see how he could afford to go to college without the army's help.

Although his home state of Kansas waives the tuition at state schools for a few veterans of foster care each year, Casey-Jack wanted to study youth ministry, a course of study not available at state universities. By combining his army benefits with a few scholarships and the federal education grants available to all low-income students, Casey-Jack figured he could earn a bachelor's degree without accumulating debt.

In October 2001, Casey-Jack signed the enlistment papers. And on June 17, 2002, three weeks after graduation from Lawrence High School, he reported for basic training at Fort Benning, Georgia.

Things didn't work out quite as he had planned.

"I Was the 'It'"

Casey-Jack is a slight-of-stature young man (in his words "scrawny") who seems to wear a perpetually sardonic grin. He's a bundle of nervous energy and rarely does just one thing at a time; if he's talking on the phone, he's probably surfing the Internet as well, and maybe even eating lunch, too. Although he generally deflects questions about his feelings with a wisecrack or a smart-alecky remark, the poetry he writes in his spare time is surprisingly revealing:

> *I am from*
> *Foodless days and foodless nights,*
> *And, once in awhile, a good meal.*
> *I am from*
> *Musty cigarette smoke*
> *Embedded in clothes, furniture and teeth . . .*
> *I am from*
> *A dark corner on the floor*
> *When everyone else got to have a bed . . . .*
> *I am from*
> *"Get your Education,"*
> *"You will never amount to anything,"*
> *"You were an accident,"*
> *"Go to your room,"*
> *"You're so cute," and*
> *"I hate you."*

For most of his life, Casey-Jack has known that if he were going to make something of himself, it would have to be without his parents' help. Caring for their five children had always seemed a low priority for his parents, he said. "I've pretty much taken care of myself since I was twelve," he says.

When Casey-Jack was five, his parents divorced. After that, the children lived mostly with their mother, who remarried and gave birth to two more boys. "Have you read *A Child Called "It"*? Casey-Jack asks, referring to Dave Pelzer's book about growing up with an abusive parent. "Well, I was the 'It' in our family. Everyone else had a bed, and my mom made me sleep on the floor. And there was a lot of physical abuse directed specifically against me. She and my step-dad would find any reason they could to whip me. Switches, hangers, metal ladles—anything they could get their hands on, they used."

In the summer of 1997, when Casey-Jack was fourteen, child-abuse investigators removed him and three siblings—fifteen-year-old twins and a twelve-year-old brother—from their mother's home. Initially, the child-welfare agency placed the children with their father. "He was a little more stable than my mom at that point," Casey-Jack explains. "He had a job and a car." But apart from the fact that Casey-Jack now slept in a bed, life with his father didn't seem to be much better than life with his mother had been.

Casey-Jack says his father abused him physically, and one night, he hit him back. "I punched him in the gut, and he fell down," Casey-Jack recalls. "Then he called the police and put on a pot of coffee to try to sober up."

That was the beginning of his five-year stay in foster care.

A New Home

Over the next year, Casey-Jack lived in an emergency shelter, four different group homes, and a family foster home. (He was pulled out of the family foster home, which he'd liked, when another resident alleged that the foster father had sexually abused him.) He was also in and out of psychiatric hospitals because of suicide threats. The frequent moves meant frequent school changes as well (he attended eighth grade in three different schools). And the distance between his hometown and some of his placements—as much as 200 miles—meant that he rarely saw his siblings, who by this time were also in foster care.

In October of his freshman year in high school, Casey-Jack was offered a spot in a group home outside of Lawrence, which would permit more frequent contact with his siblings and his mother, with whom he had supervised visits. "At first, I didn't want to look at it, because I had heard lots of horror stories about it," he recalls. "I was scared to go there. But finally I agreed to look at it. I had an interview, and they liked me. I had the option of saying yes or no. It seemed better than the place I was in in Pittsburg, so I said yes."

O'Connell Youth Ranch is a ranch-based group home that sprawls across 300 acres on the outskirts of Lawrence. The ranch has a reputation for working wonders with oppositional, defiant boys, which is the label that Casey-Jack by then carried with him, along with attention deficit disorder and placement adjustment disorder. The ranch houses twenty-four boys, ages eight through eighteen, in three separate homes, each staffed by a married couple referred to as "teaching parents." Relief workers staff the homes on weekends.

Casey-Jack liked the couple that ran the house to which he was assigned. "They seemed really cool," he says. "J. D. was an ex-navy guy, a little scrawny guy about the same size as me, with lots of tattoos and an earring. And his wife, Alex, was real nice."

Even so, Casey-Jack seemed to do his best to torpedo the placement. Every new resident starts out with limited privileges and earns more through good behavior. But within days of arriving, Casey-Jack had lost even the entry-level privileges because of bad behavior. In addition, he was suspended from high school for being disrespectful to a teacher. "By the end of the first week I was there, I was subsystem," he remembers, referring to the home's system of privileges. "I was like minus 300,000 points. I set the record of getting to subsystem faster than anyone ever did."

"Casey-Jack was very argumentative," says J. D. Kerr, one of the ranch's teaching parents. "He always had to be right, because for somebody else to be right would mean that he was wrong, which he couldn't stand. Failure is something that Casey-Jack couldn't tolerate."

The Kerrs focused on helping Casey-Jack learn to take responsibility for his actions and gain the skills he would need to live independently, including social interaction skills, which can't really be taught through textbooks. "Our kids learn all this through the experience of living with a family," J. D. Kerr explains. "Because they're sharing our home, they understand that just because my wife and I have a disagreement doesn't mean anybody's going to be hit, or somebody's going to move out, which is the experience many of them have had before."

Through a staff member at the ranch, Casey-Jack got involved with the Mustard Seed Christian Fellowship, a non-denominational charismatic church with an active youth group. "Initially, I didn't like it at all," he said. "There's lots of speaking in tongues and prayer. It wasn't like the churches I went to as a kid. But after a couple of weeks I began liking it. There were lots of pretty girls. I ended up getting involved in the youth group, and I got some of the other guys at the ranch involved, too."

During the summer after his freshman year at Lawrence High School, the ranch was invited to send two residents to the Youth for Christ Quaker Ridge Camp near Colorado City, Colorado. Casey-Jack, who had never attended overnight camp before, was selected. His week there proved to be a turning point in his life. He met a fourteen-year-old girl from Topeka, Kansas, to whom he poured out his heart. "I shared everything about my life with her," he recalls, "and she shared the gospel with me and led me to Christ. At the end of the week, they had an altar call, and sixty people went up. I was one of them."

When he returned to the ranch, Casey-Jack says he was a changed person. "I started doing really, really good," he says. "Everybody noticed. They gave me two leadership positions at the ranch. And I kept going to church, both the services and the youth group. We'd have Bible studies and do work days at Worlds of Fun and overnight lock-ins at the church—just lots of wholesome, positive fun."

Participating on the drama team of his youth group, Casey-Jack found that he had a talent for acting. "We did a video called *Taking Back Our City* about our mission trip to Lawrence," he said, "and we did another one about the Resurrection. I was one of the guys who crucified Jesus. My friends seem to think I'm a decent actor."

At school, where he was by then a sophomore, Casey-Jack was earning good grades for the first time in his life. "He went from being barely able to maintain in school to being on the honor roll, with mostly As," J. D. Kerr notes. During his prep periods, Casey-Jack volunteered as an aide in the school library, and he got involved in two clubs, the Fellowship of Christian Students and the French Club. He also served on a school-based transition advisory council, which helps design postgraduation services for special ed students (Casey-Jack was in special ed because of a behavior disorder). In that role, he coordinated some workshops and a resource fair.

In his junior year, Casey-Jack also began working part-time after school, first at a Wendy's fast-food restaurant and later at an IHOP restaurant and a day-care center. Ranch rules required him to save 80 percent of his earnings, but he could use the other 20 percent for the kinds of things that every teenager craves—CDs, name-brand athletic shoes, and outings with friends.

That summer, he was one of 240 teenagers chosen to attend the University of Kansas session of the National Youth Sports Program, a multisite collaboration of the federal government and the National Collegiate Athletic Association that is designed to provide disadvantaged youth with educational enrichment and career exposure. Casey-Jack was attached for several weeks to the local newspaper, the *Lawrence Journal-World,* where he learned about newspaper work and helped write a section devoted to teenagers. He received his first newspaper byline on a story about the determination of the program's director to make a difference in children's lives. The National Youth Sports Program gives area children the "hopes and dreams to reach for the stars," he wrote in his story.

First Wheels

At the end of his junior year in high school, two and a half years after he'd moved to the ranch, Casey-Jack was asked if he wanted to move to a foster home in Baldwin, fifteen miles south of Lawrence, for his final year in foster care. The foster father was a retired widower in his late fifties, and there would be only one other child in the home, another teenager who had once been Casey-Jack's roommate at the ranch. A major incentive to move was the possibility that he'd be able to get his driver's license and buy a car, a high priority for most soon-to-be eighteen-year-olds, and an impossibility for most youth in foster care. (Residents of the ranch weren't permitted to drive or own cars.)

After receiving assurances that he could finish his senior year at Lawrence High instead of transferring to the high school in Baldwin, Casey-Jack agreed to move. "I'd been wanting to get into a foster home for awhile, because I wanted more of a family setting," Casey-Jack says. Soon after he moved in, Frank, his foster father, taught him to drive, took him to get his driver's license, and then helped him shop for a car.

"Within a month of turning eighteen, I had a car," Casey-Jack says proudly. By combining some savings with a loan from the used car dealer, he bought a 1985 Ford Escort with more than 100,000 miles on it for $1,300. (When the car died only a few months later, he traded it in for a 1990 Escort that had seen just under 100,000 miles.) Frank also helped him find a relatively affordable insurance policy with a semiannual premium of $346, an amount Casey-Jack felt comfortable he could earn himself.

Securing His Future

Only a few weeks into Casey-Jack's senior year, terrorists seized four American passenger jets and flew them into the two World Trade Center towers, the Pentagon, and a field in rural Pennsylvania. More than 3,000 people died.

Three weeks after the attack, Casey-Jack walked into the army recruiting office in Lawrence and agreed to serve in the Army Reserves for eight years.

His older brother had enlisted in the Army Reserves right after graduating from high school, so Casey-Jack had been thinking about it as a postgraduation option for a long time. The September 11 attack was the push he needed to actually sign up. "I wanted the discipline and the leadership skills," he says, "but the main attraction was that I'd get support through college."

Among the enlistment incentives that Casey-Jack was promised was a $5,000 enlistment bonus—half to be paid after his graduation from advanced individual training the following fall, with the second half to come later. In addition, for any time during which he would be on active duty, such as the required thirty-eight days a year, he would receive active-duty pay, which would amount to about $2,400 a year.

But the education benefits were what really appealed to him. Under the Montgomery GI Bill, he could expect to receive a monthly educational assistance allowance of $272 for up to thirty-six months, plus a $200-per-month bonus for working as a patient administration specialist. And the army's Tuition Assistance Program would pay for up to 75 percent of his tuition costs, or a maximum of $3,500 a year.

For many years, enlistment in the military services was a fairly common path for young people to take upon aging out of foster care. The appeal for a young person without family support is obvious, since military service provides not just a job but food, shelter, and medical care. But with the retrenchment in the standing military that came in the 1990s, the services became more selective about whom they would accept, and it became harder for young people who have aged out of foster care to qualify. Many lack the high school diplomas or graduate equivalency diplomas that the services insist upon, and others have psychiatric histories or juvenile records that disqualify them.

When Casey-Jack learned that he'd passed the physical and been accepted into the reserves, he felt that he had secured his post-foster care future.

The Perfect Plan

During his senior year, Casey-Jack had one foot in high school and the other in his future. Besides taking a full load of classes, he was working thirty hours a week at two part-time jobs. He was active in his church's youth group and its drama team. He was serving on the new Kansas

Youth Advisory Council, which had been established to help the state's foster care agency, the Department of Social and Rehabilitation Services (SRS), figure out how to better prepare youth in foster care for independence. In addition, he was reporting for active duty one weekend a month, first in Independence, Missouri, and later in Topeka, Kansas.

Because he was less than a year away from leaving foster care, Casey-Jack had other responsibilities, too. His foster care agency required him to take Independent Living (IL) courses to prepare for living on his own and to meet regularly with his counselor. "She really helped me," he says of Jessica Hrencher, his IL coordinator. "She took me on three or four college visits, and she helped me find scholarships I could get. She gave me a lot of one-on-one help. She knew what I needed to do, and she helped me do it."

Casey-Jack also benefited from a close relationship with his longtime *guardian ad litem,* Peggy Kittel. "She was awesome," he said. "She listened to me, and she really advocated for me, and got things done. I'd tell her, 'My agency isn't doing this or that for me, like giving me my clothing allowance,' and she'd tell the judge, who'd make the agency do it. She always knew what was going on with me, more than anyone else. I could call her pretty much anytime I wanted to. I felt like she cared."

That winter, Casey-Jack applied to two private Kansas colleges, Ottawa University and Manhattan Christian College. Each offered the academic courses necessary to qualify him to work as a youth minister, though both were expensive, with Manhattan Christian's annual cost approaching $12,000, and Ottawa's, $20,000. Both his independent living coordinator and the Kerrs, his former teaching parents at O'Connell Youth Ranch, urged him to apply to some state schools as well, since Kansas in 2001 had begun waiving the tuition at state schools for some youth who have aged out of foster care. But besides wanting to pursue a course of study that the state schools don't offer, Casey-Jack was wary of the size of state schools. And he knew that since Kansas only requires each state school to provide three tuition waivers each year, receiving one was by no means a sure thing.

Both private colleges accepted him. Casey-Jack decided to attend Manhattan Christian College, which had offered him a $2,500 scholarship, giving it a substantial cost edge over Ottawa. As senior year progressed,

Casey-Jack learned that he would receive two other scholarships as well: a $1,000 grant from The Shelter, where he had spent three months four years before, and a $2,500 grant from his private foster care agency, Kaw Valley Center. By combining these grants with his expected military benefits and a federal Pell grant, he figured he'd be able to pay his bills at Manhattan Christian College without having to take out loans. "I had it perfectly planned out," Casey-Jack says. "My independent living counselor was proud of me."

At his high school graduation, he had more people in the audience applauding his accomplishment than most of his classmates, including several caseworkers, the Kerrs, his foster father and foster brother, his *guardian ad litem*, his father, and Jerry and Renita Freeman, the parents of a friend.

As a graduation gift, the Freemans threw a combination graduation and going-away party. "He didn't really have a home to have an open house in, like all the other graduates were doing, so we rented a shelter in a park, and hired a caterer, and invited everyone who had been important to him over the years," Renita Freeman explains. "When we were planning it, he was worried that no one would come. But a lot of people came, and that made him feel really loved. I felt it was the best gift we could give him."

Casey-Jack moved into the Freemans' home for the three weeks remaining until he had to report for basic training. He had often stayed at their home during his senior year when church or school activities ran late, and the Freemans had offered to store his belongings while he attended boot camp. "And we talked about him coming back here after he finished training, while he figured out what he was going to do," says Renita Freeman. "We told him he always had a place here. My husband and I have a tendency to gather other people's children. We've had several kids stay with us for months at a time."

"Welcome to Hell"

On June 17, 2002, Casey-Jack and several dozen other recruits from the Midwest boarded a plane from Kansas City to Atlanta, Georgia, where they transferred to a bus bound for Fort Benning, Georgia, the army's infantry school. "Welcome to hell, gentleman," a military police officer boomed in greeting to the tired recruits after their journey across country.

Several weeks later, Casey-Jack's battalion was finally authorized to "ship" to a different area of the base to begin the grueling training required of all recruits. "For the next nine weeks, I am God," the senior drill sergeant told the recruits in his welcoming remarks, Casey-Jack recalls.

The first week of basic training was mostly classroom work. "Traditions and rules, and discussion of the seven core army values—loyalty, duty, respect, selfless service, honor, integrity and personal courage," Casey-Jack explains. Once the army philosophy was ingrained in their psyches, the physical training began in earnest. And that's when Casey-Jack realized he was in trouble.

Since early childhood, Casey-Jack had suffered from headaches that sometimes lasted for days. He had worried about getting a headache during basic training but had persuaded himself that he'd find a way to cope. Over the years, he had usually managed to attend school or work even while he had a headache, simply because he had to. If he could just get through basic, he figured that his headaches wouldn't interfere with his one-weekend-a-month obligation to the reserves, where he would have a desk job.

But within a few days of starting basic training, Casey-Jack got a headache that wouldn't go away. It became obvious to everyone around him that something was very wrong. He stumbled on road marches. He frequently threw up. He looked pale and clammy. And though he didn't tell anyone, his vision was sometimes blurred.

"My battle buddy saw that I wasn't performing well," Casey-Jack says. "He asked me what was wrong, and I told him. And he told my drill sergeant."

Casey-Jack was placed on sick call for four days and given over-the-counter drugs, which didn't begin to touch the pain. When the four days were up, he started training again. "I tried to tough it out," Casey-Jack said.

A few days later, he had to go on sick call again. After a day of rest, he resumed training. But again, the headache interfered with his performance, and he went back on sick call. "It got really bad during rifle training," he said. "We were out in the heat in full battle-dress uniform—the camouflage fatigues with long sleeves and long pants, and heavy boots and a cap. It was 98 or 99 degrees on the thermometer, with a humidity index of probably 120. I felt like I was going to die."

This time, the medical officer barred him from any activities that required exertion of any sort. She sent for his old medical records, and after a review, she certified him for a medical discharge.

"If I'd Been Tougher"

While his discharge papers were making their way through the army bureaucracy, Casey-Jack was placed on light duty, which required him to answer the phone and run errands for the drill sergeant. No further physical training was permitted, even jogging or weight lifting.

The experience was humiliating. "The drill sergeant made fun of me," Casey-Jack says. "He'd tell me, 'You'd better just stand there. You might get a migraine.'"

Deep in his heart, Casey-Jack knew that a medical discharge was appropriate. Even so, he was hugely disappointed. It made him feel like a failure. "I knew that if I'd been tougher, I could have endured the headaches and stayed in," he laments.

It wasn't just his pride that was hurt, which would have been hard enough to endure. The way he looked at it, his whole future was now in jeopardy. Without the army's tuition assistance and monthly stipend, it looked highly unlikely that he could enroll at Manhattan Christian College the following January, as he had planned.

As is his nature, Casey-Jack affected a stiff upper lip. "I was upset, but I didn't let it take hold of me," he says. A pastor at a church near the base helped him understand that getting discharged was God's plan for him, he says.

With a lot of time on his hands while he waited for his discharge papers, Casey-Jack made frequent calls to his friends in Lawrence. Renita and Jerry Freeman told him again that he was welcome to move into their son's bedroom, which was unoccupied because he was away in the army. Their daughter, Sara, promised him the use of her car until he got his running again. And his supervisor at the service station where he had worked during his last semester in high school told him he could not only have his old job back but also move up to assistant manager.

One of the last calls that he made from Fort Benning was to his older brother, whose footsteps he had followed into the army. "It took me forever to finally get up the courage to tell my brother I failed," he recalls. "One of the reasons I had gone into the army was sibling rivalry. I wanted to prove I could do better than my brother, especially at physical training."

Finally, on September 17, 2002, two days before his battalion's graduation from basic training, his discharge papers came through. Casey-Jack boarded a plane home. Renita and Jerry Freeman were waiting for him at the Kansas City International Airport. They had readied their son's room for him, as promised.

Casey-Jack spent his first five days back in Lawrence catching up on sleep, relearning the ways of civilian life, looking up old friends, and reconnecting with his church's youth group.

On the Monday following his return, he reported for work at the service station. His pay was set at $6.75 an hour, reflecting a 50-cent-per-hour increase. That meant he could expect to take home about $200 a week.

The State Comes Through

For his first few weeks back in Lawrence, Casey-Jack didn't even think about his long-term future. Adjusting to civilian life took all of his energy. But people kept asking him what he was going to do next.

"I started thinking about what my options were," Casey-Jack said. "I knew I needed to go to school if I wanted to make anything of my life. I thought about taking classes on-line. And I thought about applying to a state school."

Casey-Jack called his former caseworker at the Kansas Department of Social and Rehabilitative Services, and she gave him a pep talk. "She told me not to let myself get down," he recalls. "She said she'd help me find a way to get to school."

A few days later, Casey-Jack met with her, and she reminded him about the new aftercare benefits for which he might be eligible, including a monthly stipend of $400 for as long as he was a full-time college student. Casey-Jack says the caseworker had no previous experience with the program, which was relatively new, but she promised to help him qualify. "I'm the oldest person in her caseload," Casey-Jack explains. "We're both learning."

Under the Chafee Act, each state is receiving about twice as much federal money as in the past to prepare older youth in foster care for independence and even to subsidize their living expenses after they leave foster care. The money first became available in 2000. The first year, Kansas received more than $1 million for independent living services, and almost $1.6 million in each of the following three fiscal years.

Kansas was slow to figure out what new independent living services to fund, and for the first few years it spent most of its Chafee allocation on other foster care programs. In an August 2001 federal audit of SRS, the federal Department of Health and Human Services criticized Kansas's slow pace in complying with Chafee. "Independent living services are not available in all areas," HHS reported. "There are concerns that children are aging out of the child welfare system without the necessary life skills training. According to stakeholders, some workers and youth are not aware that independent living services can be used for children eighteen years of age and over. Transitional planning was not always occurring for children with special needs to prepare them to live independently."[1]

Under Chafee, the states have wide discretion about how to use their federal funds to help prepare foster youth for independent living. Kansas's Chafee plan provides for a monthly subsidy of up to $400 to youth who aged out of care and are attending college full-time. But because no more than one-third of a state's allocation can be used to subsidize room and board, there's only enough money to support a small fraction of the Kansas youth who age out in a given year. In 2002, forty-eight young people in Kansas received the subsidies, out of an eligible population of 400 or so.

On October 31, six weeks after he returned from Fort Benning, Casey-Jack met again with his SRS caseworker to draw up an "achievement plan" to qualify him for aftercare benefits. The plan called for him to:

- Enroll in Manhattan Christian College by January 30, 2003
- Participate in therapy sessions through April 2003 with a therapist in private practice, with Casey-Jack paying $5 per session and SRS paying $40
- Apply for Medicaid coverage by November 30, 2002
- Remain employed
- Meet at least monthly with a community adviser and his SRS caseworker
- Work out a monthly budget

Casey-Jack felt that college was once again within his reach. He notified Manhattan Christian to expect him as a student for the spring semester. He talked to a financial aid counselor there about how to apply for the federal grants he'd need to help with tuition and room and board. And he bought himself a $1,400 laptop on an installment plan.

A Sudden Change in Plans

Casey-Jack was scheduled to move into a dorm at Manhattan Christian College on January 9, 2003. But a few days before that, he changed his mind.

The change of plans came about as a result of a revelation that Casey-Jack says he experienced on New Year's Eve. He and 20,000 other young people had crowded into the Kansas City Convention Center to mark the beginning of the new year by rededicating their lives to Christ. They were attending The Call, the fourth in a series of regional prayer events. From noon to midnight, they prayed, fasted, sang, and danced.

"While I was praying, I said, 'OK, Father, what do you want me to do with my life?'" Casey-Jack recalled a few days later. "I shut up and let God speak to me. He basically told me that it wasn't the right time to go to Manhattan Christian College. He said he didn't want me to study to be a youth minister because he hadn't called me to it yet. He told me, 'Right now, I need you to work.'"

Casey-Jack's caseworker and his community adviser have tried to talk him into changing his mind. "No one thinks it's a good idea," he admits. "They don't think I know what I'm doing. They basically think I'm acting like a little kid."

But he says his mind can't be changed.

"Everybody knows my heart was set on going to the school," he says. "It was something I really, really wanted to do. Nothing could have changed my mind except for Him. I realized I'm not called full-time to youth ministry work. I could feel it in my heart."

"Basically, I'm Broke"

So the young man who thought he'd had his future all figured out fifteen months ago is back at the drawing board, his future a blank slate.

The Freemans assured him that he could stay with them through May 2003, when their son is scheduled to return home from the army, and just pay what he can. But even without having to pay market rent, he has money problems. He has about $500 a month in fixed expenses—a car payment, car insurance, his cell phone bill, plus the installment payment on the laptop. Already, he's one month in arrears on his car payment and two months behind on everything else, with a grand total of $25 in the bank. "Basically, I'm broke," he says.

Since he's not going to be a full-time student, he's no longer eligible for the $400-a-month educational stipend from SRS. His caseworker has certified him for a transitional stipend of roughly the same amount, but for a maximum of three months. It's not enough to cover his car payment and credit card bills, let alone rent on a place of his own, so he knows he has to find work, and find it soon. His caseworker has referred him to the agency's vocational rehabilitation office for job counseling and other assistance (his history of emotional problems makes him eligible).

"What's there to worry about?" he said late in January 2003, when asked whether he's worried about his future. "I know I'm doing what I'm supposed to. I'm sure God has the perfect job planned out for me. I'm doing my part by applying and looking."

Postscript

Casey-Jack's professed optimism was sorely tested over the next nine months.

In monthly telephone conversations and periodic e-mails, he bounced from one plan to another, an indication that he had no real idea about what he wanted to do with his life.

Although he has no specialized computer skills, he thought he might be able to get a job as a webmaster at the University of Kansas, he said midway through January 2003. "They have to find out if they have money left in a grant," he said. "And they would have to find someone who'd be willing to teach me. But I'm optimistic."

By February, with no job offer from the university in sight, he was back to thinking about becoming a youth minister and was talking about applying to college in California. "It's where I feel my ministry is supposed to be," he wrote in an e-mail. "It'll be a nice life. I want to be out of my comfort zone, and that's well out of it." Nothing came of it.

Over the next four months, he says he put in job applications all over Lawrence. "The economy sucks," he said in early spring, "but I'm still optimistic I'll find a job. My [social] worker still thinks I should be in school somewhere, but she doesn't seem to understand that I have about $500 a month in bills that I'm not going to be able to pay if I'm in school full-time and only working part-time."

In May, he finally found a job as a clerk for the city water department. "I love my job," he reported by e-mail.

Two weeks later, he was fired.

Not much else in his life was going well either. His debts were, as he put it, "out the wazoo." His church had made him leave the youth group because he had started a relationship with a sixteen-year-old girl whose mother objected. And because the Freemans' son needed his bedroom back, he had lost his housing. "Everything is crashing down," he reported in May. "My life is hell right now."

With no income and no other friends offering him a spare bedroom, he moved in with his father. "It's hell, but it was my only option," he said. He began thinking about trying to reenlist in the military. "I'm on medication now for my headaches, so I think I'd do OK," he said.

In early June, he started training as a certified nurse's aide. "After I finish, I'll be able to work in a hospital," he wrote in an e-mail.

Two weeks later, he quit.

Soon afterward, he got a job as a sander in a factory. But he was fired after four days.

"I sit in my room all day basically doing nothing," he said in July, when asked what he did with his time. "I'm on the computer a lot." He was writing poetry and spending a lot of time sending instant messages to friends. He was also working on a novel about a rape.

Late in August, Casey-Jack checked in again by e-mail. "Sorry it's been awhile," he wrote. "Still going through hell. It sucks, but whatever. I wound up getting a job at Kwik Shop. Then my car died, and I can't get there, so I can't work there."

Two days later, he sent e-mails to all fifty-seven people in his on-line address book. In a not-too-subtle plea for help, he wrote that he had a lead on a local job, but that to get to it he needed $800 to buy a car. "Please pray that I will have the funding available to me," he pleaded. "I really need a car! I really need a job! Thank you!"

Within a week, his plans had changed again. "I have made the decision to go ahead and go to school this fall at Ottawa University," he wrote in an e-mail. "I just now am taking the step towards it. I'll start real quick like."

In a telephone conversation, Casey-Jack explained that after months of indecisiveness, he had realized that he had no future without further education. "I've wanted to be in school for a while," he said.

"As indecisive as I am and how many different things I've told you, I know it's hard to believe. I really have. But so many other people were telling me, 'You can't, you can't, you can't' for so long about the things I wanted to do, and I'd been telling myself 'I can't' too. I finally woke up and said, 'Piss off if they don't like what I want to do.' I can't have a family without a career, and I can't have a career without an education. I won't be able to do anything with my life unless I go to school."

An admissions counselor at Ottawa, a Baptist college, helped him line up grants and loans to supplement the $3,500 in scholarships that he had been awarded by two child welfare agencies. But when he called in September to ask how to claim one of the scholarships (for $2,500), he found out that he had missed the deadline for claiming it, and it had been given to someone else. That means he's had to borrow about $5,400 for the 2003–2004 school year, which worries him, since he's already amassed about $7,000 in consumer debt since aging out of foster care.

In early September 2003, Casey-Jack moved into a dorm at Ottawa University. He plans to major in communications, with the goal of becoming a journalist. That summer journalism experience he received in 2000 appears to have accomplished one of its intentions: to give children the "hopes and dreams to reach for the stars."

Transitions have always been hard for him, and for the first few weeks at Ottawa, he was miserable. He talked about transferring to another school as soon as he could. But by late October, he seemed to be adjusting. He still had plenty of problems—creditors badgering him to make payments on his debts, a broken computer, a roommate who he says doesn't like him, and Ds in two subjects. And his girlfriend's mother was still refusing to allow anything but minimal contact.

But the state vocational rehabilitation agency was giving him a living stipend of $450 a month, plus about $250 a month for gas. (He qualified on the basis of his emotional problems.) The agency had also bought him a reliable car and paid his insurance for a year. And the adviser to the college newspaper had asked him to serve as co-editor.

By spring 2004, the news was still mixed. His first semester GPA had turned out to be a dismal 1.3, and he was on academic probation. He was still strapped for cash, and in an effort to save money had foolishly moved out of the dorm and into the home of an adult of questionable character. On the positive side, his second semester grade point average, though still below 2.0, was rising. And he was doing well in his part-time job as a research assistant with the Kansas Appleseed Center for Law and Justice, a Lawrence-based advocacy group interested in foster care. His boss had already given him two raises, bringing his pay to $9.50 an hour, and offered him a full-time job during the summer of 2004.

As the semester was drawing to an end, Casey-Jack was weighing whether to return in the fall or transfer to a college in Oklahoma or Tennessee. In June 2004, he was to turn twenty-one, which will end his eligibility for most of the special services available to young people who have aged out of care.

"Life pisses us a horrible brick sometimes, but it goes on," he said in his characteristic way. "I've got a lot going against me, but I've got a lot going for me, so I'm not letting it get me down."

For relaxation,
Casey-Jack likes
to play the drums.

Casey-Jack Kitos
cites religion as a
source of strength.
Left, he worships
at a charismatic
church in Lawrence.

Monica Romero with her
daughter, Amber

"I WAS TIRED OF LIVING THAT LIFE"

Monica Romero, San Antonio, Texas

By age sixteen, Monica Romero was skipping school and spending her allowance on drugs. She and her foster mother fought constantly.

By seventeen, she had dropped out of high school and run away to Mexico. For seven months, her foster mother had no idea where she was.

And by eighteen, Monica was pregnant. For four months after her baby's birth, she depended on the kindness of friends—and sometimes strangers—for a place to stay. The low point in her odyssey was surely the night she and the baby spent in the home of a stranger who'd offered them a ride.

Many young people become parents not long after aging out of foster care. Within four years, 42 percent have given birth to or fathered children, a study by the Westat, Inc., research organization has found.[1]

For too many young women who become mothers while they're still teenagers, giving birth marks the end of aspiration. They are much less likely to attend college than their peers. About one-fourth give birth to a second child within two years, and 28 percent of them remain poor through their early thirties, four times the rate for women who delay childbearing.[2]

But Monica has defied the odds. Becoming a mother proved to be a turning point for her. She vowed that her baby would have a better life than she had had. And she also promised herself that she would never put her feelings for a boyfriend ahead of her devotion to her child, as she believed her mother always had. "Seeing what kind of mother my own mom was made me know that that's not how I wanted to be," Monica says. "I saw what drinking and partying did to her, how they took her attention from her children, and how men took her attention away from us, too. That's not how I wanted my daughter to grow up."

One and a half years after her daughter's birth, Monica is a model mother, a conscientious student, and a devoted granddaughter and sister.

Monica got on the right track because a lot of people believed in her—strangers who opened their homes when she didn't have a place to stay. The social workers at the private agency that supervised her foster placement. The psychologist in whom she confided for twelve years. The case manager at a program for homeless mothers and children. Her sisters and grandmother.

But Monica wouldn't be where she is today if she hadn't also begun to believe in herself.

A Grandmother Steps Forward

Although many children in foster care spend years wondering why they were taken from their parents, Monica always knew that it was for her own safety. She may have fantasized about returning to her mother, but deep inside she knew that if she and her sisters had not been placed in foster care, at least one of them might not have survived childhood.

That's because she and two sisters had seen their mother's boyfriend beat their two-year-old sister, Emily,[3] so badly that she nearly died. And Monica had endured numerous beatings herself. "I got beaten up a lot because I was the oldest," Monica says matter-of-factly. "He'd hit me with his shoe, or a belt, and he'd slam me against a wall. One time he hung me by my wrists in the closet."

After Emily nearly died, the abuser was prosecuted, convicted, and sent to prison for twelve years. When Emily recovered, she was placed first with a foster family and then, a few months later, with her maternal grandmother. Child-protection authorities kept Monica and two other sisters in a children's shelter for a few months before allowing them to go home to their mother, along with a new sister who had been born three months after the incident in which Emily was injured.

However, the girls' mother wasn't able to maintain a stable home. She failed to take the parenting classes that a judge ordered and often left the three younger girls in the care of Monica, who was only eight. None of the girls' fathers was in a position to care for them, so the three oldest girls were all sent back to the children's shelter until social workers could find them foster homes.

It's hard to find foster families for a large group of young siblings, and it looked for a while as though the sisters would have to be split up. Putting them up for adoption was discussed. Their maternal grandmother, Maria Romero, then fifty-two, didn't want to see the family broken up. She was already caring for Emily and was willing to take care of the three oldest girls, too, but she couldn't see how she could afford to on her income from her disability check and her late husband's Social Security income. A state caseworker told her the state couldn't help. She told Mrs. Romero that she was eligible only for a monthly welfare payment of $60 for Emily and nothing for the three other girls.[4]

A few weeks later, however, the state caseworker learned about a private foster care agency that was getting started in San Antonio and planned to specialize in placing children who required long-term foster care. Casey Family Programs is a Seattle-based operating foundation that provides long-term foster care and kinship care services to children in more than a dozen states. Public agencies sometimes look to Casey to find foster homes for children they are having trouble placing, such as large sibling groups, like the Romero girls. The state pays Casey a monthly fee for each child the agency places in one of its licensed foster homes,[5] and Casey, in turn, passes on the state fee to the foster parent, as well as a supplement. Casey uses income from its endowment to provide additional support services to the children in its caseload, such as summer camp, music lessons, tutoring, individual and group therapy, and outings, and the agency pays some college-related costs as well.

"I heard that Casey was looking for a family to help and that they could provide me with enough assistance so that the girls could even go to college," Mrs. Romero said. "I realized that if I let them be adopted, I wouldn't ever know anything about them when they're older. I thought I might as well take them. I don't know if it was the right thing, but it's what I did."

In the fall of 1991, Mrs. Romero completed a training program and became a licensed foster parent to the four oldest Romero girls. (Because she had recently had surgery on her wrists, she felt she couldn't care for the baby, who was adopted by one of her daughters.) Casey Family Programs provided Mrs. Romero with a monthly stipend for each of the girls, as well as medical insurance.

"Financially, we were OK for the first time in a long time," she says, with obvious gratitude. "The money allowed me to be a full-time mother to the girls, and I could buy them what they needed."

"Get Out of My Life"

Because she took her role as a licensed foster parent very seriously, Mrs. Romero ran a tight household. She rarely made a decision about the girls without consulting with their caseworker. And she was careful about how she disciplined them. "Raising kids who are in foster care, even if they're your grandkids, is not the same as raising your own kids," Mrs. Romero explains. "When I was raising my own eight, I would get after them when they did something bad. I might even spank them, though I didn't like to. But as a foster mother, you can't spank them."

Throughout elementary school, Monica seemed to thrive in this protective and loving environment. As expected, she struggled with what caseworkers call "birth family issues"—in particular, why she couldn't see more of her mother or father and why a social worker had to supervise the visits they had. But otherwise, she was a typical little girl. She did well in school, helped out at home, attended summer camp, and participated enthusiastically in the social activities that Casey organizes for children in its foster homes. At Palo Alto Elementary School, she chaired the beautification committee and was selected as "citizen of the week" several times and "Queen of Palo Alto" in fifth grade.

But as Monica moved into her teens, she became surly and disrespectful. She was feeling increasingly guilty about Emily's injuries, which had left Emily with chronic health problems that required multiple surgeries. "My other sisters and I had been jumping on the bed, laughing and playing, and the next thing we knew, one of them pulled the curtains down," she says of the incident that preceded the abuse. "We told Rudy [her mother's boyfriend] that [Emily] did it because we thought he wouldn't beat her since she was little. But he did."

Monica was also burdened with anger toward her mother. "I was angry at her because it seemed to me like she'd made no effort to try to get us back," she says. "She always put men before us. I wanted her to stop picking men over us so we could all be together and be happy."

And Monica also began resenting her grandmother. Instead of loosening her grip on Monica's life as she entered puberty, Monica's grandmother tightened it. In Monica's eyes, she became more of a jailer than a surrogate mother. "She was really strict," Monica remembers. "I was trying to be like other kids. I wanted to be able to go to the movies and sleep over at my friends' houses and go to the mall, and my grandmother wouldn't let me. It made me depressed. I'd shut myself up in my room and turn on the radio and turn off the lights."

Mrs. Romero's protectiveness was partly due to her strict interpretation of the foster care rules, some of which make it hard for children in care to participate in normal social activities (like sleepovers). But she had other reasons as well. Her husband had been shot to death in 1976 during an argument. Also, several of her own children had had rough passages through adolescence, and she knew all too well what unsupervised teenagers might get in to. "She didn't trust the people out there," Monica says. "She was afraid of something happening to us. Most of her daughters, including my mom, had their first kids when they were teenagers. My grandma especially wanted to keep us away from boys so that we could complete our education before we had kids. She didn't want us to struggle like they have."

Although Monica now speaks with understanding of the reasons for her grandmother's rules, at the time she complained about her grandmother whenever she met with her Casey caseworker or with her psychologist, her case files show. She also used any opportunity she got to complain about Casey's involvement in her life.

"I hated Casey while I was growing up," she admits. "I hated them being in my life. It was always like their way or no way. I hated that my grandmother had to report everything I did to Casey, and constantly fill out progress reports.

"They were a pain. They were always in my business. I had no freedom to do anything. I would tell them, 'I just want to be a normal, regular kid. Get out of my life. Leave me alone.'"

More Problems At Home

In February 1998, when Monica was sixteen and a half, Mrs. Romero discovered a boy in her bedroom. She threw him out and she told Monica that she was free to leave, too. The next day, Monica ran away. She sought refuge at the boy's home and refused to return home.

Monica's caseworkers decided that both Monica and Mrs. Romero would benefit from a respite from each other, and they found her another foster home. But within days of moving in, Monica disappeared again. This time, she hid out in her mother's house.

Monica was going through a phase common to many adolescents in foster care. Until recently, she had been so angry with her mother that she rarely spoke to her when they met for a supervised visit. "One time, when she was at my grandma's, she told me to go to bed." Monica recalls. "I told her, 'Don't you ever tell me what to do. You're not raising me. It's your fault we're in foster care. It's your fault we're unhappy. It's your fault [Emily] is the way she is. How could you let this happen?'"

But now, as she approached adulthood, she wanted to have more contact with her mother than her caseworker would allow. "I didn't want to be in a foster home any more," Monica says. "All I wanted was for my mom and me and my sisters to be able to live together again and be happy. I wanted us to be a family again."

The Casey worker tracked Monica to her mother's house. She told her that the court would never permit her to live with her mother, who had lost her parental rights. Monica returned reluctantly to the new foster home. After a brief stay, Monica went back to her grandmother's.

Hiding Out

The truce between Monica and her grandmother lasted just over a month. One night late in June 1998, Monica failed to come home after finishing her shift at a restaurant, and Mrs. Romero reported her missing. Two days later, the police found Monica and brought her home in handcuffs. She wouldn't say where she'd been.

Later that same night, Monica ran away again. After a month with no word, Casey hired a private investigator to look for her, but he had no luck. For seven months, Mrs. Romero had no idea where she was. "I was so worried about her," Mrs. Romero remembers. "I cried all the time. Sometimes, I thought the worst, really. One day the police came and told me that they'd found a body that might be Monica's. For a whole day, I didn't know if it was Monica or not."

For the first few months, Monica now admits, she lived with Richard, the boyfriend who'd been discovered in her room, and his mother, Sally.[6] "The cops came to his house once, but I was elsewhere," Monica says.

The "elsewhere" was just the kind of environment from which Mrs. Romero had been trying to protect her. "I was always out partying," Monica says. "My boyfriend ended up going to jail, and me and his sister spent all our time doing drugs. Coke, crank, whatever you could sniff, and marijuana."

Monica got something from drugs that she couldn't get anywhere else: insulation from her feelings. "I really loved being on cocaine," she says. "It was like no one could touch me. No matter what anyone said or did to me, it wouldn't matter. I was so tired of people hurting my feelings, and that was the one way no one could."

Monica's mother knew where she was staying and feared that the private investigator was closing in on her, so in September 1998, she arranged for Monica to hide out in Mexico with the relatives of a man she had married not long before. She promised Monica that she'd come and get her in December.

The man's family lived in the village of El Saladillo, a day and a half drive from San Antonio. "The family was really nice to me," Monica recalls. "They bought me this and that to make sure I was comfortable. I ended up making friends there. We'd go to the dances together, and I got a job picking chilies for 10 cents a bucket. I'd work all day and make a few dollars. It was a really different life."

When December arrived, there was no sign of Monica's mother. "I was like, 'Mom, where are you?'" Monica recalls. "And when she finally called, she told me she wasn't going to be able to come for me until March."

Monica was devastated. "I was tired of being in Mexico," she says. "I was tired of being a runaway. I didn't want to do drugs or party any more. I wanted to go back to school and graduate."

One day in late December, a visitor to her host's home mentioned that he was heading to San Antonio later that day. Monica was in the middle of doing laundry but didn't hesitate before asking him for a ride. "I left all my wet clothes and went off with this perfect stranger," she says. "All I took was my radio and the few clothes that were dry."

A Home with "Grandma Juanita"

By now seventeen and a half, Monica did not want to return to her grandmother's home. Nor did she want to live in another foster home. She moved in with her mom and her new husband.

Early in the new year, she called the psychologist she'd been seeing since she was eight and told her, "I'm tired of this life. I want to go back to school. I don't want to hide any more."

With the psychologist's help, Monica enrolled in January 1999 at South San Antonio Academy, an alternative school at which students progress at their own paces. At the urging of the psychologist, Monica called her social worker at Casey Family Programs, which was still her legal guardian, to let her know where she was. Her worker told her that she couldn't live with her mother while the agency still had legal custody of her. She would either have to go to court to seek emancipation from foster care or remain in the agency's custody, live in an approved home, and receive services aimed at preparing her for independence. The conversation ended without a resolution.

Over the next month, relations between Monica and her mother deteriorated, as they usually did whenever the two spent much time together. "It seems like every time she's with a man, it doesn't work out between us," Monica says. Monica made plans to move back with Sally, the mother of her former boyfriend, who had sheltered her the previous summer. But her social worker objected to this arrangement.

Finally, in March, Monica and her social worker reached a compromise: Monica would live with Sally's mother, a woman she calls "Grandma Juanita," whom she had gotten to know the summer before. Juanita Sandoval was a widow in her mid-seventies who had raised eleven children and was grandmother to thirty-two and great-grandmother to "too many to count." For much of her life, she'd been opening her two-bedroom home to children who needed a place to stay.

"I felt sorry for her not having nobody," Mrs. Sandoval says of Monica. "She was having a hard time with her mother, who would lock her out when she got mad at her. And she wasn't getting along with her grandmother. She had no place to go. So I said, 'Why not?' I prayed with her and talked to her like I would to my own granddaughters."

Because Mrs. Sandoval wasn't licensed as a foster parent, Casey could not pay her a monthly stipend. But the agency gave Monica $35 a week for food to lessen the burden on Mrs. Sandoval, whose only income was Social Security.

Monica got along with Mrs. Sandoval in a way that she had been unable to get along with her grandmother. Four years later, Monica still thinks of Mrs. Sandoval as an important influence on her life. "She's a great example of a Christian woman," Monica says. "Everything she does is out of the kindness of her heart."

On June 1, 1999, Monica graduated from high school a year ahead of her class. Working at her own pace at the alternative school, Monica had managed not only to make up for the semester she had missed while in

Mexico but also to get ahead. Her grandmother and sisters were there to celebrate her success, as was Mrs. Sandoval, her daughter Sally, and a caseworker from Casey Family Programs.

After graduation, Monica took a waitress job at a family-style restaurant. Although she still harbored bitter feelings toward the foster care agency, she began to take advantage of some of the transition services that Casey offered to emancipated and soon-to-be emancipated youth. An aide from the transition program helped her enroll at San Antonio College, a community college. "He picked me up and even waited in line with me to register," Monica remembers with gratitude. "And he got me a loan from Casey for my books."

A Place of Her Own

Because she was enrolled in college, Monica became eligible after emancipation for a new supported housing program that Casey was offering to its foster care alumni. The agency was renting apartments for youth who had aged out of foster care, a dream come true for Monica, who was still living with Grandma Juanita.

Liz Cruz, a caseworker with Casey's transition services center, helped Monica find an apartment and signed the lease, with the agency as the leaseholder. Monica recruited some friends to help her move in. Her stay there lasted exactly one night. Her friends made so much noise that the landlord terminated the lease the next day.

Monica returned to Grandma Juanita's home in self-imposed exile. She was so embarrassed by what had happened that she cut off contact with Casey Family Programs for most of the next year. "I had messed up so bad, losing the apartment after just one day, that I didn't think they'd want to help me again," she says. "I thought they'd just think I'd mess up again."

But Cruz says the agency shares some of the blame for what happened with the apartment. "Monica wasn't the only client for whom the program didn't work out well," she says. "At the time, there was not a lot being offered in San Antonio to help prepare youth for emancipation. We had some training in independent living skills, but it wasn't much. It certainly wasn't enough."

An Unexpected Crisis

Soon after the apartment fiasco, Monica got involved with Patrick,[7] a guy at work. "He was funny," she says. "He made me laugh." Monica soon moved into a house he shared with two other young people.

Unlike her previous boyfriend, Patrick didn't use drugs, which was part of his appeal. Monica had been clean for a month and was intent on giving up drugs. "One night, I looked at myself in the mirror, and I was ugly," she explained. "I realized I was tired of living that life. Patrick helped me stay away from drugs. He told me that I had to have strong will."

Although Monica was ready to give up drugs, she wasn't ready to get serious about her future. Her life revolved around working and spending time with Patrick.

Late that fall, she dropped out of college. "Patrick would work until midnight, and then come home, and we'd stay up all night," she explains. "We wouldn't sleep, so I was too tired to go to school."

By mutual consent, the relationship ended early that winter, although both continued to live in the same house. "I still had feelings for him, but we broke up because he was still immature and not ready to settle down," Monica says.

A few weeks after they broke up, Monica found out she was pregnant. By this time, Patrick had another girlfriend. Although many eighteen-year-olds in her position would have been devastated, Monica says she was happy about the pregnancy. "I wasn't really thinking then about how I would take care of a baby," she said. "I just wanted to have my baby, and knew it would somehow all work out. I think it's because when my sisters and I were younger we used to stay awake late at night talking about how we wanted to be moms, and I always pictured myself as a single mom, without the dad in the picture."

Monica moved out of the house in which Patrick was still living and, after a few days with her mother, moved in with the manager of the restaurant where she worked. After two months there, she had saved up enough to rent her own apartment.

Initially, she managed to keep up with her bills. But money became tight after she gave up the restaurant job to work as a cashier at a Target store because it was closer to the apartment. "Taking the job at Target ruined everything," she says. "I was making minimum wage, and I didn't earn enough."

Money wasn't her only problem. Soon after moving in, she had let two other teenagers move in with her. The first was Sally's eighteen-year-old son. "I told him, 'No drugs,'" Monica says, "but he walked all over me. It ended up getting out of control."

Then Sally prevailed upon Monica to let her boyfriend's fifteen-year-old daughter move in. Monica consented because she felt beholden to Sally for taking her in twice. Thus, at age eighteen, Monica was the de facto grown-up in a household of teenagers.

"They were like kids," Monica complains. "Give me $10 for this, and $5 for that. My money was going here and there. I couldn't save anything. And they had people coming in and out of my apartment all day long while I was at work. I'd come home and find out that they'd eaten everything in the house and left all the dishes in the sink."

By midsummer, Monica was two months behind in her rent. On August 6, three weeks before her due date, she was evicted.

No Place to Go

Nine months pregnant, Monica sought refuge in the house where she and Patrick had lived together the previous winter. One complication was that Patrick was still living there, along with a new girlfriend. That bothered her, but she had nowhere else to go.

When she went into labor on her due date, David, another resident of the house, took her to the hospital and stayed with her until an aunt arrived to coach her through the birth. Amber Lynn was born on August 26, 2000, weighing seven pounds, five ounces.

Monica brought Amber back to the house, where they occupied the room next to the one Patrick shared with his new girlfriend. Three weeks later, Patrick and his new girlfriend got married, dashing any hopes that Monica harbored about reconciling. "In a way, I guess I had been hoping that we would get back together, that he would give us a chance to try being a family so that she could have both of her parents in her life," Monica says. "But he was in love with someone else."

With Patrick's marriage, the living situation soon grew intolerable. When Amber was six weeks old, Monica packed up their things and moved to her mom's house. But living together had never worked out before, and it was clear to Monica that she couldn't stay there long. "She locked me and the baby in the house, behind security gates, when she went out," Monica says. "I couldn't stand it."

Nor could Monica return to her grandmother's house. Although Monica and Mrs. Romero got along better than before, staying there for more than a few days wasn't an option. For one thing, Mrs. Romero believes that once a granddaughter becomes a parent, she has to take responsibility for herself. "It's not because I want to be mean," she explains. "But I have thirty-six grandchildren, and eighteen great grandchildren. I don't want them to think they can depend on their grandmother to raise their kids. Going on their own is better. It makes them take responsibility."

For another thing, Casey Family Programs probably wouldn't have allowed Mrs. Romero to take in Monica and her baby. In many states, including Texas, foster care rules make it difficult for foster families to allow emancipated youth to live in the home—even if, like Monica, they're related. "Nobody's supposed to come and stay here who isn't on my license," Mrs. Romero says. "One time I asked if a grandson could stay with us, and they told me no."

In desperation, Monica called Jessica,[8] a friend who had moved with her husband to Killeen, a military town about 150 miles north of San Antonio. "When she heard about the problems I was having with my mom, she said, 'Move in with us,'" Monica says. Monica again packed her bags, and she and Amber moved into the couple's mobile home. Monica found a job at a telemarketing firm.

This arrangement lasted two months. Monica began to feel that her presence was causing problems between Jessica and her husband and that it would be better for them if she moved out. Though she didn't have an alternate plan, she set out on foot for the telemarketing firm, where she hoped she might talk one of her co-workers into taking her in.

She was trudging along the side of the road, carrying Amber in her car seat, when a passing motorist offered her a ride. When they reached the telemarketing firm, it was already closed. The motorist took Monica and Amber to his home so Monica could use the phone to call local shelters, but none would take her. "None of them could take me because I wasn't battered or anything," Monica says.

It was one of the lowest points in Monica's life. "I actually thought of leaving Amber on the shelter's doorstep," she says. "I felt that if they didn't take me in, that at least they would take my baby and provide for her better than what I was providing for her at the time. I felt like the worst mom in the world."

Feeling sorry for them, the stranger let Monica and Amber spend the night in a spare bedroom. "Luckily, he was actually a good guy," Monica says. "God was watching over me."

More Good Samaritans

As Monica had hoped, a co-worker took pity on her when she showed up at work with Amber the next day. The co-worker arranged for Monica and Amber to spend the next few nights at the home of her brother, who made it clear that the arrangement was only temporary. Fortunately, yet another co-worker, Angela, persuaded her grandparents to let Monica and Amber move in with them. She and her own baby were also living there.

Again, Monica managed to land in the hands of Good Samaritans. Jose and Elida Mendoza, both in their late sixties, had taken in Angela after she'd become pregnant at fourteen, and were helping her raise her baby. They were also raising a ten-year-old grandson, whom they'd adopted.

"I wasn't real happy when Angela called and said she wanted to bring someone home," recalls Jose Mendoza, a retired military man. "But my wife feels sorry for kids like this, and so do I, because I had a bad childhood also. I didn't have a father, and I went from aunt to grandmother to friends. At that time, there was not much help out there from the government. And being a minority made it still harder. I basically raised myself.

"I told Monica, 'If you're going to stay here, you're going to have to follow my rules,' and she did," Mr. Mendoza continues. "She listened to us. And she took good care of the baby. She never went out except to work or to buy things for the baby. She was a sweet girl." The Mendozas bought formula and diapers for Amber, and Mrs. Mendoza even took care of her while Monica worked.

About five weeks after Monica had moved in, Mr. Mendoza told her that he would be passing through San Antonio on his way to visit his son. He offered Monica and Amber a ride. It was almost Christmas, and Monica was ready to go home.

When Mr. Mendoza left Monica at her grandmother's home on Christmas Eve, he told her, "I want you to take care of this baby. Don't let anything happen to her."

Stepping Forward

Although she was just nineteen, Monica had grown up a lot in the four months since she had become a mother. Having someone else to care for made her understand the need to secure stable housing and begin to think about the future. "I had been moving around too much," she says. "It wasn't fair to Amber. I didn't want her to grow up like that."

Monica's grandmother cautiously welcomed her back into the family fold. But for the same reasons as before, Mrs. Romero couldn't let Monica and Amber stay for more than a few days. Monica got back in touch with her friend David, her old housemate in the house where she'd lived in the months immediately before and after Amber's birth. Once again, he made space for her. By this time, Amber's father and his wife had moved to El Paso, where he was stationed with the army.

Monica's grandmother urged her to get back in touch with Casey Family Programs, which she knew was expanding its services to emancipated foster youth. But Monica still felt ambivalent about Casey and was reluctant to approach the agency for help. She did feel close to one of the case aides, though, and called him. He told her about Stepping Forward, a Salvation Army shelter for homeless mothers and their children.

The Salvation Army launched Stepping Forward in 1993 after recognizing that the established network of services in San Antonio wasn't meeting the needs of homeless women and children. Although Stepping Forward was not set up to serve young women who have been emancipated from foster care, they constitute a majority of the clients. "We've inadvertently become a safety net for girls aging out of foster care," says Victoria Bernal, the program's caseworker. "The fact that they're coming to us means they didn't get the skills they needed to make it on their own. While they're in foster care, the system tries to shelter them so much that they don't get the skills they need to survive. And then once they're eighteen, it's bye-bye.

"It's a lot to ask of an eighteen-year-old. Most eighteen-year-olds are living in a college dorm or with their parents or other relatives. When you're eighteen and on your own, it's very scary."

At first, Monica was put off by the notion of living in a shelter. "I didn't want to hear anything about it," she says. Bernal says Monica's initial reluctance is common. "Nobody really *wants* to be in our program," she says. "That's the truth. But for most of them, it's the best option they have. They can continue to couch-surf or come here and learn the steps they have to take to make it on their own."

After weighing her options, Monica decided to give Stepping Forward a shot. "I decided I was going to move in there and play by the rules," she says. "I needed to straighten out my life and get some stability in it, for my daughter's sake." On March 22, 2001, she and Amber moved in.

Taking Care of Business

The Stepping Forward program occupies a low-slung building on the Salvation Army's sprawling Peacock Village campus, the site of a former military academy. From the outside, all that distinguishes the residence from the office buildings on the site is the small playground out front.

Eight mothers and their children can live here at one time, with each family in a private bedroom. They share a communal living room and kitchen, where each mother prepares her own family's meals. Stepping Forward residents must attend weekly parenting classes and comply with fairly strict house rules, including an 8 P.M. bedtime for children over age one. "I didn't have a problem with the rules, and I got along fine with the other girls," Monica says. "They were pretty much like me. I liked living there."

The Salvation Army charges no rent for the first three months because it typically takes that long for someone who has been homeless to get her affairs in order and begin bringing in income. In the second quarter of her stay, a resident pays 5 percent of her earnings as rent, and then 9 percent in the third quarter, 12 percent in the fourth quarter, and so on, with a cap of 30 percent. It's a form of enforced savings; if a resident leaves the program in good standing, she gets back 40 percent of the rent she's paid.

Like all new residents, Monica had to meet regularly with a caseworker from a family preservation program. That program's goal is to help residents develop the budgeting and parenting skills necessary to live on their own. The caseworker spent a lot of time talking with Monica about her finances and Amber's developmental needs. "He helped me with anything I needed help with," Monica recalls. "Like I needed to renew my driver's license, and he took me to do that, and paid for it and everything. And when I was feeling down, he would take me out to eat, and we would talk about what was going on."

Managing her personal finances was clearly one of Monica's biggest problems. She still owed $780 to the apartment complex from which she'd been evicted and $209 to the phone company. She'd had no income since she'd left her job in Killeen three months before.

Rather than accept the first low-paying full-time job that comes along, Stepping Forward encourages residents to attend college so that they can gain the skills they need to qualify for good-paying jobs. Most residents also work part-time and supplement their earnings with welfare. Monica reenrolled at San Antonio College, financing her education with a federal Pell grant of about $2,000 per semester and a work-study program grant of up to $2,535 a year. She also began receiving $180 a month from TANF (Temporary Assistance to Needy Families), plus $248 a month in food stamps.

At Bernal's urging, Monica also enrolled in Project Quest, a local workforce development program that helps low-income people with education costs. Project Quest paid for her books, bought her $300 worth of school clothes, and helped her plan a course of study likely to lead to a job as a computer information specialist, a growing field in San Antonio. Monica wasn't really interested in that field as a career but was persuaded to view it as a way to support herself while she was earning a degree in the field of her choice. In her spare moments at work in the college Career Center, she had researched career options and had concluded that she wanted to become a speech pathologist. "One of my sisters had a stuttering problem when she was young, and another one had certain speech problems related to the abuse," Monica explains. "I know from their experiences how much good you can do in that job."

By the fall of 2001, Monica had managed to pay her debts, buy a used car, and even amass some savings. She was doing well at the community college, where she was taking mostly computer courses, and her parenting skills were beyond reproach. "She's a wonderful mom," Bernal says. "She is so patient. And it shows in Amber. She's such a happy baby."

Residents can stay at the shelter for up to two years, but after Monica had been there only eight months, the staff felt that she was ready to move on to the Salvation Army's Scattered Site Apartment Program. This federally financed program provides subsidized furnished apartments, financial assistance for groceries, utilities, and clothes, and case management services for up to two years to thirty-two formerly homeless single parents and their children. In November 2001, Monica and Amber moved into a one-bedroom unit in a garden apartment complex in south San Antonio.

"I didn't want to let her go," Bernal says. "She was a good role model for the other residents."

"I See Such Growth in Her"

Finally, sixteen months after she'd been evicted, Monica had her own apartment again. Although less than 600 square feet in size, it's perfect for Monica and Amber. It includes a spacious living room, a small kitchen, a bedroom, and a bathroom. The apartment is part of a two-story complex featuring a small swimming pool and several grassy areas, and the neighborhood is safe. The market rate for the apartment is $460 a month, an amount Monica could never have afforded on her own. Instead, Monica pays $120 a month, 30 percent of her current income, and the program pays the rest. And if she does everything the program asks of her for two years, the entire amount she's paid for rent will be given back to her when she completes the program. Most clients receive at least $1,500 when they move on.

With her housing stable, a semester of college behind her, and a good record at her work-study job, Monica finally felt confident enough about herself to reestablish contact with Liz Cruz, one of her old caseworkers at Casey Family Programs. "Before, I hadn't wanted to ask for help because I figured they'd still be mad at me for what happened with the apartment," she says. "So I waited until I finished a full semester of school."

By this time, early 2002, the agency was offering much more comprehensive transition services than when Monica had last sought help. Under a contract with the state, Casey was now providing services to all Bexar County teens in their final years of foster care—about 250 adolescents—in addition to 150 young adults who have recently aged out of the system. The agency operates a transition center in an office building near San Antonio College where young people can come to use computers, meet with a vocational specialist, get help with a crisis, or simply play pool. Scott Ackerson, the center's coordinator, describes it as "a home base for youth who don't have a home or adult guides to help them through this period and answer their questions. It's one-stop shopping for a whole continuum of services."

Monica was initially interested simply in getting information about scholarships that would help her become a speech therapist. When she met with Liz Cruz to talk about scholarships, she was surprised to learn that even more help was available—a monthly stipend from Casey for up to one-third of her living expenses.[9] With Cruz's help, Monica prepared a six-month budget, which showed her falling about $2,100 short of her anticipated $6,325 in expenses. Casey offered her a monthly stipend of $359, around the maximum that the program's guidelines permit. "Our intention is to provide an amount that makes things more comfortable, so that they're not so stressed by money problems," Cruz said.

In return for the stipend, Monica committed to doing some serious thinking about her strengths, concerns, and long-range goals. The process was designed to help her realize that she held her future in her own hands.

Cruz was thrilled to welcome Monica back to Casey. "She's changed so much, even her appearance and the way she carries herself," Cruz says. "I see such growth in her. It's really nice to see."

Cruz said it's common for young people who have aged out of foster care to want nothing to do with their foster care agency for the first year or so after emancipation, only to return for assistance once they see how difficult it is to live on their own.

With Cruz's help, Monica has worked out a detailed timetable for achieving her educational and career goals. After completing community college, Monica plans to work as a computer help-desk technician until she can enter a degree program. She'll probably only be able to attend college part-time, so it is likely to be 2006 before she obtains a bachelor's degree.

Cruz has also helped Monica take the steps necessary to obtain child support from Amber's father. She and Amber underwent DNA tests a few months ago, as did Patrick, and a hearing on her petition to establish paternity and child support is coming up soon. Based on Patrick's military salary, Monica has been told that she can expect to be awarded a little over $200 a month, which will be a big help as she weans herself from welfare in the coming year.

"She Went the Right Way"

Although progress in relationships is always harder to measure than educational progress, it's clear that Monica is making strides in that realm as well. She's outgrown her hostility to her grandmother, and the two now seem to have a close relationship. "We have our ups and downs, but that's normal," Mrs. Romero says. "She listens to me more than before. I'm real proud of her, finishing high school and now going to college. She went the right way."

For her part, Monica regrets having caused her grandmother and sisters so much worry. "I was too busy thinking about myself," Monica says. "I wasn't thinking about my sisters and my grandma and their feelings. I know now that we were better off living with my grandmother because my mom would have let us do what we wanted to do."

Monica has also reestablished her close relationships with her sisters. One of them lives in the same apartment complex with her toddler, and she and Monica often watch each other's child. Another sister will soon graduate from high school and head off to a four-year university in Florida. Emily, the sister who was nearly beaten to death when she was two, still struggles with physical and emotional problems stemming from the abuse, and requires further surgery. Monica worries about her constantly. "[Emily] means as much to me as my own daughter does," Monica says. "When she's older, she wants to live with me, and I want her to. I'd do anything for her."

In yet another sign of personal growth, Monica has even come to realize that the caseworkers at Casey Family Programs were trying to act in her best interest, even though she still disagrees with some of their decisions. "Two of us sisters have graduated from high school, and one more will soon, which probably wouldn't have happened if Casey hadn't been involved in our lives," she says. "And I understand now that the money they gave to my grandma is what made it possible for us to live in a nice house, and to go on vacations. Plus I got to go to camp every summer, and even on a trip to Idaho.

"But being in foster care could have been better. I think if they would have listened to what I had to stay, and let me have more space to grow, I wouldn't have run away."

Her relationship with her mother is still complex. Monica sees her frequently, and sometimes she even lends her money that she should be saving for her own needs. The mother-child bond is, after all, very strong. Even so, there's constant tension in the relationship. "I guess I'm still mad at her," Monica says. "All through childhood, I wanted us to be a family again. She was trying to work on it, but then she'd screw up because of a boyfriend. No matter what, she'd always find a way to screw up. She never learned. The way I see it is to this day, she would choose a man over her kids.

"But I forgive my mother. I want her to know her granddaughter. I'm letting her be a part of her life. I'd never let Amber stay with her, but the people who are supposed to be important in her life, I want them there for her."

Monica gained some insight into her relationship with her mother recently when she read about a famous experiment with monkeys. In the experiment, the researchers created "monster" surrogate mothers for infant monkeys—wire models that catapulted the infant monkeys from their arms or blasted them with compressed air or stabbed them with sharp spikes. Yet no matter how the monster surrogates had treated them, the monkeys kept trying to approach. "I thought when I read it, 'It's exactly the same with humans,'" Monica says. "That's just how I am with my mom. Despite all that's happened between us, she's still my mom, and I can't stay away from her."

Monica's feelings about men are muddled as a result of the abuse that she and her sisters suffered at the hands of their mother's boyfriend. Since she became a mother, she's found it even harder to trust men. "I have trouble going with a guy, because I feel like I don't know what his past is," she says. "I'm always worried about what he might do to my daughter. I don't want my daughter to go through what I did."

"She is my motivation for everything," she continues. "I pray to God to be a good mother. I don't want to ever choose a man over my kid. I don't want anyone to hurt her. I'm trying to protect her from the world, from people who are going to hurt her. I don't want her to make the mistakes I did. I see the world. I know what goes on.

"When I was younger, I used to always get scared about having a kid. People would say to me, 'Don't you know that if you were abused as a kid, you'll abuse your kid?' I always said I was going to prove that wrong.

"And now people tell me, 'You can't protect her from everything.' Well, at least I can try."

Postscript

When we caught up with Monica again in the spring of 2004, there was a lilt in her voice that hadn't been there before. By then twenty-two, she was noticeably more confident and more optimistic about her future than she had been two years earlier. And she seemed to have good reason to be. Her life is on track.

She and Amber's father worked out an agreeable visitation and child-support schedule, and she is glad that Amber is able to have a relationship with him. Amber, three, is attending a Head Start program and flourishing.

Since October 2003, Monica has been working as a customer service representative and insurance agent for USAA, a Fortune 500 insurance and financial services company. With a night-shift differential, the job pays almost $15.00 per hour and provides benefits. "Liz, my caseworker at Casey, told me about the job, and I was really surprised to get it, because there was a lot of competition," Monica said. "It's a great company. I'm really excited to be working there."

Her satisfaction with her job and positive feedback from her supervisor have started her thinking about pursuing a career in insurance rather than speech pathology. Her employer will provide tuition assistance for relevant classes. The company also has offices in Arizona, California, Colorado, Florida, and Virginia, and Monica is thinking about asking for a transfer to one of them after the requisite eighteen months on the job.

Except for the time she was hiding out in Mexico, she notes, she's spent her entire life in San Antonio. "I want to see what's out there," she says.

Monica completed the Salvation Army's Scattered Site Apartment Program in November 2003 and received a rebate of more than $2,000 from the rent payments she had made. She moved into a larger apartment so that Amber could have her own room.

And she is involved in a committed relationship with a young man who seems just as focused on his future as Monica is on hers. He, too, attends San Antonio College. He also works full-time for a telecommunications company. Most important, he's nice to Monica and Amber.

The first few years after foster care were rough, Monica acknowledged. "But the way I see life is that everything happens for a reason," she says. "Certain things had to happen in my life in order for me to mature and face reality. I had to go downhill to learn to accept certain things the way they are, to appreciate what I have, and to learn from my mistakes.

"Sometimes I get down, but when I look at my life, I can see that the whole time I've been moving forward. I don't regret anything that happened to me."

Right, Monica Romero teaches her daughter, Amber, to count. Below, she works the phone in the career center at her college.

In His Loving Memory

REGGIE KELSEY

Born
February 14, 1983 – Minneapolis, Minnesota
Died
May 28, 2001 – Des Moines, Iowa

Reggie Kelsey

MENTALLY RETARDED, MENTALLY ILL, AND ON HIS OWN

Reggie Kelsey, Des Moines, Iowa

From the time Reggie Kelsey entered foster care as a fourteen-year-old, just about everyone who met him doubted that he would ever be able to live on his own.

Although Reggie had an endearing personality, he functioned on the level of a third grader. Test after test found him to be mentally retarded, and as he moved into his teens, signs of mental illness emerged as well. He was bedeviled by hallucinations and frequently unable to distinguish what was real from what wasn't. His therapists gave him labels ranging from depressed to psychotic, and, as he grew older, wrote increasingly urgent reports about the need for his legal guardian—the Iowa foster care agency—to arrange for supportive services in anticipation of the day when he would become too old for foster care.

Reggie also worried about how he'd survive once he left foster care. As his eighteenth birthday approached, he told a school social worker that he sometimes thought about killing someone, because at least in jail he would "have a place to stay and three meals a day."

Under Iowa law, Reggie would have been eligible for foster care until he was twenty, since he hadn't finished high school when he turned eighteen. He could also have qualified for adult services, including a supervised residence and day-treatment program. But his state case-worker failed to take the steps necessary to open either option to him.

A week and a half before his eighteenth birthday, Reggie Kelsey was thrown out of his last foster care placement. His independent-living-skills counselor dropped him at a homeless shelter. "Reggie failed to help himself," he wrote in his discharge report.

For three months, Reggie bounced from one shelter to another while a loose-knit coterie of people tried to help him qualify for federal disability benefits and adult services. On the nights when the local shelters were full or the voices in his head wouldn't quiet down, he camped out with other homeless youths in an abandoned warehouse or under a bridge.

On Memorial Day 2001, Reggie's body was pulled from the Des Moines River. Three and a half months after he had aged out of foster care, he was dead.

Although Reggie's story illustrates the worst-case outcome for youth who age out of foster care, the personal limitations that contributed to his problems were by no means unique. The federal government estimates that of the 100,000 youth age sixteen to twenty in foster care, one in five has a disability.[1]

"That's Just Reggie"

Reggie was born in Minneapolis, Minnesota, on February 14, 1983. Little is known about the first five years of his life. His official history begins in 1988, when he and his younger brother and sister were placed in an emergency foster home in a suburb of Des Moines because their biological parents, who were mentally disabled, were unable to take care of them.

Their foster parents were Steve and Helen Campbell,[2] who were also raising two biological children and three adopted children, all under the age of ten. Over the previous four years, the Campbells had cared for thirty children, mostly for just a few weeks at a time.

Reggie and his siblings were supposed to stay with the Campbells for just a few weeks while social workers looked for a long-term foster home that would accept three siblings. But social workers couldn't find one, and after six months of caring for them, the Campbells decided to adopt them. Helen Campbell told a social worker that she thought the trio would be good candidates for adoption because they hadn't moved around a lot. The adoptions were finalized in February 1990, bringing the size of the Campbell family to ten.

As a young child, Reggie was by all accounts adorable. Photographs show a slight little boy with wide-set eyes and an appealingly lopsided grin. However, he was a slow learner. He was held back in kindergarten, and he was ten years old before he learned to ride a bike.

The Campbells divorced in 1994, when Reggie was eleven, and Helen Campbell received primary custody of the children. As Reggie moved into puberty, he became hard for her to manage. He had always had a problem with lying and stealing, his adoptive mother told a social worker, and now he began sneaking out at night, threatening his siblings, making costly calls to telephone sex lines, and getting into fights at school. His mother complained that his school didn't take his behavior problems seriously because he was otherwise so likable. She complained that they'd say dismissively, "That's just Reggie." She told the social worker that "she tried grounding, writing sentences, time-outs, and taking TV away, but nothing seemed to help."

The household was already under considerable stress by the time Reggie started acting out. He was "fourth in a line of problem teenagers," a social worker observed. The couple's oldest adopted child, Tony, had run away to live with his biological grandmother. When the next-oldest adoptive child, Angela, had begun stealing, the Campbells had returned her to foster care. Not long afterward, they also returned the third oldest adoptive child, Luke, to whom Reggie was especially close. Steve Campbell later told a social worker that he and his former wife had "reached their burnout point" and had come to realize that their adopted children had problems that required more than just a home.

Late in 1997, when Reggie, then fourteen, threatened to kill himself, Helen Campbell took him to a hospital in Des Moines for an inpatient psychiatric evaluation. The therapists there recommended a combination of day treatment for Reggie and in-home counseling for the entire family.

But Helen Campbell wouldn't go along with the treatment plan. She told the therapist she didn't want Reggie to live with her any more. Instead of taking Reggie home, she took him to an emergency youth shelter.

Youth Emergency Services and Shelter (YESS) operates forty-four emergency beds for children who are having problems at home. Most of the 800 or so children who spend time there each year eventually go home. Not Reggie. After his adoptive mother took him to YESS, he never lived with a family again.

"A Child in Need of Assistance"

The Iowa Department of Human Services (DHS) formally took custody of Reggie on December 5, 1997, after a juvenile court judge in Des Moines declared him a "child in need of assistance." He stayed at YESS for four months while his state social worker, Karin Ford, looked for a suitable placement.

While at YESS, Reggie was wracked by feelings of abandonment. "Despite consistently receiving the message that [his adoptive mother] refused involvement with him, he never fully believed she would not be back for him," a social worker observed at the time. "In fact, he reported often hearing her apologizing voice regarding her abandonment of him."

A psychiatrist recommended that Reggie be placed in a therapeutic setting where he could get professional help with his feelings of worthlessness. In mid-April 1998, he was admitted to Orchard Place, a 118-bed psychiatric medical institution for children. DHS contracts with Orchard Place and nine similar facilities to provide residential psychiatric treatment for children in state custody who have serious emotional problems. In 2002, the state paid facilities like this $147 a day, or $4,416 a month, for each child in their care. Although expensive, this is less than one-third of the cost of a psychiatric bed in a community hospital. The setting is also more homelike.

At the time Reggie entered Orchard Place, he was already hallucinating and exhibiting distorted thinking. A psychiatrist diagnosed attention deficit hyperactivity disorder (ADHD), post-traumatic stress disorder with psychotic features, and borderline mental retardation. Reggie began taking medications for the ADHD and the psychotic symptoms and participating in regular therapy sessions. He seemed to adjust to Orchard Place's routines, though he continued to hold out hope that he would be reunited with his adoptive family. That August, he wrote his brother and sister, "I'm sorry that I just disappeared like that. I know that life is tough without me, and you need to hang in, because I'll see you guys again, but I don't know when it will be. Say Hi for me to Mom."

Reggie initially attended the facility's on-campus school, but in the fall of 1998, he was allowed to enroll in the local public school. From the start, other students at Lincoln High School harassed him. Within the first two months, he was suspended for three days for acting as a lookout while another student sold marijuana. He returned to the school at Orchard Place.

An IQ test administered around this time showed that his verbal IQ fell into the low-average range, with his performance IQ in the mentally retarded range. "The practical ramifications to be aware of . . . [are] that Reggie presents as able to understand situations and navigate the basics in life much better than he actually does," an educational consultant explained to the staff at Orchard House. "It is recommended that those involved in the care of helping this young man realize self-sufficiency frequently check with Reggie as to how he is perceiving and if he understands whatever the situation is at hand."

Federal law requires that children in foster care be placed in the least restrictive environment possible. For that reason, in late October 1998, seven and a half months after Reggie entered Orchard House, he was transferred to Youth Homes of Mid-America, a sixty-year-old residential treatment and counseling agency that sprawls across forty-three acres in Johnston, a suburb of Des Moines, and provides several different levels of care, from highly supervised group-home living on site to independent living opportunities.

The discharge letter from Orchard Place recommended that Reggie continue his psychiatric medications and treatment. It also warned: "Although Reggie [speaks] of moving toward independent living, in fact, this young man will most likely require adult living services in order to maintain basic functioning."

"Big Heart and Giving Nature"

At Youth Homes, Reggie lived with five other boys in a highly structured cottage with round-the-clock supervision. He attended the on-campus school, and counselors worked with him on anger control and assertiveness training. Staff members reported to his state social worker that he frequently lied and stole, that he was confused about sexuality, and that he "struggled to understand what are normal and what are abnormal thoughts and behavior." His new psychiatrist added oppositional defiant disorder, a common label for adolescent males in foster care, to his list of diagnoses. The psychiatrist also took him off the antipsychotic drugs that his previous psychiatrist had prescribed.

After six months at Youth Homes, the staff reports on Reggie's behavior became more upbeat. He was said to be "taking a much more realistic view of his life" and to have made "many improvements" in his behavior. The staff reported fewer instances of lying and stealing, and "much more normal thoughts, feelings and ideas relating to sexuality."

In October 1999, after spending ten months in the on-campus school, Reggie was moved to a nearby public high school, where he received instruction in a self-contained special ed classroom with four other students. He apparently settled in easily; by the end of his first month there, his teachers reported a "growing ability to stay on task" and to "handle frustration in a positive manner."

Since Reggie seemed to perform best in one-on-one interactions, Youth Homes found him a mentor, Dave Beamer, who worked there as an independent living counselor. Beamer frequently took Reggie off campus, and helped him get a part-time job as a doorman at a local movie theater. The two seemed to have a great relationship. "The mentor program gives Reggie great joy," according to a progress report dated November 1999, eleven months after he had arrived. "The positive male role model has given Reggie a renewed self-concept. Reggie also enjoys the ability to talk openly with his mentor."

Reggie was also deriving pleasure from a regular exchange of letters and phone calls with his biological siblings and with Luke, one of his adoptive brothers, as well as supervised visits with his biological brother, Chris, who by then had also been returned to foster care by the Campbells. "Reggie shows a great deal of interest in all their lives," the progress report noted. "He shares his pride in them with everyone and works hard at being a positive role model.

"Overall, this has been a positive report period for Reggie," the report concluded. "Reggie has shown emotional growth and leadership skills. He continues to struggle with the ability to be assertive. Reggie's big heart and giving nature make it easy for him to be taken advantage of."

Planning for the Future

With Reggie's seventeenth birthday approaching, his state worker, Karin Ford, began looking for a less structured placement. She first looked for a foster family, and when none could be found, she decided to seek a spot for him at Boys and Girls Town, the well-known residential care facility near Omaha, Nebraska.

However, officials at Boys Town turned Reggie down, saying that they didn't think they could meet his needs. That spring, Ford came up with a new transition plan for Reggie. She instructed the staff at Youth Homes to help him apply to enter Job Corps in the fall of 2000. Reggie seemed excited by the idea, mainly because he thought he'd see more of Luke, who was already in the Job Corps training program in rural Denison, Iowa, about ninety miles west of Des Moines.

The Job Corps initially accepted Reggie but withdrew the acceptance late in the summer of 2000 after learning that his behavior had worsened. In his cottage at Youth Homes, he was again lying and stealing. He was also shouting at the other residents, talking about violent sexual fantasies, and masturbating publicly. And at summer school, his

teacher reported that he was "continually very moody and lacks concentration in class."

Yet Another Plan

With the Boys Town and Job Corps options now ruled out and his eighteenth birthday just months away, Ford and the Youth Homes workers
began focusing on preparing Reggie to live on his own. In October 2000,
Youth Homes moved him to Bracewell Group Home in Des Moines, a
less restrictive setting than the cottages on its main campus.

The move meant that Reggie had to change schools for the fifth time
in three years. This time, he enrolled at Roosevelt High School, a public
school with 1,600 students on Des Moines's north side. He was again assigned to a self-contained special ed classroom for students with behavior disorders.

Reggie did not adjust well to either change. Soon after moving to
Bracewell, he was caught shoplifting a videotape from a store in a mall.
Then he stole a lighter and a map from a convenience store. "All the recent changes may have prompted this behavior," Ford wrote in an annual case report filed around this time. "In the past when Reggie is busy
with school work and the cottage milieu, he is successful. Hopefully, he
will find a routine which will provide him with stability."

Ford noted in her report that staying in foster care past the age of
eighteen would be an option for Reggie, since he had not yet finished
high school. But she did not indicate whether she had discussed that option with him. Some youths are reluctant to stay in state custody past age
eighteen because they want more freedom than group- or foster-home
living allows.

Ford registered her concern about Reggie's ability to live on his own.
"This writer believes that Reggie will need continuing support as an
adult and will pursue a case manager in Adult Services," she wrote.

However, there's no record of her filing the paperwork necessary to
make that happen.

"Reggie Failed to Help Himself"

Six weeks after Youth Homes officials moved Reggie to Bracewell, they moved him again, this time to an agency-controlled apartment in a residential neighborhood in Des Moines. The apartment is one of several that Youth Homes maintains for youth in its Apartment-Based Independent Living Program, which the organization's Web site notes is intended for youth who are "physically, mentally, emotionally able to handle apartment-based independent living." Clients who are not suitable for the program include those who are "severely emotionally disturbed, requiring intensive medical or psychiatric care; suicidal; mentally retarded or developmentally disabled," according to the Web site.

Dave Beamer, Reggie's paid mentor for the previous two years, took on a new role as Reggie's independent living counselor. He began devoting ten to fifteen hours a week to helping Reggie with such activities as filling out employment applications, washing clothes, and completing homework.

The move was a disaster almost from the start.

The morning after Reggie moved in, he arrived at school in what a teacher described as "a drunken-like state." He regularly stayed out past curfew, and his apartment was a mess. He cut himself with knives, gave away his psychiatric medication, and set several Barbie dolls on fire, putting other residents of the building at risk. He complained repeatedly of hallucinations. A therapist who had worked with him for three years wrote a report questioning whether Reggie was capable of living on his own. He characterized Reggie as a threat not only to himself but also to the community.

Ten days after Reggie moved into the apartment, he took a knife to school. The Des Moines public school system, like most others, has a "zero tolerance" policy for weapons violations. School officials suspended him for five days, with a recommendation for expulsion. But because he was receiving special ed services, the Individuals with Disabilities Education Act required that a "manifestation determination" meeting be held to determine whether his behavior was a manifestation of his disability (if it was, he couldn't be expelled). Pending that meeting, Reggie was allowed to return to school on February 2.

Later that afternoon, however, he was caught stealing a meat cleaver from the school's kitchen and was suspended again. This time he was arrested and taken to Meyer Hall, the city's juvenile detention facility, for processing. As a result of the arrest, the Youth Homes management refused to allow him to return to his apartment. Ford, Reggie's state caseworker, directed Beamer, his independent living counselor, to take Reggie to Youth Emergency Services and Shelter, the same emergency children's shelter at which his mother had left him four years before.

In Reggie's discharge summary, Beamer wrote that Reggie "needed more supervision and wasn't ready to live on his own."

"Through the month of living in this apartment, Reggie deteriorated rapidly," Beamer wrote. "This counselor encouraged Reggie to turn things around many times, and warned him if he didn't that he may be discharged. Each time, Reggie assured me he would, but he did not follow through. Despite my efforts, Reggie failed to help himself. He often talked of planning to improve, but his behavior only got worse."

No Bed Available

On February 7, the school district held the manifestation determination meeting, one of the steps mandated before the district could expel Reggie from Roosevelt High School. At the meeting, Reggie worried aloud about being able to live on his own after he turned eighteen the following week. "He was very apprehensive that he did not have the skills to take care of himself and live on his own," the school psychologist wrote in a report on the meeting. "His eighteenth birthday was in one week, and as of that date he would be on his own completely, and he had no idea what to do and no place to live."

School employees recommended that Reggie be permitted to return to school so he could undergo a psychological and educational evaluation. The evaluation was scheduled for February 14, his eighteenth birthday, so that it could serve as the basis for qualifying him for adult serv-ices. (Every minor who has been diagnosed with a disability has to be reevaluated upon reaching adulthood in order to be considered for adult services.)

February 14 was also the day that Reggie had to leave the youth shel-ter because its license limits it to housing minors. That morning, Reggie turned up at Roosevelt with all his belongings in a plastic bag. Among the treasures he crammed into it were a Bible and a photo album containing pictures of the family he once had. Later that day, Karin Ford, Reggie's state worker, wrote on his file: "Reggie reached majority. Closed case."

"A Little Cutie"

At Roosevelt, it fell to Emily Burroughs, the school's part-time social worker, to figure out what to do with a homeless, mentally disabled eighteen-year-old. She knew that the options were limited, since Des Moines, unlike San Francisco and Denver and a few other cities, doesn't have a homeless shelter expressly for older teens and young adults. Al-though the adult shelters in Des Moines accept eighteen-year-olds, Burroughs was reluctant to refer Reggie to any of them because his lim-itations made him so vulnerable.

Burroughs had previously referred students in similar circumstances to Iowa Homeless Youth Centers, which operates a variety of programs for homeless youth and young adults, including the Buchanan Transitional Living Center in Des Moines. Burroughs called over there and explained Reggie's circumstances. "She really cared about him and she wanted to find him some place to stay," recalls Jena Sigler, the youth services worker who took the call. "But she didn't know what to do with him."

From what Burroughs told Sigler of Reggie, he didn't sound func-tional enough for the transitional housing program, which is intended for young people with the potential to become self-sufficient. But the Buchanan Center keeps an extra bed for emergencies, and Sigler got per-mission for Reggie to use it for a few days while the staff evaluated his suitability for the transitional living program.

When Reggie arrived at the shelter, Sigler's heart melted. "I loved him from the start," she says. "He was a little cutie. I don't know what made me care so much about him, except that I could tell that no one had ever spent any time teaching him anything. I could tell that he needed someone."

Diane Martin, the center's volunteer services coordinator, remembers thinking at first that Reggie was too young for any of the center's programs, which are meant for youth age eighteen to twenty-three. At eighteen, Reggie was both small in stature and juvenile in his behavior. Martin thought he looked about fourteen.

"He was childlike," she recalls. "You could tell just from looking at him that he was limited, and when I talked to him, he came across like a third or fourth grader. Everyone on the staff was asking each other, 'What are we going to do with this kid?' We had to start from scratch figuring out who he was and where he came from. And the more we found out, the sadder and sadder his story seemed."

Mitch Henry, the center's case manager, has worked with many youths who grew up in foster care, and he couldn't understand why Reggie's caseworker had not arranged for him to receive adult services as soon as he turned eighteen. "Everyone in foster care is supposed to have a discharge plan," he says. "There should have been a plan, and it should have been implemented. But we couldn't figure out what the plan was for Reggie."

The staff began trying to piece together Reggie's history and identify services to which he might be entitled. On February 15, Sigler called Ford, Reggie's state caseworker, for details about his past. Sigler says that Ford told her that she had nothing to do with Reggie any more. "She told me that he was eighteen, his case was closed, and somebody else was going to contact me and tell me what to do," Sigler says.

A few more days passed before Reggie received a letter from a caseworker with the Adult Services division of the Department of Human Services. The letter instructed Reggie to appear at the agency's office on February 28, two full weeks after his eighteenth birthday, to begin the assessment process for adult services.

Settling In

By all accounts, Reggie loved the atmosphere at the Buchanan Center. During the day, most residents work or attend school, but at night, when they're all around, there's a lot of activity. The residents jostle for access to the microwave or the telephone, scout around for card partners, or do homework as *Survivor* plays on the TV in the shared living room. The atmosphere is very much like that of a small college dorm, though with lots more supervision.

"Life was very simple for Reggie," Sigler says. "If you gave him a pop and put him in front of a TV, he'd tell you he was having the best day of his life. Just being around people seemed to make him happy."

Although he was no longer officially involved with Reggie, Dave Beamer, Reggie's former counselor at Youth Homes, occasionally dropped by to see him. He also gave the staff at the Buchanan Center several hundred dollars in savings that Reggie had amassed from his movie theater job and recommended that they dole it out in $20 increments. "Every time I'd give Reggie $20, he was delighted," Sigler recalls. "He would go to Walgreen's and come back in half an hour, and he would have blown the whole $20 on a bag of lighters, and candy and gum and pop. He'd buy five or ten of everything. And the next day he'd do it again."

During the day, Reggie reported to his special ed classroom at Roosevelt High School. There, the school psychologist began a comprehensive evaluation, which included both extensive testing and subjective evaluations by Reggie's special ed teachers.

A new IQ test found that Reggie functioned in the borderline range of cognitive ability, with particular delays in nonverbal problem-solving skills. An adult basic learning test showed him functioning at the third to fourth grade level in all areas. And social-emotional-behavioral assessments prepared by the two teachers who knew him best noted significant learning and interpersonal difficulties, including inappropriate sexual remarks. The findings meant that Reggie met Iowa's definition of mentally disabled.

On February 21, another incident at school ended any possibility of Reggie's continuing there. He again brought a knife to school, and this time he threatened to hurt a student who had called him gay. Reggie told the vice principal that he felt like he was about "to do the worst thing I have ever done." When Burroughs, the social worker, questioned him further, he threatened to kill someone, saying, "at least in jail he would have a place to stay and three meals a day," she reported. He also told her "he had a horrible life" and "just wanted a family."[3]

To avoid arrest, Burroughs persuaded Reggie to commit himself to a psychiatric hospital for an evaluation. He was admitted to Lutheran Hospital, which has an inpatient ward as well as an adolescent partial-day program that combines outpatient psychiatric treatment with schooling. The admitting psychiatrist prescribed an antidepressant along with Haldol, a more powerful antipsychotic drug than the one he'd been on before. The diagnoses: post-traumatic stress syndrome, with psychotic features; major depressive disorder; and reactive attachment disorders.[4]

"Something Needed to Happen"

At Lutheran Hospital, the public school teacher assigned to the adolescent treatment unit recognized Reggie from a previous stay at another psychiatric unit where she'd once worked. Although hundreds of children in crisis had passed through her classrooms in the years since, Reggie had left an indelible memory.

"At the time I first met him, he was heartbroken because his adoptive mother had dropped him at a shelter and told him, 'You will never have another birthday or Christmas present from us,'" recalls Pat Glassell, the teacher. "I never got over wondering how someone could say that to a little boy."

As she does with all newcomers to her classroom in the day-treatment program, Glassell gave Reggie a fill-in-the-blanks questionnaire so she could learn more about him. His answers reveal a child mourning the loss of his adoptive family and anxious about his future.

No one should be without
a mom and a dad.

The worst news I ever heard was

my separation of my parents.

The thing that is hardest for me to do is

be without a mom and dad.

The most hopeless thing you can try to do is

jump off a bridge.

Despite the depression suggested by those answers, Glassell found Reggie a joy to have in her classroom. "He was very endearing," she says. "I admit I've sometimes been accused of being a Pollyanna and looking for the bright side in all of our kids. But this one just had something about him, a childlike innocent quality, though admittedly with psychotic features. When he was in a structured environment, he did real well. His behavior was appropriate. He was never a problem here."

Glassell took an interest in Reggie's welfare that went far beyond her teaching responsibilities. She took him to get a photo ID, since he'd been discharged from foster care without one. And while Reggie attended therapy sessions or worked on life-skill-based lesson plans, she worked the phone to explore educational options that would permit him to pursue a high school diploma or a GED.

"Given the knife incidents, it didn't seem as though he was going to be able to continue in a regular school," she says. "This is a kid who was on Haldol, for Christ's sake. He would have been a perfect candidate for a therapeutic high school, but we didn't have one in Des Moines yet. I looked into the local community college, though it was pretty clear that he didn't have the skills for something like that. And he was almost too low-functioning for vocational rehabilitation. A sheltered workshop probably would have been the right level."

Why did Glassell get so involved with Reggie's plight? "I guess it's because I believe that part of being a human being is that you do things for other people," she muses. "Somebody was dropping the ball for this kid. Something needed to happen for him, and that was why I was doing it. It was clear to all of us that we were dealing with an individual who would always be a young child intellectually and emotionally."

"Nowhere Else . . . to Go"

All this time, the clock was ticking on Reggie's stay at the Buchanan Center. The center's federal funding limits stays in the emergency bed to three nights. The staff worried that by allowing Reggie to continue to stay on, they were jeopardizing funding for all of their programs.

They tried to figure out how they could accelerate Reggie's certification for adult services, including supervised housing. Sigler called John Hoehne, the adult services caseworker to whom Reggie had been assigned, and he told him that it would expedite matters if Reggie filed applications for food stamps, Medicaid, and Supplemental Security Income (SSI, the federal cash assistance program for the low-income disabled) before their meeting on February 28.

The catch was that to apply for any of those benefits, Reggie had to present copies of a Social Security card and a birth certificate, neither of which he had been given before being discharged from foster care, a common problem. Diane Martin figured that Reggie's adoptive father might have copies of those documents, and she helped Reggie place calls to him. But he repeatedly hung up on Reggie.

Finally, Martin left a message explaining Reggie's need for the documents, and Reggie's adoptive father agreed to tape an envelope containing the documents to the front door of his home in a Des Moines suburb.

It was clear to the staff at the Buchanan Center that Reggie wasn't capable of filling out the applications for SSI, food stamps, and Medicaid by himself, so Sigler did it for him. She also took Reggie to his meeting with Hoehne, though she wasn't permitted to sit in on it. When the meeting ended, Reggie couldn't tell her what the outcome had been. "He didn't understand anything that had been said to him," Sigler says.[5]

The more time that Sigler and Martin spent with Reggie, the more persuaded they were that the Buchanan Center was not the place for him. "He needed a lot more than we ever could give him," Sigler says.

"He needed supervision every minute of the day. He could not function out in the world by himself."

On March 5, another homeless youth needed the emergency bed at Buchanan Center. Reggie had been staying in it for almost three weeks, and the staff reluctantly told him he had to leave. They tried to get him in at the YMCA men's residence, but there was no vacancy. So they took him to a 150-bed dormitory-style adult shelter. "It's like the worst shelter in the city," Martin says. "There's a lot of fighting. It's not safe for someone like Reggie. But there was nowhere else for him to go."

Reggie was back at the Buchanan Center early the next morning. He told the staff he had been too scared to sleep.

"Noncompliant" or Incapable?

The next day, Pat Glassell, Reggie's teacher at Lutheran Hospital, convened a meeting of all the people who were working on Reggie's situation. Most had only talked with each other by phone, and Glassell felt it was important to sit down, face to face, to try to break up the bureaucratic logjam.

Among the people in attendance were Sigler and Martin, of the Buchanan Center; Reggie's longtime therapist, Jeff Kerber; and the social worker for Roosevelt High School, Emily Burroughs. All of them were fond of Reggie and worried about his future. Also attending were several people who had only recently met Reggie: John Hoehne, Reggie's new caseworker from the adult services division, and Jodi Steenhoek, an intake counselor for Golden Circle Behavioral Health Services, an agency that provides service to the chronically mentally ill in Polk County.

One by one, those in attendance spoke about the efforts they were making in Reggie's behalf and their frustration with the lack of progress. When Hoehne's turn came, he blamed Reggie for the impasse, labeling him as noncompliant for missing meetings and failing to get his paperwork in order.

Hoehne's characterization of Reggie infuriated Martin. As the mother of an autistic teenager, she understood better than most people how children with mental disabilities function, and she couldn't understand why Hoehne seemed to be blaming Reggie for not doing something that he was actually incapable of doing. "I often looked at Reggie and thought, 'He could have been like my Nick, who's a big love, if he'd just have had a supportive family,'" she explains.

By the end of the meeting, it was clear that Reggie was no closer to having a place to call home. "There were so many people trying to do the right thing, but there were also so many others who kept slamming doors in our faces because he was eighteen, or they didn't have the funding," Sigler recalls. "We felt like we had done everything we could do, short of take him home with us."

As the group left, Martin said aloud: "We're all going to go home to dinner with our families, and Reggie will be on the street. This kid is going to end up dead."

Missing

That night, Reggie didn't show up at either the Buchanan Center or the adult homeless shelter where he had stayed the previous night. The next day, he also failed to report to Glassell's classroom at Lutheran Hospital.

Finally, two days later, Reggie called Glassell from Lincoln High School, where he had briefly attended ninth grade. He told her that he had gotten lost on his way to the hospital and had ended up clear across town. Glassell drove over and picked him up. Months later, she still remembered being shocked by his appearance. He hadn't bathed for days, and his clothes were filthy. She also noticed that his bright yellow winter coat was missing. "I said, 'Reggie, where's your coat?'" she recalls. "He said, 'I gave it to someone who needed it, but they gave me a sweatshirt in return.'" At that time of year, the temperature in Des Moines is often in the low teens.

Glassell pressed Reggie about where he had slept for the previous two nights. He was vague, telling her he had stayed one night with "some people I met downtown" and the next night at the home of some friends of his adoptive brother Luke, who by this time had left the Job Corps and returned to Des Moines.

During their drive back to the hospital, Reggie appeared distracted and unfocused. He said he hadn't slept in a long time and didn't know where his psychiatric medication was. And he admitted to hearing voices and hallucinating again. As they drove over a bridge, he became visibly agitated. "Don't like them bridges," he told Glassell. When they arrived at the hospital, Glassell arranged for him to be admitted to the locked adolescent inpatient unit for the weekend.

The next week, a bed finally opened up at the YMCA men's residence, and Glassell drove Reggie over and checked him in. This wasn't an appropriate place for Reggie to stay for more than a few days, since residents are supposed to be able to work and take care of themselves, and their average age is forty-one. But it was better than letting him wander the streets, Glassell thought.

"Well, at least it will be warm and clean," Reggie said.

A New Advocate

In the meantime, Reggie's file had landed on the desk of Deb Thompson, a case manager at Golden Circle Behavioral Health Services. Thompson went over to Lutheran Hospital's day program to meet him and became an immediate convert to his cause.

"Reggie was great," she says. "He was a very likable kid, and it was clear that he'd had a pretty rotten shot at life. He really wanted to please people, to be approved of."

Thompson was disturbed to learn that Reggie had been discharged from foster care to a homeless shelter, but not surprised. "Reggie's one of hundreds that are out there," she says. "The ideal is that there's a seamless transition from foster care to adult services for someone like him, but it doesn't always happen." She was particularly distressed to learn that his foster care caseworker had not filed an application for him to receive SSI months earlier so that he would have had a monthly income when he turned eighteen.

Since the Buchanan Center staff had already helped Reggie apply for SSI, Thompson could tackle his need for permanent housing. His income and diagnosis of mental retardation made him eligible for Medicaid, which meant that there would be money for a supported housing program. "Living in an apartment on his own hadn't worked for him before, and I didn't want to set him up for failure," she says. "But I thought that if we got him set up in a residential facility, he would learn enough living skills to eventually make it on his own."

Thompson arranged for Reggie to be admitted to Westminster House, which operates two fifteen-bed group homes for the adult mentally ill. Each home occupies an attractive, low-slung brick building in a pleasant residential neighborhood. Residents have their own rooms, and meals are served communally. Residents receive training in cooking, budgeting, anger management, hygiene, cleaning, social skills, community resources, and medication management, but they are largely free to come and go as they please. Reggie moved in on March 15. For the first week, Thompson visited him every day.

Sigler, the Buchanan Center youth worker who had befriended Reggie, wasn't sure that Westminster was a good fit for Reggie. Whenever she visited, he seemed unhappy, Sigler says. "I'd tell him I was coming at 4:00 P.M., and he'd be waiting on the corner for me when I pulled up," she recalls. "And when I got up to leave, he said, 'Please take me back home with you.'"

Sigler was particularly concerned about whether the facility provided the intensive level of supervision that she believed Reggie needed. Residents of Westminster House are supposed to be "capable of participating in a community day program and learning to use public transportation," according to the organization's Web site. They're also supposed to "have the ability to complete activities of daily living with a minimum number of prompts," something Reggie had proven unable to do in the past. The last time that Sigler visited him there, she says Reggie "reeked of body odor, and his room was a disaster," which indicated to her that he didn't know how to care for himself.

"A Threat to Himself"

On March 28, the Roosevelt staff recommended to the Board of Education that Reggie be expelled from the Des Moines public schools because of the second knife incident. The staff also included what amounted to a distress call about Reggie's future.

"Reggie needs an extensive support system which includes multiple agency involvement for adult services, now that he is eighteen," the staff report said. "He is mentally handicapped, and there appear to also be significant mental health issues, which put both Reggie and the larger community at risk if he is unsupervised and on his own. Reggie does not have the prerequisite skills for independent living and is not ready to handle those responsibilities without extensive support and assistance. Reggie needs a supervised living situation which supports his emotional and adaptive behavior needs to function adequately without him being a threat to himself or the larger community."

Thompson, Reggie's case manager at Golden Circle, began looking for alternatives to public school, such as community-based life-skills training or a job in a sheltered workshop. She also began trying to identify a responsible adult who could serve as Reggie's guardian and payee for the federal disability benefits for which he was expected to qualify. "Reggie does not have the skills to manage his own money to meet his basic needs," she wrote in a case report around this time.

Another Crisis

It sometimes seemed to Thompson that as soon as she came up with a solution to one of Reggie's problems, another arose. On the night of April 4, Reggie sneaked out of his room at Westminster House and returned to his old apartment, where he banged on the windows and bothered the residents. He told them that he was "high on crack and needed money."

When confronted the next day, Reggie denied sneaking out. But the Westminster House director found footprints leading away from his window. As a result, he was transferred to Westminster House's other facility across town, where the windows were higher off the ground.

Four days later, the staff detected the smell of a lighted match coming from Reggie's room. Smoking isn't allowed in the bedrooms, so they told him that he'd have to turn his cigarettes in to the office, speak to a staff member when he wanted one, and go outside to smoke. He complained to Thompson that he "was being treated like a five-year-old" and wanted to move out. She urged him to give her more time to find an alternative.

Later that night, he threw some belongings into a backpack and signed himself out of Westminster House. He went to a mall and called Howard Matalba, the outreach worker for Iowa Homeless Youth Centers, who picked him up, got him something to eat, and took him to a homeless shelter. After one night, he was asked not to return because he made a mess in the bathroom.

Living on the Streets

For the next two and a half weeks, Thompson and the staff at Buchanan Center did their best to keep track of Reggie. He occasionally checked in with Thompson by phone, and sometimes he'd drop by the Buchanan Center to pick up bus tokens or food, or just hang out.

On Thursday and Sunday nights, Reggie would sometimes show up for the free dinners that Iowa Homeless Youth Centers hosts for street kids. The dinners, prepared by volunteers, consistently draw 80 to 125 young people to a former storefront in downtown Des Moines.

"From the first time I met him, I worried that he was going to become a victim of the streets," says Matalba, the outreach coordinator who presides over the dinners. "He did not have what it takes to survive on the streets. It would be like if you took your eight-year-old child and put him on a street corner and said, 'Go. You're on your own.'"

At the dinners, Reggie would sometimes be in the company of his adoptive brother Luke, who was also homeless, or with two young women, sisters, who had befriended him. The older sister, Jessica, nineteen, had been homeless since being discharged from foster care eighteen days before her eighteenth birthday. The younger sister, Michelle, who was seventeen, had recently run away from her adoptive home and joined her sister on the street. Reggie and the sisters spent their days "just walking around downtown until we found something to do," Jessica says. "Sometimes people gave us money, and we'd go get something to eat. Or we'd go into stores and look around. I wanted to shoplift once, and Reggie wouldn't let me. He said he didn't like people who did that."

At night, Jessica said, she and Reggie and her sister slept either in an abandoned warehouse or under one of the bridges that span the Des Moines River. Reggie called Michelle his girlfriend and liked to hold her hand while they slept, Jessica says. "He always told me he wanted to get married and get a house and have kids, but that he had to finish school first," she recalls.

"He was really nice," Jessica continues. "If you put someone down when you were with him, he'd say, 'Don't do that. It's not nice.' He protected whoever he was with, as much as he could."

In late April, Michelle decided to return to her adoptive home, and Jessica went to stay with her biological mother. Reggie called Thompson and told her he was hungry. She picked him up in downtown Des Moines, bought him some food, and tried to talk him into letting her find him another place to live. As usual, he loved riding with her in her car. "He wanted to roll down the windows and scoop the Loop so that everyone could see he had a friend with a car, even though it was a mom in a minivan," Thompson recalls with a laugh.

Reggie told her that he was "tired of living on the streets and being beaten up every day" and was willing to give Westminster another try. His main problem at Westminster had been boredom, he told her, and she promised to try to speed his entrance into a supported employment program. But she warned him that, unfortunately, the earliest appointment she could arrange with the state Department of Vocational and Rehabilitative Services was six weeks in the future.

Before he could change his mind about returning to Westminster House, Thompson drove him over to meet with the director. The director told him that she would give him another chance, as long as he agreed to follow the house rules.

This time, Reggie stayed two days at Westminster House before he checked himself out again.

On the Move Again

On April 30, an obviously contrite Reggie called Thompson again. He knew she'd be disappointed in him for leaving Westminster House and apologized. He told her "it just wasn't the place for him," she recalls. He asked her to send him his birth certificate so he could prove that he was old enough to stay at a homeless shelter for adults. After they hung up, Thompson called the directors of several of the homeless shelters near downtown and asked them to notify her whenever Reggie showed up so she could keep track of him.

On May 2, Reggie checked into the Churches United Shelter. Matalba, the outreach worker for Iowa Homeless Youth Centers, went over to see him. "He said he wasn't in the mood to talk, just very sleepy and still sick," Matalba wrote in his daily report.

On May 4, Reggie tried to stay at the Door of Faith Mission and was turned away. The director called Thompson to report on the contact and explained that he had told Reggie that he was "not appropriate for their program."

Later that week, Reggie showed up at the Buchanan Center. From his appearance, staff members concluded that he was sleeping outside. "He was so dirty that I got him soap and shampoo and took him upstairs and made him take a shower," Jena Sigler recalls.

After he had showered, Reggie came down to Diane Martin's basement office and plopped himself down in the chair in front of her desk. "There was a box of staples on my desk, and he put a handful in his mouth," she recalls. "It was like something a two-year-old would do. I told him, 'Reggie, don't do that. Spit them out.'" His odd behavior led her to believe that he had stopped taking his antipsychotic drugs. "He was even more disconnected than before," she says. "He was probably using [street] drugs to some extent. And he was sick. He had the worst deep cough."

Thompson heard from Reggie on May 10. They arranged to meet at the Churches United Shelter. The first thing he did when Thompson arrived was to show her a star-shaped tattoo that he had etched into his forearm with a needle and ink. "He was so proud of that darned tattoo," she recalls.

Thompson told him that she was hopeful that he would soon begin receiving a monthly Social Security disability check of about $532, which would increase his options. "And I told him that I'd try to get some money to set him up in an apartment with some supportive living services," she says. "At that time, there was enough money in the state budget to get him a few hours a day of help at home. I was also going to try to set him up in a day program that would keep him occupied most of the time. I felt that he could be successful with a lot of support."

Thompson urged Reggie to be patient. "I thought we could have everything lined up within a month," she says.

Thompson recalls Reggie seeming strangely uninterested in the options she described to him. "This is so hard to say, but I think by that time he was committed to the lifestyle that goes with living on the street," she says. "By this time, the weather was nice, and he didn't mind sleeping outside. Plus I think he liked coming and going and not having anyone tell him what to do. It made him feel like he was in control. Once they turn eighteen and they no longer have a legal guardian, kids like this typically want to experience life a little bit."

Before they parted, Thompson reminded him of an appointment she had made for him with his therapist for May 16. She told him she would send a cab to pick him up.

The next day, Reggie dropped by Howard Matalba's office. "He was looking worse," Matalba recalls. "He was dirty, and he had gotten really skinny. He told me he was selling himself on the gay loop by the river, and I told him that wasn't a healthy choice he was making. I talked to him about AIDS. But Reggie couldn't really grasp what I was saying.

"I said, 'Reggie, this doesn't look like it's working for you. Let me take you to a shelter.' But he didn't want to go. He'd been in placements most of his life, and he didn't want to be in one any more."

On May 16, Reggie failed to show up for the appointment with his therapist. Thompson called around to the shelters where he sometimes stayed and even searched a warehouse where she knew he sometimes slept, but she couldn't find him.

A Memorial Day Outing

On Memorial Day 2001, three men in their mid-twenties decided to take advantage of a day off from work to fish for smallmouth bass in the Des Moines River. They set out in a motorboat from a launch point about five miles downstream from downtown Des Moines.

Because of recent rains, the water level was high and the current strong. Here and there, piles of debris were caught up on fallen trees.

While casting toward a logjam, the men noticed something suspicious. They maneuvered the boat close enough to see what it was. It turned out to be a body that was caught on a tree root. They motored to a wastewater treatment plant on the eastern riverbank to call for help.

Three hours later, Des Moines police brought the body to shore. It was nude from the waist down and in an advanced state of decomposition. A metal tape measure was wrapped tightly around the neck.

During an autopsy two days later, the pathologist noticed an amateurish star-shaped tattoo on the left forearm, as well as two distinctive scars. Local media were asked to put out an appeal for help in identifying the body and to mention the tattoo.

Deb Thompson heard the news bulletin while she was driving to work. She called the police the minute she got to her office. She told them that the description of the tattoo fit the one she'd seen on the left forearm of her client, Reggie Kelsey, whom she'd last seen almost three weeks before.

Dental records confirmed the identification. Reggie Kelsey was dead at the age of eighteen. The coroner attributed the death to suicide by drowning. Reggie's champions believe that he was more likely the victim of an accident or foul play.

Goal: "Not One Child Lost"

The people who had tried so hard to help Reggie over the previous few months were both saddened and outraged by his death, and they made sure that his story came to light. In a front-page article on June 17, 2001, the *Des Moines Register* told the sad story of his life.[6] A subsequent series of editorials called for more assistance for youth after they turn eighteen. The paper devoted an entire page to the many letters it received from readers, which it ran under the headline, "We Can Do Better."

As a result of the public outcry, three Iowa legislators asked the Iowa Citizens' Ombudsman, the legislature's investigative arm, to look into the actions of all the public agencies with which Reggie had contact in the months before he aged out of foster care.

After a seventeen-month inquiry, the ombudsman concluded that the Department of Human Services and Reggie's longtime caseworker, Karin Ford, had violated both Iowa law and the department's policies in their handling of Reggie's transition from foster care. The report found no fault with any other agencies.

Ombudsman William P. Angrick II wrote that Ford's biggest mistake was approving Reggie's move to the apartment-based independent living program, despite substantial information in his case file regarding his likely inability to take care of himself. The ombudsman found that Reggie did not meet five of the agency's nine criteria for eligibility for independent living and that he did not have the capacity to function outside a group-care setting.

Angrick also found that Ford failed to refer Reggie to the Polk County Transition Committee when he turned seventeen, as agency rules required. The committee would have worked with Ford to develop an effective transition plan for Reggie, Angrick noted. He also faulted her for failing to refer Reggie to her department's Adult and Family Services unit in a timely manner.

In a formal response to the 186-page report, Ford wrote that she had "used all available resources (as limited as they were) to make decisions to best help Reggie succeed with his quality of life. These decisions were made by me without adequate supervision or adequate resources. The unfortunate reality is that our community does not embrace our children in foster care."

Sally Titus Cunningham, the department's interim director, wrote in her response that the department agreed with the ombudsman that DHS "should have done a better job in planning for and helping with

Reggie's transition from the child welfare system." But, she added, "Caseloads around the state, and particularly in Polk County, create a serious challenge to meeting these standards and the needs of the people we serve. It is becoming increasingly difficult to provide the type of casework that the vulnerable children of Iowa need and deserve. Having said this, it must also be recognized that no matter what resources are available, not every tragedy can be averted."

The ombudsman reserved the last word for himself. "Rather than recognizing fatalistically that 'not every tragedy can be averted,' our state should strive towards the goal of 'not one child lost,'" he wrote.[7]

Postscript

Reggie's death sparked a period of extended soul-searching by Iowa children's advocates and policymakers. In April 2002, Iowa governor Tom Vilsack signed a bill requiring the Department of Human Services to involve counties and private social service providers in planning the transition of children from foster care to independence, beginning at age sixteen. "Iowans have learned how high the cost is to foster children when we do not provide good transition planning for their move into the adult world," Vilsack said, referring to Reggie's death.

About the same time, the Department of Human Services contracted with the Iowa Aftercare Services Network, a new network of nine social-service agencies around the state, to provide transition services to young people who age out of foster care. Youth and Shelter Services, the parent agency of Iowa Homeless Youth Centers, one of the agencies that tried to help Reggie in the months after his emancipation, is the lead agency. By April 15, 2004, the network had served 250 young people.[8] The network helps young people set personal goals, find safe housing and health care, attend college or get job training, receive counseling, and connect with other community resources and opportunities. It also makes "vendor payments" of up to $1,000 per participant per year for expenses such as a down payment on an apartment or a utility bill. The state's Chafee grant, at $1.55 million per year, pays for the $800,000 in aftercare services. The rest of the money goes for self-sufficiency training for the 2,500 youth age sixteen to eighteen in foster care.

In another development, the Jim Casey Youth Opportunities Initiative chose Polk County, which includes Des Moines, to participate in a pilot study of the Youth Opportunity Passport, an asset-building tool for youth in transition from foster care. Through 2006, up to 225 youth in the county will receive a dollar match for every dollar they save (up to $1,000 a year). They'll also receive financial education and exposure to opportunities to learn about careers. "Iowa foster kids need all the help they can get, and this program offers generous help by both teaching kids and providing them with dollars to build assets," the *Des Moines Register* editorialized about the program. "Equally important, the program strives to change the way communities view the children in foster care. The public should feel a sense of responsibility and desire to do all it can to help these youngsters get on track. This initiative is leading Iowa toward that goal by example."[9]

In memory of Reggie, Iowa Homeless Youth Centers opened an after-hours coffeehouse for homeless youth in downtown Des Moines in July 2003. Reggie's Place provides a refuge from the streets from 9:00 P.M. to 2:00 A.M. three nights a week for the estimated 700 youth who sleep in homeless facilities, cars, abandoned buildings, or makeshift camps in Des Moines. While there, young people can get help with shelter needs, employment, and medical and dental problems.

"Before, there was nothing. Now, there's something," said George Belitsos, chief executive officer of Youth and Shelter Services, referring to the new aftercare services. "Reggie's death was tragic, but some good has come of it."

Giselle John and her sister Roxanne

8

"THERE IS LIFE AFTER ABUSE"
Giselle John, Brooklyn, New York

When Giselle John was discharged from New York City's foster care system at the age of twenty-one, she already had a year of college behind her and an interesting job. She had an apartment waiting for her, $5,000 in the bank, and a network of friends and church members whom she could call upon day or night.

She was a published writer and a highly regarded advocate for youth in care. Her foster care agency had posted her picture on its wall as an inspiration to other children in foster care.

In other words, Giselle John had a lot more going for her than most young people do when they leave foster care.

Even so, Giselle's journey to self-sufficiency hasn't been easy. In the years since she aged out of foster care, she has struggled with finances, at times working three jobs to make ends meet. And she has wrestled with memories of her past. Finally, with help from a therapist, she's come to realize that her childhood experiences will shape her life for decades to come.

Giselle has also made a conscious decision to make sure that those experiences don't just have negative effects on her life. "Life is what you make of it," she says. "If I hadn't had those bad experiences, I would never have met some of the wonderful people I've met. I've had a lot of people who took an interest in me and kept me on track."

Giselle works full-time for an advocacy and training organization. She is also working on a bachelor's degree in deviant behavior and social control at John Jay College of Criminal Justice in New York City and is expecting to graduate in December 2004. Eventually, she hopes to earn graduate degrees in both social work and law so that she can better advocate for abused children. An immigrant, she dreams of someday returning home to start a child-abuse prevention program.

"I used to want to be a lawyer so I could put people like my father in jail," she said. "But as I've grown older, I've lost the zest for that. Instead, I want to represent children. I believe that somebody's got to stand up for children and fight for them."

An Idyllic Early Childhood

Giselle was born in the Republic of Trinidad and Tobago in August 1978. Her father had two other daughters from a previous relationship, but she was her parents' first child together.

As an infant, Giselle was sent to live with her mother's sister's family in Parlatuvier, a picturesque village about an hour and a half from her parents' home. Giselle says such child-rearing arrangements are common in Trinidad and Tobago. During the early years of their lives, her brother and sister, born one and seven years later, respectively, lived apart from their parents as well.

Giselle recalls a happy childhood as the youngest child in a household that included twelve cousins. She called her aunt "Mommy Lucy." "Since I was the baby in the family, I was my aunt's prize," Giselle says. "She let no harm come to me."

There were few telephones or televisions in the village, and the roads were dirt. Life centered on the sea. Most of the men worked as fishermen, and their schedules set the pace for the entire village. "All the little kids would help pull in the seines, and for our work, we'd get a bucket of fish," Giselle says. "We'd go to the standpipe, clean it off and then take it home for dinner."

Shortly after she turned ten, Giselle's parents brought her home so that she could attend Standard 4, the local school system's equivalent of sixth grade. Her parents wanted her to prepare herself for the secondary school entrance exam that children in many Caribbean countries take after finishing Standard 4. Only students who do well receive a free education in secondary schools.

Giselle received a high score and was admitted to a good secondary school where she became a model student, a runner, and a singer in the choir. Publicly, she was a star. But privately, her life was a nightmare.

Soon after she moved home, her father began molesting her. Giselle didn't know how to get him to stop or where to seek help. "In Tobago, child abuse is very, very common, but it's not a subject people talk about," she says. "It's like the elephant in the room. There's no help for a child. It's family first. You do not put your parents in a position where they might lose their job or go to jail or lose face."

Initially, she begged her mother to send her back to her aunt's home, without telling her why she wanted to return. But her father refused to allow it, so she endured his abuse for four years. "I just didn't talk about it," she says. "My parents argued all the time, and he beat on my mother and my brother. My mother had bad nerves, so I didn't want to make things worse for her. And other than molesting me, he never did anything to hurt me. He also could be so nice. I think that maybe he really had two personalities."

The abuse might have continued longer if a teacher at her school hadn't questioned her about rumors she'd heard. Giselle wouldn't talk to her, so the teacher went to see her mother. When Giselle got home from school that day, her mother asked if the teacher was telling the truth. Again, Giselle remained silent for fear of angering her father. "I knew he had a bad temper and it would take nothing to make him hurt any of us," she says.

But Giselle's little sister, Roxanne, who was then eight, spoke up and told their mother that the rumors were true. "Mother cried," Giselle remembers. However, she initially did nothing to protect her daughter. "She had to walk in and see him with me on three different occasions before she decided she was going to take action," Giselle says. "That's when she started planning to send me away."

Little Help in the Islands

The Republic of Trinidad and Tobago has a population of fewer than 1.2 million people and occupies two islands, together the size of Delaware. Tobago, the island where Giselle lived, is smaller than some American cities—less than 200 square miles—and has only 50,000 residents. There was nowhere on the island where Giselle's mother could send her so that she could be safe from both her father and the rumor mill.

Nor could Giselle count on protection from Tobago's rudimentary social-services system. "At one time, what I call a bootleg social worker came to the house and sat us all down and said, 'Now tell me about it,'" Giselle recalls. "I realized right away that she was a buddy of my father's. I knew I was not going to get any protection from her."

Even if she had trusted the social worker, the islands' child-protection system didn't have much to offer her. "The best they could have done was to send me to an orphanage in Trinidad, where I would have gotten abused worse," she says.

Giselle's mother came up with a radical solution: She would send Giselle to New York City, where she had an acquaintance with whom Giselle could live.

Giselle had never been to New York. In fact, she'd never been out of the Caribbean before. "But if my mom had asked, 'Do you want to go to Mars?' I would have gone," she says. "I had spent five years trying to separate my mind and body. I came here to protect myself. Sending me to the States was the safest thing my mother could do."

Giselle's mother flew with her to New York early in August 1993. When they got off the plane at Kennedy Airport, Giselle, then a few days short of fifteen, looked around for a big apple. "I used to hear people on my island talk about going to the Big Apple," she says. "I didn't really know what that meant. I literally expected to see a big apple."

"I Never Complained"

Giselle's mother took her to the home of her acquaintance, Winifred, a native of Grenada who had once lived in Trinidad. Winifred lived in a two-bedroom apartment in the Flatbush area of Brooklyn with her five-year-old daughter and an eighteen-year-old niece. Giselle's mother agreed to pay room and board.

Giselle's mother left it to Winifred to enroll Giselle in school. But summer turned into fall and fall into winter, and still Giselle wasn't enrolled. Instead, she spent her days cleaning the apartment and baby-sitting the five-year-old. "I'd wash dishes, scrub floors, wash the clothes, and iron that woman's clothes by the bagful," Giselle recalls. "I never complained, because I was living in someone else's house."

When Giselle still hadn't been enrolled in school by January 1994, five months after she'd arrived, Giselle's mother returned to New York and took her to register. The local high school was full, so Giselle was assigned to Prospect Heights High School, an hour and a half by bus from Flatbush. To get to school by 8:15 A.M., she had to rise every morning at 6 A.M. Often, she wouldn't get home until 6 P.M., when the housework would be waiting for her.

Although Giselle had been a good student in Tobago, she fell in with the wrong group of kids at Prospect Heights and did poorly in school. "I kept getting low grades because I was cutting and not doing the work," she says. "Sometimes I would just go home and sleep, or I wouldn't even go to school at all. There was no one looking over me, so I did what I wanted. Winifred was too busy with her own life to pay attention to mine."

Giselle's living arrangement began fraying a few months after she started school. For one thing, her mother was having trouble paying the room and board. Giselle got a baby-sitting job and tried to make up the difference. But the biggest problem was Winifred's niece, a bully who did her best to make Giselle's life miserable. "Finally, I couldn't take it any more," Giselle says. "I wanted out."

Giselle then did what many teens in unhappy circumstances do: She found herself a new home. Late that spring, she moved in with a classmate and her older sister, who were also from Tobago. In return for room and board, Giselle took over all the housekeeping. "I knew how to clean house," she says. "I knew how to cook. I knew how to iron. That's how I paid my way."

That living arrangement might have lasted through the next school year if Giselle's father hadn't come for a visit toward the end of the summer. She doesn't want to talk about what happened then. Whatever it was, it resulted in her removal from the home by New York City child-abuse investigators.

Another Home

Unfamiliar with America's child-protection system, Giselle worried at first that she was in trouble with the Immigration and Naturalization Service. She had received a three-year, multiple-entry visa when she arrived the preceding August, but she hadn't left and reentered the country after six months, as required.

But the child welfare authorities didn't care about her immigration status. What they were worried about was what to do with yet another sixteen-year-old who needed an out-of-home placement at a time when the New York City child-welfare system was so overwhelmed that it was setting up cots in its offices for children for whom no foster homes could be found.

Once again, Giselle found herself her own home. Earlier, she had met a woman in whom she had confided about her unhappiness. Judith was a Trinidadian in her forties who worked as a maid at a fancy Manhattan hotel. She had told Giselle to contact her if she ever needed a place to stay. Remembering her offer, Giselle now asked child welfare authorities to call Judith and see whether she was still willing to let her move in. Judith agreed to seek guardianship of Giselle, which had the benefit, from the authorities' point of view, of keeping Giselle out of the overburdened foster care system.

After a three-week stay at a diagnostic center in Queens, Giselle moved into Judith's apartment in East Flatbush just before school started in the fall of 1994. Over the telephone, Giselle's mother made a deal with Judith: She would help Judith's children in Trinidad obtain visas to the United States if Judith would look after Giselle and help her attain permanent residency in the United States. Giselle's mother agreed to send Judith money to hire an immigration lawyer for Giselle, plus room and board. Giselle again assumed the role of housekeeper.

"Someone Who Thought I Was Valuable"

Meanwhile, back at Prospect Heights High School, Giselle began to take school seriously. She credits her turnaround to the relationship she developed with her English teacher, Pamela Stanford Odle. They ate lunch together nearly every day.

"I could talk to her about anything that bothered me," Giselle says. "She took an interest in my life, and I felt special. I had found someone who thought I was valuable. We developed a good relationship. I began to settle down and go to school more often."

Research on the resiliency of at-risk adolescents has found that many do well, no matter how difficult their family situations, if they have a caring relationship with an adult. Mrs. Stanford, as her students called her, became that person for Giselle. "She realized that I had nobody, and she wanted to be that somebody for me," Giselle says.

Mrs. Stanford recommended that Giselle take Honors English, which made Giselle feel smart. "It meant that I had potential," she says. "I wanted to get good grades and be on the honor roll. She gave me encouragement to use the talents I had." Mrs. Stanford also saw to it that Giselle had access to opportunities that many youth in foster care miss out on. "When camps were coming up, she'd do all the paperwork in order for me to be able to go away," Giselle recalls.

And with Mrs. Stanford's urging, Giselle got involved in school activities. A strong swimmer from the years in which she'd lived just a stone's throw from the Caribbean, she joined the boy's swim team at her high school (there was no team for girls). "In swimming, I found something I liked," Giselle says. "It began to motivate me, even more than I already was, to be an outstanding individual. I had to keep my grades up in order to participate, and I got addicted to high grades. Getting a high average made me feel good about myself."

Her new self-confidence brought her new friends. "They were kids who were hard workers," she notes. "My new friends were looking toward the future, and so was I. Instead of hanging out and cutting school, we were studying to pass an exam and to stay on the honor roll."

Mrs. Stanford also introduced Giselle to a new religion: Seventh Day Adventism. Mrs. Stanford was the youth leader at her church and invited Giselle to services. "We'd go to church together on Saturday morning, and then I'd go to her house for lunch and just hang out," Giselle said. "When I first starting going to church with her, I'd sit right next to her. It was like I was stuck to her. But she introduced me to other people there, and I got to know many of them."

Giselle, a Baptist by upbringing, joined the Seventh Day Adventist Church in 1995. Over the next few years, the church was to become a stabilizing influence in her life.

"It's Always About Money"

While Giselle was blossoming at school, things weren't going so well in the home she shared with Judith.

Giselle wanted Judith to be a mother figure, but Judith wanted only to be Giselle's landlady. "I was doing well in school, getting ninety averages, and I was mad because there was nobody at home to show my grades to, nobody to be proud of me," Giselle says.

Giselle also objected to some of Judith's habits. She borrowed Giselle's clothes without asking, and she brought men home to spend the night. "She had a wild side," Giselle says.

For her part, Judith began to resent Giselle's involvement in the Seventh Day Adventist Church. Because the church's period of worship extends from dusk Friday until dusk Saturday, Giselle says, "I wouldn't iron her clothes for her on Saturday any more, and she told me, 'I don't like this Adventist stuff.'"

In addition, both Giselle and Judith were upset with their financial arrangement, though for different reasons. "My mother had sent her a lot of money to use to work on getting my green card," Giselle says. "Well, I didn't get my green card through her, and I never saw that money. And then when my mother missed a few months because there was a fire at home, and then two deaths in the family, my Mommy Lucy and my grandfather, Judith went ballistic. She thought it was a trick. She wrote a letter to my mother saying that she wasn't living up to her end of the bargain.

"And she said to me, 'You're out. The longest rope has an end. I can't take it any more. You've got to go.'

"One thing you learn when you live with strangers: It's always about money," Giselle says.

"No Place Else to Go"

Once again, Giselle had to find another home. Mrs. Stanford arranged for her to stay with their church's choir director for two weeks. Then Giselle reluctantly decided to ask the city's child-protection agency, the Child Welfare Administration, to put her in foster care.

"I didn't have a choice," she explains. "I had no place else to go. I couldn't go back with Judith. You can't imagine what it's like to live with someone who's always threatening to throw you out. And I didn't want to go home. If I had to sleep on the streets, I was going to stay in the United States. But without a green card, I couldn't take care of myself."

The agency placed Giselle in a temporary foster home pending a hearing. The judge ruled that Giselle was entitled to the protection of the Child Welfare Administration. "When the judge announced her ruling, she said she believed that I was going to do well, that I would make a fine citizen one day," Giselle remembers with pride.

With that ruling, Giselle's lawyer told her, she was entitled to petition immigration court for special juvenile immigrant status. That status can be granted to an unmarried person under age twenty-one who has been declared a ward of a court because a judge has found that it would not be in the child's best interest to be returned to his or her home country. About 5,000 such petitions are granted each year.

Giselle didn't understand all the legalese, but she got the main point. She was no longer going to have to find herself a place to sleep. The Child Welfare Administration would take care of her.

Into the System

In 1995, the year Giselle went into foster care, more than 42,000 children were in foster care in New York City, more than in most states. Although the Child Welfare Administration recruited and supervised some foster homes directly, it also contracted with more than sixty private agencies to provide foster care to abused and neglected children. The administration paid agencies a per diem rate for each child it placed in one of their licensed homes, and the agencies, in turn, paid their foster parents a fee intended to cover their costs. Giselle's case was assigned to Talbot Perkins Children's Services, a not-for-profit agency that, at the time, was providing foster care for almost 600 New York City children.[1]

Giselle's first foster home was in Queens, far from her high school, but Giselle didn't want to switch schools midway through the year. The school had been one of the few constants in her life. She was still on the swim team and was taking Advanced Placement classes in English and U.S. history, which would mean she'd leave high school with some college credits. And Mrs. Stanford was still serving as her de facto mentor. Giselle therefore committed herself to getting up before dawn every morning and taking two trains and a bus to get there.

Giselle's foster mother was a sixty-five-year-old woman who told Giselle to call her Grandma. Grandma was paid about $16 a day for each of the five girls in her home, or a total of about $29,200 a year, assuming a full house. Besides the five girls, ten other people lived in the house: Grandma, her husband, a daughter and her four children, and three adopted children.

Grandma ran her home like an institution. She wouldn't allow the girls to have their own keys. She was stingy with food, serving only two meals a day. If she caught a resident eating a bowl of cereal between meals, she would accuse her of stealing. "If you missed dinner, there'd be no food," Giselle says. "And if you weren't up when breakfast was served, too bad. I used to buy food and keep it in my room, and she didn't like that either. She was afraid of mice."

That's not all. Besides their bedrooms, the only room in the house that the foster children could use was the kitchen, and then only at mealtimes. They could use the front yard, but not the backyard. They could shower only once a week, and only on a certain day.

In addition, Grandma apparently kept some of Giselle's clothing allowance for herself. "She'd tell me that I only got $65 every three months for my clothing allowance, but I found out that she actually got $200 every three months for me," Giselle says. "In the whole year I lived there, I can count on my hands the things she bought for me."

Most galling of all from Giselle's point of view was that Grandma gossiped about the girls in her care. Giselle kept quiet about her resentment, as she had during the years of abuse by her father. Even though Grandma's house didn't feel like a home, she decided to stay, largely because she couldn't face the prospect of changing homes again.

A Diet of Gum and Water

A few months into her stay at Grandma's, Giselle began to lose weight. She had weighed about 140 pounds when she moved in, just about right for a 5'-5" adolescent who's a long-distance swimmer. But through the fall of her junior year, the pounds fell off. By the end of her first six months there, she had dropped twenty pounds.

With mealtimes at Grandma's so rigid and in-between snacks all but banned, Giselle simply stopped eating. At that point in her life, she had never heard the term "anorexic," but that's clearly what she had become. "I'd get home from swimming, and there would be no food for me, so I'd just do my homework and go to bed," she says. "I decided I wasn't going to let anyone use food as a weapon, so I trained myself not to eat. Eventually, I couldn't be bothered with food. I lived off gum and water."

When Giselle lost another ten pounds, Grandma finally noticed. "She started making me eat, and I started throwing up," Giselle says. Another ten pounds fell off.

With much of her body fat gone and little muscle mass left either, Giselle soon gave up swimming, one of her main joys in life. "After a while, I stopped going to practice because I didn't have the energy," she says.

Midway through her junior year, Giselle called her caseworker in despair. "I told her I couldn't take it any more and just wanted to die," she remembers.

The "Good Girl"

The caseworker arranged for Giselle to be admitted to a hospital psychiatric unit, where she was diagnosed with post-traumatic stress syndrome, a common diagnosis for victims of severe abuse. A psychiatrist prescribed counseling, to which Giselle agreed, and antidepressants, which she refused to take.

Before she was discharged from the hospital, Giselle asked her caseworker to move her to a different foster home. "I couldn't imagine going back to Grandma's," she says. Giselle's worker found her a home with the Tangs,[2] a family in Brooklyn. The parents in the household were both from the Caribbean, Mrs. Tang from Barbados, and her husband from Jamaica, so Giselle felt more at home there. The couple had two girls of their own, Jennifer, fourteen, and Jeanette, nine. Jeanette moved into Jennifer's room, and Giselle took over hers.

Initially, Giselle liked the Tangs. They gave her keys to the house, something she'd never had in her previous homes. She and the mother and girls would often bake cookies or watch movies together. "As time went by, I began to feel welcomed into the family," she says. "I felt as if I belonged. I fell in love with this house and the people who live in it."

As had been her practice in her previous homes, Giselle did her best to make the Tangs like her. "I got in the habit of doing all the cooking and cleaning, just to be a good girl," she says. "I used to iron Mr. Tang's clothes. At first I did it as a favor, and then it became my assigned chore. And I cleaned the toilets."

Another positive aspect to the placement was the neighborhood, which was close to her church and to the home of her best friend, Nikki. She spent most of her out-of-school hours either at church or at Nikki's home.

The Tangs had been informed about Giselle's eating disorder and tried to keep a close watch on her. Giselle also attended regular counseling sessions at a special eating-disorder clinic at New York Hospital, where she and the therapist worked out meal plans.

But she soon figured out how to outfox the Tangs and the therapist. "I would sit down and eat with my family, but I wasn't promising I was going to keep it down," she says. When the Tangs realized what she was doing, they tried to make sure that she was never in a room by herself. Again, Giselle outwitted them by vomiting into a Ziploc bag after they thought she'd gone to bed. She'd dispose of the bag on her way to school.

By the summer after her junior year, it was clear to everyone around Giselle that she was getting thinner and thinner and sicker and sicker. The physical symptoms of advanced malnutrition were obvious even to untrained eyes. She had dark circles under her eyes. Her fingers were always cold, and sometimes the tips were blue. Her hair had thinned, and a coat of down-like hair covered the rest of her body, a telltale sign of anorexia. She no longer menstruated, and her teeth ached all the time. "My friend at church would tell me she was afraid that if she hugged me I would break," Giselle remembers. "I wore a size 4, and it was big on me."

The therapist persuaded Giselle's agency that her condition required hospitalization in an inpatient program. Giselle fought it, but in retrospect she admits, "That was the only way to get me settled down."

On the August 1996 day on which Giselle was admitted to the hospital, she weighed ninety-eight pounds.

"I Can Control It"

For most of her first two weeks in the hospital, Giselle refused to take part in therapy. The program used a combination of therapies to help its patients confront their eating disorders, which are among the hardest of all psychiatric syndromes to treat. Giselle hated them all. "Cognitive behavioral therapy, dialectical behavior therapy, group therapy, private therapy—you name it, and they made me do it," Giselle says. "I told everyone, 'I'm fine. I can control it.'"

She also refused to eat. "They'd put a full plate in front of me and tell me, 'That's your dinner,'" she says. "But I ate nothing, even when a lady said to me, 'If you don't eat, they're going to tube you.' I didn't care. I didn't think anything was wrong with me."

Finally, after two weeks, Giselle admitted that she had a problem. "I remember sitting in a corner during a therapy session when suddenly it just dawned on me that I really did have a problem," she says. "Once I learned what I was fighting, I decided I wanted to get better, and I started eating a little."

Giselle spent six weeks in the hospital and then returned to the Tangs' home. With outpatient therapy and encouragement from the Tangs, Giselle began to gain weight. "The hardest part was allowing myself to gain the weight," she says. "I had come to associate being skinny with being happy. Once in a while I'd still throw up, or just not eat."

Five years later, she admits she still has to fight the desire to purge. "I try to tell myself I'm fine the way I am, but it's hard," she says. "If somebody says something about my weight, I lose my mind. I think I'll probably have to struggle with this all my life.

"But I'm becoming stronger. Most of the time, I accept the fact that this is how I am. I'll never be skinny. I'll never be huge. I'll just be me."

"Write for Us"

After she got out of the hospital, Giselle returned to school. Missing the first semester of school during her first year in the United States had left her two courses short of the graduation requirement, so she hadn't been able to graduate with her class the previous June. She completed the necessary classes in the fall of 1996 and received her diploma at a ceremony in February 1997. She ranked twelfth in a class of 305.

Neither of her foster parents came to the ceremony. However, one of the elders from her church took time off from work to come. "I had told him that nobody was coming, and that I was so sad," she says. "So he came and cheered me on and took pictures. I wouldn't have gone if he hadn't come."

After the ceremony, Giselle had no place to go. No one had offered to take her to a celebratory lunch or to host a party in her honor. She couldn't look for a job, because she didn't yet have her green card. Nor could she enroll in college, since permanent residency in the United States is a requirement for most financial aid.

The one thing she didn't have to worry about was being homeless. Although most states force youth to leave foster care once they turn eighteen or graduate from high school, New York permits them to remain in care until they turn twenty-one, which meant Giselle was assured of a home.

While she was casting around for a way to spend the rest of her day, Giselle remembered hearing about an organization called Youth Communication, which provides journalism training to youth in foster care and publishes their pieces in a semimonthly magazine. "Some of the editors had come to talk to one of my independent living classes, and I used to see the magazine around the agency," she says. "I remembered seeing an ad on the back of the publication that said, 'Write for us,' and I'd heard that they would give me $35 for every article they published. My English teacher used to tell me that I was a good writer, so I thought, 'Why not?'"

Still wearing the smart red suit that she'd bought for her graduation, Giselle took a subway to Youth Communication's headquarters in Manhattan's fur district. Within moments of arriving in the shabby newsroom, Giselle knew that she had found a new home. "And I just kept going back," she says.

"I Just Kept Writing"

Keith Hefner, a former magazine editor, founded Youth Communication in 1980 after becoming concerned that the voices of youth were unrepresented in journalism. That May, Youth Communication presented the first issue of a youth-written publication called *New Youth Connections*, to be published seven times a year. Hefner worked out an arrangement with the public schools so that students could receive either academic credit or an honorarium for contributing articles to the publication, which has since grown to a circulation of 70,000.

In 1993, Hefner started another youth-written publication, *Foster Care Youth United*,[3] with dual aims: to give youth in foster care a place to express their opinions and to educate people who work in the system about how well—and how poorly—it meets youths' needs. Since then, *Foster Care Youth United* has published more than 1,300 stories written by more than 300 youth. Several full-time editors help the young writers produce the best work that they can.

"The main motivation for the kids is to help someone else who's in the same situation," Hefner says. "I've often heard them say that they wanted to tell their story so that someone else could benefit. They have some awareness that they've been through the mill, and they want to say something about it. Although it's not intended to be therapeutic, I think that working on one story can be worth three years of therapy."

With stories like "Are Foster Kids Overmedicated?" and "When Your Staff's a Playa," *Foster Care Youth United* has become a must-read for administrators of New York City's foster care system. The agency buys 2,000 copies of each issue for distribution to staff and youth in care. "We are read," Hefner says. "There's no doubt about it."

At the time that Giselle was getting involved with the publication, the editor was Al Desetta. Or, as Giselle describes him fondly, "Al from Hoboken, with that red hair and those big glasses." Desetta has been with Youth Communication since 1985 and had previously edited *New Youth Connections* and a newsletter written by inmates at a juvenile justice facility.

As he does with all recruits, Desetta asked Giselle to first write a few short essays so he could assess her ability. He recalls her dashing them off with little apparent effort. "Right from the start, her writing was very high quality," Desetta says. "And it was clear that she understood that the goal was to help other young people. So we let her plunge right in."

Giselle's first published article was "Listen Up, Let's Talk." "I thought the story was finished, and I turned it in, but Al didn't think it was finished, and I had to rewrite it over and over again," Giselle recalls with a laugh.

The piece was an unabashed plea to foster parents and caseworkers to listen more carefully to children in foster care. "They fail to listen to the cries of the child who has been pushed to and fro in the system," she wrote. "Many times it's because adults have the impression that we don't know what we want or what is good for us."

Next came "Would You Place Your Child There?" an account of a weekend she spent in an emergency foster home in Manhattan. "As I looked around the living room, I saw broken down chairs and all types of junk," she wrote.

> The shelves were coated with dust, as if they had not been cleaned for years. The kitchen had dishes piled in the sink, and there were uncovered plates of food on the counter. I saw roaches crawling over the counter and going into open cans of food. I turned to my social worker, held onto his hand, and said, "Get me out of here." He said to me, "Don't worry. It's only for the weekend . . . ."
>
> As I look back on the days I spent in that house, I believe no one should have to live in a situation like that. Why did my social worker leave me there after he saw the mess the house was in? Was it because there was no alternative? Was it because he did not care, so he pretended he was blind to the existing conditions? Or was he just too busy to look for another home for me? . . .
>
> If that's the best the system can do, then I don't want to see the worst . . . There is no legitimate excuse for any home to be so dirty, whether there are foster kids there or not, whether the stay is temporary or not. To me, an unsanitary home is an unsafe home, and that's that![4]

And then "Youth Must Have a Voice," "Hang IN There! An Education Is Worth the Fight!" "The Way It Should Be," and so on, dozens of articles in all, most on topics of her choosing.[5] "I just kept writing and writing until I got everything out of me," she says. Although she sometimes wrote about her own experiences in the system, she was more guarded than many of the publication's other writers about what had happened to her in her birth family. "Giselle was somebody who wrote more about problems in the system than her own problems," Desetta observes.

Through her writing, Giselle came to the attention of Nicholas Scoppetta, whom then mayor Rudy Giuliani had appointed in 1996 to try to fix the Child Welfare Administration,[6] which had been rattled by the deaths of several children in foster care. Scoppetta made Giselle the only youth member of his Foster Care Advisory Board, a role that put her into contact with many of the movers and shakers in New York City's foster care system.

All in all, writing for *Foster Care Youth United* served several purposes for Giselle in the interregnum between high school and college. It gave her a place to hang out with other youth who were growing up in foster care, an experience that can easily become isolating. It helped her process her own foster care experience. And it made her feel good about being able to help other young people.

"She was a real leader in the group," Desetta says. "Whenever there was conflict between kids, or tensions arose, she was always the person who would try to calm things down. She befriended many of the writers, and mentored them. In my memory, I can still see her trying to help others write their articles or deal with the emotions that the articles were raising. She was one of the best young people I've worked with."

Saving for Self-Sufficiency

In May 1998, Giselle finally received her green card. The green card not only entitled her to permanent residency in the United States and the right to apply for citizenship after five years, but it also gave her the right to work and to apply for financial aid for college.

More practical than many young people her age, Giselle knew that she was going to need to save as much as she could if she was going to be able live on her own when she aged out of foster care. "The card wasn't going to get me a place to live," she said. "But I figured if I saved $50 per week until my twenty-first birthday, I'd have a decent amount of money."

Through someone she met at Youth Communication, she found a twenty-hour-per-week job at Dress Barn, which paid $5.15 an hour. She also began attending every class in independent-living skills that her agency offered because she wanted the $40 stipend that she was paid for attending. She kept her savings in a shoe box.

In her spare time, Giselle drew up sample budgets to help her figure out how much she was likely to spend each month after leaving foster care. "I also started paying attention to how people who already had apartments of their own lived, and even how they furnished their homes," she says. No matter how conservative she tried to be, the numbers she came up with shocked her. She set a goal of saving $5,000 by the time she turned twenty-one.

For months, saving money was all she thought about. It was harder than she expected. Because she was working in a clothing store, she faced temptations to spend every day. "I found myself spending a lot of my hard-earned money on clothes," she said.

In the fall of 1998, Giselle started classes at John Jay College of Criminal Justice. She received a financial aid package of $2,300, mostly from a Pell grant. She put some of it into savings, along with a $1,000 scholarship she received from *Foster Care Youth United*. The balance rose to $2,700, putting her more than halfway to her savings goal.

Within months, however, her savings had shrunk to $1,000. Softhearted by nature, she had lent money to friends and relatives, including her mother, who by this time had separated from her father. "If someone I knew was in need, I just gave them money," she said. "I felt like since I had money saved up, I needed to help those close to me. I temporarily forgot that the day would come when I'd really need that money to fall back on."

Rather than get discouraged, Giselle took another part-time job working sixteen hours a week at the day-care center at John Jay College.

"I was senior writer at *Foster Care Youth United*, and I still had my Dress Barn job, too, so I was working three jobs at once," she says.

"The impetus for me was the fear of being homeless. I couldn't see myself living on the street."

"I Want Out"

About the same time that Giselle began to plan in earnest for life after foster care, she began to find life with her foster family confining.

She was by then near the end of her second year in the Tangs' home, taking a full load of college classes and working three jobs. Yet the Tangs still treated her like a child, scolding her for staying out late and even trying to ground her. "I was getting older," she said. "I wanted to be treated like an adult."

Another problem was that Giselle believed the Tangs weren't giving her her entire clothing allowance, the same problem that she'd had at Grandma's. "I don't know what they were doing with it, but I wasn't seeing it," she says.[7]

And then there was the lack of privacy. The Tangs had asked Giselle to move into their basement family room so that each of their daughters could have their own rooms. Because the family's fifty-two-inch TV was down there, Giselle was displaced whenever anyone wanted to watch something. "I couldn't even go to bed when I wanted to," Giselle recalls. "It was just driving me bananas."

Because the atmosphere seemed tense whenever she was around, Giselle began spending less and less time at home. "In my mind, I was staying out of my foster mom's hair," Giselle says. "I thought if I stayed out of her way, she'd stay out of my way, and we'd be all right."

But Giselle's absences from the home meant that she was less available for housework, which Giselle says irked Mrs. Tang. "I stopped cooking, because I was at work over dinnertime," Giselle says. "And I stopped ironing Mr. Tang's clothes, too, so he had to iron for himself."

One day, Mrs. Tang demanded her keys back. Giselle went to a friend's house and called her caseworker. "I told him, 'I want out,'" Giselle recalls. "I was sick of living in somebody's house and not feeling a part of it."

Moving On

Giselle was psychologically ready to leave foster care. But she was entitled to another year in care, and she still hadn't saved enough to live on her own.

Most older children in foster care in New York City live in group homes or large institutions because there are few foster families willing to care for them, so Giselle's caseworker warned her that that would probably be her fate, too. However, Giselle was pretty sure she'd be happier in a family setting. Thus, just as she'd done when her informal placements hadn't worked out, she found a replacement family: Mr. Tang's sister, whom she called Auntie Cherry, and her husband, Uncle Keith.

"She was a foster mother for my agency, and I had gotten to know her through the Tangs," Giselle explains. "I was working most of the time, so all I wanted was a place where I could sleep, eat, and feel comfortable. I was hardly going to be there at all, so how much trouble could I be?"

Auntie Cherry and Uncle Keith agreed to give Giselle a home for her last year in foster care. They had no children of their own but were foster parents to two young boys. At their house in the Canarsie area of Brooklyn, Giselle got a real bedroom of her own. And the couple didn't seem to mind that she was hardly ever home.

"Time for Me to Go"

On August 7, 1999, Giselle turned twenty-one. For many youth growing up in America, turning twenty-one means little more than an excuse to get drunk. But for Giselle, turning twenty-one meant that she was at last going to be on her own. She was one of about 1,000 young people in New York City who aged out of foster care that year. Each received a $750 emancipation stipend from the Administration for Children's Services. Giselle used hers to buy a set of bedroom furniture.

When she said good-bye to her foster parents, no tears were shed. Nor did they invite her to come back and visit or to spend the holidays with them. "They didn't even say, 'It's been nice to have you,'" Giselle says. "From all our perspectives, I guess, it was time for me to go."

Although Giselle was scared about being on her own, she felt she was now ready both financially and psychologically. She had achieved her goal of saving $5,000. And she didn't have to worry about becoming homeless. Sharon Andall, a pen pal of her mother's, had rented her the basement apartment in her small brick house in a quiet residential neighborhood in Canarsie. She had agreed to charge Giselle only $450 a month, less than the market rate.

"Renting to Giselle seemed the right thing to do, even though I could make more renting to someone else," explains Ms. Andall, an immigrant from Grenada. "She's been through a lot, and her story touched my heart. I've seen her struggle to take care of herself, and all the responsibilities she's taken on. I want her to finish school and be what she wants to be."

Before she moved in, Giselle's friends helped her clean the apartment. Some members of her church gave her unneeded furniture and household items. Others gave her housewarming gifts. "They had been there for me while I was in foster care, and they were still there for me when I went out on my own," Giselle says appreciatively.

By middle-class standards, the three-room apartment is modest. It's at the bottom of a rickety staircase that is accessed through Ms. Andall's garage. There's little natural light; the sole window looks into a covered window well.

But from Giselle's point of view, it's a castle. It's the first place she's ever lived where she makes the rules. And there's no one to tell her she can't have her own key.

"A Perfect Transition"

Not only did Giselle finally have an apartment she could call her own, but in the months before she left foster care, she had lined up a prestigious ten-month apprenticeship. The arrangement came about through a national nonprofit organization called Public Allies, which partners with community-based organizations and Americorps to provide young people with opportunities to work full-time on projects that improve or expand the partner organizations' services.

Besides receiving real-world experience, Public Allies apprentices benefit from training seminars and team-building exercises, and after concluding their stint, they receive an education award of $4,725 from Americorps. Twenty-one young people from eighteen to thirty were selected for Public Allies' inaugural class in New York City in 1999. Giselle was one of them. Only one other apprentice had been in foster care.

Accepting the Public Allies apprenticeship meant taking a year off from college, but Giselle saw the program as a way to gain leadership skills while supporting herself and gaining money for college. In addition to paying each apprentice a stipend of $1,500 per month, the program provides health insurance, something Giselle had worried about paying for after she left foster care. "It was really a perfect transition for someone coming out of foster care," Giselle says of the program.

Giselle was matched with a local development corporation in East New York, where she organized and ran a program that provided computer-training and job-placement services for neighborhood youth. She also helped local residents apply for jobs connected to the 2000 census.

Her projects went well for seven months. Then the organization's administrative assistant quit and Giselle was expected to take over her duties as well, leaving her insufficient time for her real work. Giselle expressed her unhappiness to her boss, who fired her.

Public Allies agreed to try to find her a new placement for her final three months in the program. In the meantime, Public Allies assigned her work at its office.

As she's demonstrated over and over again, Giselle has never been inclined to wait for other people to come up with solutions to her dilemmas. Instead, she asked Keith Hefner whether Youth Communication would join Public Allies' program and accept her as an apprentice.

As it turned out, her timing was fortuitous. A few months before, Youth Communication had given free office space to a nascent youth advocacy and leadership-training program called Voices of Youth. Voices of Youth was about to start offering advocacy training sessions for youth in foster care, with the dual goals of teaching them to advocate for themselves and helping the system become more responsive to their needs. Who better to train youth in foster care to speak for themselves than someone like Giselle?

Getting Help

While Giselle was waiting for Voices of Youth and Public Allies to process the paperwork necessary to enter into partnership, she slipped into a deep depression. Her confidence had been shaken by the problems she'd had at the community development agency. And she had continued to be haunted by memories of her father's abuse.

One Saturday in March 2000, Giselle washed down a bottle of Tylenol capsules with a bottle of cough syrup. Then she slashed both forearms. "I just didn't want to be bothered with life any more," she explains.

When Giselle failed to appear at church, the pastor came to her apartment to check on her. He took her to the emergency room at King's County Hospital, where her stomach was pumped. She was admitted to the psychiatric ward, her sixth hospitalization for emotional problems since going into foster care.

After a few days there, the hospital agreed to release her to the custody of a nurse whom Giselle knew from church. Giselle spent a month at the nurse's home. She also agreed to begin taking antidepressants, something she'd resisted before, and to go back into therapy.

"She's a Natural"

While Giselle was recovering from her overdose, Voices of Youth held the advocacy-training job open for her. Giselle came on board late in April 2000. Just over a week later, she made her first public appearance for the project—at the annual meeting of the California Youth Connection in Sacramento, California, where she was one of several young adults who discussed their lives since leaving foster care.

"She's a natural," said Jennifer Nelson, Giselle's boss. "She can read an audience and know what to emphasize and what not to emphasize. I think it's a coping skill from being in foster care. Plus, she has a lot of God-given talent. She's articulate and insightful."

Giselle also relates well to the youth who wander into the tiny Voices of Youth office, just down the corridor from the *Foster Care Youth United* newsroom. She is personally familiar with the conflicting emotions that they are experiencing as they made the transition to adulthood—hope, fear, anger, frustration—and, as they begin to enjoy some successes, even contentment and optimism. And she knows how important it is for young people without a supportive family to create their own support network. Because she sometimes had no one to celebrate important milestones with her, she makes sure that none of the organization's clients ever mark important events, such as birthdays or graduations, alone, even if it means giving up her day off.

But not only is Giselle perfect for the job, the job is perfect for her. It provides a supportive workplace, an important benefit for someone who suffers from clinical depression. "You don't usually age out of care and go into a job where they understand what you've gone through so well," she says. "A lot of employers don't understand what it's like for someone coming out of care. Dealing with authority is an issue for a lot of us, since we've had people telling us what to do all our lives. And we may not be as consistent as they need us to be, since some of us are homeless, and even if we're not, we have a lot of other things on our minds.

"I was depressed, and there were some days I wouldn't make it to work. I'd just stay in bed. And at the beginning, I had low self-esteem, so when I didn't know how to do something, I felt it would be stupid to ask. I'd just sit in meetings without saying anything. Voices of Youth gave me a place I could work on those issues."

When the Public Allies apprenticeship ended in July 2000, Voices of Youth found the money to keep Giselle on part-time as executive assistant. Nelson worked out a flexible schedule so that Giselle could resume classes at John Jay College.

Besides being Giselle's boss, Nelson, nine years older, became something of a big sister to her. If she senses that Giselle's refrigerator is empty, she'll drop by with a bag of groceries. When Giselle needs something special to wear to a Voices event, Nelson raids her mother's designer wardrobe or buys Giselle something with her own money.

Nelson has also helped Giselle get control of her finances. Like many people her age, Giselle had run up some debts—$1,000 for a cell phone bill and $1,500 on a credit card. "The minute you enroll in college, you get all these offers for credit cards," Giselle explains. "Even though I had one with a $500 limit, I somehow ran it up to $1,500 because of interest. I didn't know anything about credit or how interest worked. No one had ever taught me anything about that. Jennifer took me to get my bills consolidated, which helped me pay off most of my debt."

And Nelson has made sure that Giselle continues in therapy. "Her philosophy is that you can't be a good employee unless you're a healthy employee," Giselle says. "She told me, 'You pick your therapy time, and we'll work your schedule around it.' And she really encouraged me to do things that would make me healthy."

After trying out several therapists, Giselle finally found one with whom she feels comfortable. He's both a licensed psychotherapist and a Seventh Day Adventist pastor.

New Responsibilities

Late in the summer of 2000, Giselle took on a major new responsibility. At the age of twenty-two, she became the guardian for her fourteen-year-old sister, Roxanne, because she feared she would be molested if she stayed in Trinidad and Tobago. "Here, she can go to therapy, like I did," Giselle says. "Here, she can have a life."

The many people who care about Giselle worried that taking on the responsibility for her sister would put additional stress on an already fragile psyche. Giselle admits that it's been harder than she expected. "Sometimes, I want to send her back," she says. "As much as I love her, sometimes I want to be selfish and not have to worry about taking care of anybody."

Feeding and clothing another person on an income that hovers around $20,000 a year is proving to be a challenge. When money got really tight a few months after her sister arrived, Giselle took a second job on the night shift at a Dress Barn store. "It would be easier if I didn't have to split my paycheck two ways," Giselle acknowledges. "It's digging a deep hole in my pocket."

But perhaps the hardest thing of all for Giselle is knowing that she's the person upon whom her sister depends for advice and moral direction. "I'm still struggling with what to do in life, and here I am in a role where I'm supposed to be advising her how to live her life," she says. "I feel so useless sometimes. She asks me what to do in a certain situation, and I don't know if I'm giving her the right advice. Other times I fool myself that I'm making a difference by having her live with me."

Whatever the difficulties in the arrangement, there are clearly benefits for Giselle as well as for her sister. With another person at home, it's less easy for Giselle to fall into as deep a depression as the one she suffered in the spring of 2000.

And she also has the gratification of knowing that as long as her sister is living with her, she's not being abused.

"It Toughened Me Up"

Reflecting on her five years in foster care, Giselle is grateful for the safe environment it provided, even though there were difficulties of one kind or another in each of her foster homes.

"I needed foster care," she says. "I had nothing else. And it's because I was in foster care that I got with *Foster Care Youth United,* which sent me on the path I'm on today. So in essence, I'd have to say that foster care was a positive experience. It was good for me. It toughened me up."

Giselle is particularly grateful for the three extra years in care that New York allows young people who are enrolled in school or training programs. Had she been forced to go out on her own at eighteen, the age at which foster care ends in most states, she fears she might have ended up on the street. The years between eighteen and twenty-one were important growth years for her, as they are for most young people. They were years in which she transformed herself from a shy, insecure teenager to a poised, self-supporting young woman.

In 2002, Giselle was promoted to the job of youth organizer at Voices of Youth. She got both a raise in pay and health benefits, which will help her afford antidepressants and continuing therapy. (Her coverage by New York's Medicaid program ended when she turned twenty-one.) Although the job is full-time, the schedule is flexible enough to allow her to continue her studies at John Jay College.

To her, the promotion was a concrete affirmation of her self-worth. "I'm really happy about it," she says. "For somebody like me, with just a high school diploma and three years of college, the money's pretty good. Other people who aged out at the same time as I did are serving food at Popeye's, and here I am working in this organization that's helping me grow."

When young people who are in transition from foster care ask her for advice, she tells them that it's important both to believe in themselves and to find themselves a support system. "I had a network of support outside of foster care," she says. "I had a swim team. I had a church. I had friends. I had a teacher who believed in me. Even today, if I have a problem, I'll call her up. She's always telling me she's proud of me and urging me to go for my dreams. She's like my personal cheerleader.

"At work, I have a boss who takes a very personal interest in me and helps me out. And I have a landlady who really looks out for me, who provides me with housing and someone to talk to. Nobody can do a better thing for you than provide a roof over your head.

"I don't take all the credit for my success. I had the goal to be happy and do well. But there have also been a lot of people out there working hard to keep me on track."

Postscript

In January 2003, Giselle went back to Tobago for a two-week visit. The trip ended up being much more than a vacation. It became a symbolic triumph over her past.

While she was there, she conducted two dozen workshops and public meetings on sexual abuse, most of them at schools. Reports on the events were broadcast nearly every night on the island's only television station, Tobago News Channel 5. "I was told that people were rushing home from work to see it," she says.

Giselle's public appearances came about as a result of a call she made to the TV station to request a copy of a program the station had run about incest. A reporter told her that the station would like to do more reporting on the subject but that no victims would speak out. She told them that she would.

"Incest is my island's silent killer," she says. "But it's always been something people didn't talk about. I've been raising awareness about other issues in the United States, and I wanted to raise awareness about what I think is a big issue in my home country. I'd always had the burning desire to talk about the problem, and suddenly, I had the opportunity."

The experience was rewarding, but emotionally wrenching. "The hardest part was meeting the victims who came forward while I was there," she says. "Many of them told me that I was the first person they had talked to. In the middle of the second week, I went to bed and just cried and cried because I was so overwhelmed by how many people were walking around holding these problems in."

Giselle's message to the children of Tobago was straightforward. "I told the young people that if this was happening to them, it was not their fault," she says. "I told them that it's the person who's doing it to them who's at fault, not them. They don't need to feel guilt and shame, as I did.

"I also urged them not to keep it to themselves, but to talk to somebody they trusted. I said, 'Don't wait five or six years before you talk about it, because it's like a cancer, and eats away at you.'

"And I told them, 'There is life after abuse. You can survive this.'"

While Giselle was in Tobago, a close friend from childhood came over every night to watch the TV news with her. They caught up on what had happened in each of their lives in the years since she'd moved to the States. When she returned to Brooklyn, they continued to talk by telephone. By the time she went back for another visit in July, they were in love, an emotion Giselle had feared she'd never be able to experience. They're planning to get married in the spring of 2005.

"I think that being able to go back there and make those presentations made it possible for me to love somebody," she says. "It gave me closure. Because I had taken my experiences and used them for good, I had room to invite somebody else into my life."

A bumper sticker posted over her desk bolsters Giselle John's confidence when she's feeling insecure: "Speak your mind, even if your voice shakes."

Below, Giselle prepares for work in the basement apartment she shares with her sister.

CONCLUSION
What We Must Do

Teenagers can be stubborn and headstrong. They can be obnoxious and annoying. And they often seem hell-bent on making choices that those of us with more maturity and experience recognize as doomed from the get-go.

As others before us have observed, Americans regard teenagers as the least lovable of our children. A 2001 survey of research on the public perception of teenagers reported that the public holds largely negative perceptions of teenagers—lazy, spoiled, irresponsible, and materialistic are a few of the descriptions commonly offered up—and overestimates their involvement in crime and sexual activity.[1] One opinion poll found that only 16 percent of Americans think that people under thirty share most of their ethical and moral values.[2]

Can we really hope to generate public support for enhancing the prospects of a subset of America's least lovable children?

We think so. In early 2003, the Jim Casey Youth Opportunities Initiative, which Gary Stangler heads, commissioned a research project to explore public opinion about foster care, transition issues, and promising intervention strategies. The project found that most people have never even thought about the issue and, in fact, know little about foster care. But when asked to reflect on the transition to adulthood, those polled drew on their own experiences as parents and as former teenagers themselves. And they expressed surprise and dismay when they were told of the outcomes for this population.

Among the most interesting findings:

- Most people said the age at which the average young person is completely independent is twenty-three; one-third of respondents said twenty-five or older.
- Most people (70 percent) expected youth leaving foster care to experience more challenges during the transition to adulthood than other youth.
- Almost all of those polled believed that transition programs are important (70 percent said "very important," and 23 percent "somewhat important"). That it's the "right thing to do" was a common comment, as was, "Pay now or pay later."
- Ninety-seven percent said transition programs should connect youth with caring adults to help them become self-sufficient and contributing members of society.
- Equally strong support was expressed for programs that teach young people how to manage and save money and for efforts that involve local businesses, community institutions, and schools in helping young people make connections in the community.[3]

The public's preferences echo those expressed by the young people profiled in *On Their Own*. Over and over, in so many words, each of them told us that they benefited—or would have benefited—from permanent, family-like connections with adults, meaningful preparation in life skills (especially in money matters), and engagement with the community, as a contributing citizen or as a leader.

What We Can Do in Our Communities

When pressed to think about how they might help mitigate social problems, too many Americans are quick to conclude, "Nothing works." However, this is less true now than ever before. In recent years, we have seen significant progress in what have long been regarded as intractable social or public health problems (for instance, teen pregnancy, infant mortality, long-term welfare dependency, and even national smoking rates). Improving the prospects for young people who are aging out of foster care is by no means an impossible challenge. As we've noted before, the number is manageable—not more than 25,000 a year—and there is a known set of strategies that can make a difference.

Three decades of research on how to improve economic and life outcomes for at-risk youth provide us with guidance about what is most likely to work with this particular group of at-risk youth. In 2003, the Manpower Demonstration and Research Corporation (MDRC), one of the nation's leading nonpartisan social policy research organizations, reviewed the research on programs that serve at-risk youth to determine the most effective strategies for helping disaffected young people improve their prospects. The MDRC researchers concluded that the most successful efforts "focus on building social networks as well as human capital, giving young people the leadership skills and resilience to derive the best from and resist negative influences in their peer cultures."

Before devising new services or programs for at-risk youth, the MDRC advised government agencies, private funders, and communities to:

- Recognize the heterogeneity of the population. As we saw in the previous chapters, some young people are highly resilient (remember Patty Mueller and Lamar Williams), and some loiter on the margins of functionality (Reggie Kelsey and Alfonso Torres). Most are stuck somewhere in the middle, with low or intermittent motivation and few supports (Casey-Jack Kitos and Raquel Tolston).
- Emphasize youth engagement and work hard to maximize it.
- Work with local officials to develop clear, compelling, and achievable goals.
- Invest in building public will and in changing youth policy and the systems that deliver services.[4]

Although the MDRC guidance was directed at programs that target at-risk youth in general, it clearly addresses the needs and deficits of youth leaving foster care. And it aligns closely with the preferences expressed in the public opinion poll and with the lessons we derive from the lives of the young people in *On Their Own*.

From Empathy to Action

For those readers who are ready to move from empathy for the individuals they've met in these pages to action on behalf of the many thousands of others like them, we would like to suggest some specific strategies and actions that can be undertaken at the community, neighborhood, and even personal level. For young people who are naturally tenacious, such as Lamar Williams and Patty Mueller, there may be an immediate payoff. But as Raquel Tolston's story shows, we must also prepare ourselves for a more gradual payoff for those young adults who have low motivation and few natural supports. Remember what one caseworker said about Raquel: "She didn't believe she could do it. But we kept after her, like a protective parent would."

In devising these recommendations, we found it useful to think in terms of the specific economic and life outcomes that we want to impact, while recognizing that no action is isolated from any other action (in fact, integrating or coordinating efforts generally maximizes impact). As you work with this group of young people, you should keep in mind that transition is a process, not a program. Each individual's path to adulthood proceeds at a different pace, and what helps one young person move forward won't necessarily help another.

We propose specific strategies in five outcome areas—education, employment, housing, health care, and personal and community engagement.

Education

As a group, young people who have aged out of foster care have serious educational deficits.[5] Because of chaos at home, many were already performing below grade level when they came into foster care and then dropped even further behind because of the trauma of being separated from their families, as well as the frequent moves and school changes while in care.

They score fifteen to twenty percentile points lower in statewide achievement tests and are twice as likely as other youth to have repeated a grade or enrolled in special education programs.[6] Whereas 86 percent of all American students graduate from high school, the only national study of foster care alumni found that 54 percent who stayed in foster care through age eighteen failed to earn high school diplomas.[7] The high school graduation rate found in smaller, localized studies ranges from 63 percent in Wisconsin and West Virginia to 65.2 percent in New York City to 72.5 percent in the caseload of Casey Family Programs, a private agency.[8]

As we all know, securing a good-paying job today usually requires more than high school completion. Yet the college attendance rate of young people who have aged out of foster care is estimated at only 10 percent, compared with a graduate rate of 60 percent of all adults twenty-five and older. Paying for college is a problem for many students, but it is an even bigger challenge for youth in foster care. Few are able to save much money while in care, and most don't have family members they can tap for financial support.

In recent years, some states have begun providing targeted educational aid in recognition of the special challenges facing youth who have aged out of care. Some states are using money from their Chafee allocations to defray the costs of housing while attending college, although the money available isn't enough to meet the demand.

Another source of educational aid for youth who have aged out of care is the new Education and Training Vouchers program, established through the Promoting Safe and Stable Families Amendments of 2001. Since October 2003, Congress has annually given money to the states to use to provide education and training vouchers of up to $5,000 a year to youth who have aged out of care or were adopted out of care at age sixteen or older. Some states were slow to develop protocols, and the vouchers weren't widely available until fall 2004. Funding rose to $44.7 million for fiscal 2004 and $46.6 for fiscal 2005, and President George Bush was seeking $60 million for for fiscal 2006.

Targeted financial aid is welcome, but the cost of college is by no means the only barrier to higher education for young people who have aged out of foster care. Inadequate academic preparation is a major problem. Many youth in foster care lack the college preparatory courses required for admission to four-year universities. In addition, for those without relationships with adults who can help them, the application process can appear daunting.

It's important for individuals and community groups that care about the future of children in foster care to provide support while they are still in elementary and secondary school and to help them compensate for any educational deficits after they leave. Besides advocating for increased funding for tuition aid, concerned individuals and communities can take the steps discussed below.

Provide educational liaisons or advocates.   All children in foster care could benefit from an educational advocate, or liaison, who could help them penetrate the school bureaucracy, choose classes, arrange tutoring, and obtain school records, as well as accompany them to disciplinary hearings or individual education plan (IEP) meetings or just show up when needed. (Some foster parents and caseworkers play this role.) One community-based model for providing such assistance is a Seattle-based nonprofit organization called Treehouse, which has been offering individualized tutoring and school advocacy services to hundreds of children from the foster care system since 1994. And in Santa Clara County, California, Social Advocates for Youth provides trained educational mentors to ninety youth, including many in foster care.

Help them engage in school life.   Youth in foster care often lack the money to participate fully in school life. The first national overview of the well-being of children age six to seventeen living in child-welfare placements found that 39 percent had low levels of engagement in school, and 28 percent were not involved in any extracurricular activities, such as sports, scouts, clubs, or lessons.[9] Individuals and community groups can facilitate engagement by connecting youth in care with local resources for activity-related purchases, such as musical instruments, athletic uniforms, or prom expenses. Through its Little Wishes project, Treehouse provides funds so that children in foster care can participate in fee-based school and community activities. Most large cities have similar organizations that welcome donations for that purpose.

Broaden their horizons. Many youth in care lack exposure to their community's cultural or natural resources and to opportunities that would permit them to make the connection between learning and a particular career. They can benefit from organized college trips, such as those organized periodically by the California Youth Connection, that expose them to institutions besides the local community colleges and vocational schools that are familiar to them.

Help them get into college. The paperwork associated with registering for tests such as the SAT and ACT and applying to college is often beyond the understanding of youth in care or even their independent living counselors. (It is difficult even for highly educated parents to help their children wade through all the forms they must file, and many pay admissions consultants to help them.) Communities can pair college-bound youth with private educational consultants or trained volunteers who have specialized knowledge of financial aid opportunities. Treehouse offers a Coaching to College program in which trained volunteers assist high school students to get into college. And in the Los Angeles area, the Early Start to Emancipation Preparation program provides mentoring, tutoring in math and reading, and training and practice in everyday living skills to young people age fourteen to sixteen in foster care.

Help them stay in college. Once a youth has begun college, it's important to provide continuing assistance. Remember that many have no one to call upon for advice about what courses to take or which meal plan to choose, let alone a place to stay over school holidays, when dorms often close. In California, 67 percent of emancipated youth who enroll in college drop out before graduation. To improve retention, several California community colleges match students who have aged out of foster care with peer mentors,[10] and at some other California campuses,

Americorps volunteers play that role. On twenty campuses in California and Indiana, the Guardian Scholars Program, a project of the Orangewood Children's Foundation of Santa Anna, California, provides academic advising, housing and job assistance, tutoring, financial aid and mentoring to students who were in foster care. Nationally, the Orphan Foundation of America sends several thousand care packages each year to college students who aged out of foster care and also pairs several hundred of them with "virtual" mentors who provide encouragement and education and career advice via e-mail.

Employment

Many young people who age out of foster care have trouble finding pathways into the workforce. They often lack the documents necessary to establish eligibility for employment, such as a Social Security card or a birth certificate. And because frequent moves while in care made it difficult to hold part-time employment, many have no work history or marketable skills. "I've never had a legitimate job," Alfonso Torres laments. "When [employers] ask about experience, I don't have anything to tell them about."

A 2002 report from researchers at the Chapin Hall Center for Children gives us the most recent picture available of the employment experience of children who aged out of foster in three states, and it's depressing. The researchers looked at the work experiences of youth who aged out of foster care in California, Illinois, and South Carolina during the mid-1990s and found that no more than 45 percent had earnings during *any one* of the thirteen quarters covered by the study. The young people who were most likely to work after aging out of care were those who had worked before their eighteenth birthdays. And even those who were employed did not earn much. They averaged less than $6,000 a year in wages, well below the 1997 poverty level of $7,890 for a single individual.[11] Their findings were similar to those of the earlier Wisconsin transition study, which found that three-fifths of young people who had aged out of foster care were not employed twelve to eighteen months later.[12]

One predictable consequence of joblessness is welfare dependency. Not surprisingly, young people who have aged out of foster care are far more likely than other young people to go on welfare. A study of 11,060 youth who aged out of foster care in California between 1992 and 1997 found that about one-fourth of the females drew welfare benefits in each of the six years immediately following emancipation, compared with about 6 percent of all California females in the same age group. Fully one-half of the young women who had aged out of care relied on welfare benefits at some point in the six years after leaving care.[13]

The implications for direct action are clear. We must help these youth before they leave care; some strategies are discussed below.

Expose youth in care to the world of work.   Many youth in care have no direct experience with adults who go off to work every day, so they have no idea how to dress appropriately, let alone how important it is to show up on time and leave personal issues at home. Helping youth in care understand the culture of the workplace can help them get and retain jobs. One model is Project Paycheck, a fourteen-week work readiness program in Cheyenne, Wyoming. Youth learn how to dress appropriately for job interviews, participate in several mock interviews, and attend a career fair. Each participant is connected to an adult role model, often a local business or agency representative, who provides ongoing encouragement and advice about workplace expectations.

Help youth in care get jobs.   Several studies have found that part-time work while in foster care is a strong predictor of educational and economic success. According to one study, working part-time while in care makes a young person four times more likely to graduate from high school.[14] (In our own small sample here, the two young people who graduated from high school on time—Lamar Williams and Casey-Jack Kitos—both worked part-time.) Connecting young people in foster care to part-time jobs is a small effort that can yield major dividends. To this end, community volunteers can help youth in foster care identify job opportunities, fill out applications, obtain work permits, and overcome transportation issues (remember, few have driver's licenses, let alone access to a car). Each community's employment situation will dictate the

best approach. Lamar benefited from a model program, Work Appreciation for Youth (WAY), that combined paid employment with mentoring,
financial literacy training, and a matched savings program. Another
promising program is The School to Career Partnership, which provides
youth in or recently emancipated from foster care in eight cities with
paid employment and learning experiences.[15]

Expose youth to career options.   The daily lives of youth in foster care
do not expose them to a variety of careers. How do they know they could
become a welder, a nurse, or a banker if most of the professional role
models they come in contact with are connected with the child welfare
system? For youth who are not likely to attend college, it's important to
help them understand that with some skill training, they may be able to
qualify for high-wage jobs with clear career paths.

Holding job fairs and career days, organizing field trips to work-
places and job-shadowing opportunities, and creating internships and
apprenticeships are all valuable strategies that often require very minor
time commitments. Around the country, examples abound of creative
approaches to this challenge. For instance, Our Piece of the Pie operates
six small businesses in Hartford, New Britain, and Bristol, Connecticut, to
give youth in foster care and the juvenile justice system experience in entrepreneurial skills and adult peer mentoring.

Connect youth with proven programs.   Government-sponsored programs such as Job Corps, the Urban Youth and Conservation Corps, and
Americorps, and private programs, such as Youthbuild and the Quantum
Opportunities Initiative, have proven track records for helping disadvantaged young people gain educational, vocational, or community service
experiences. For some young people, the military services provide an attractive option.

Educate youth about money.   Money management is the number one
skill deficit cited by youth raised in foster care. Although many agencies
provide "financial literacy" training, it can amount to little more than

watching a video or attending a single class. Without any connection to their lives or the world, the information is abstract and doesn't stick. Literally hundreds of financial literacy curricula are available, many as on-line learning courses. This training should be provided while a youth is still in care. (As the stories told by Casey-Jack, Lamar, and Giselle show, young people commonly run up thousands of dollars in credit card debt within a few years of leaving care.) Financial training must be appropriate to a youth's stage of development, and it must be culturally appropriate. It should allow for mistakes and learning. The best training connects learning to earning, like the WAY program in which Lamar took part.

Some specific actions could include:

- Helping youth open checking or debit (paperless) accounts. (For minors, this will almost always require an adult to co-sign.) With their own account, youth with earnings from part-time jobs can begin to learn money management in a real-world setting.
- Encouraging savings. Building up assets is crucial to rising above poverty, as mounting evidence demonstrates. But as we see with our own children, they are not likely to save without constant pushing from an adult or a responsible peer. Among the effective tools are savings clubs, peer support groups for saving, and financial incentives to save (such as matched savings accounts [Individual Development Accounts, or IDAs] that restrict withdrawal of savings for "asset" purchases, such as a home, post-secondary education, or investments).

Housing

As our stories demonstrate, finding and keeping a roof over their heads is a major problem for many young people who have aged out of foster care. Homelessness is widespread, and even many who don't think of themselves as homeless, such as Monica Romero, survive by couch-surfing (staying with friends until they wear out their welcomes). In a 1991 study, between one-eighth and one-fourth of emancipated youth reported being homeless within eighteen months of leaving care;[16] in a 2003 study, 42.2 percent of 1,087 respondents reported being homeless at *some point* after leaving foster care.[17]

For such youth, the main barriers to safe and stable housing are cost, lack of availability, the unwillingness of many landlords to rent to them, and their own lack of knowledge about how to be good renters. (Many young people who have grown up in their own families face similar barriers, but more of them have their housing needs met in college dorms.) In devising housing options for young people who have aged out of care, it's important to take into account the tension between the desire of most individuals this age to be independent and their lack of preparedness for total independence.

The Chafee Act removed the prohibition against using federal independent-living funds for room and board, and as a result, the options for subsidized housing have recently increased in some states. Some states are now using sizable portions of their Chafee allocations—up to the 30 percent maximum—to subsidize room and board costs for those who are eighteen to twenty-one. And the Department of Housing and Urban Development's Family Unification Program now gives priority for Section 8 vouchers to youth who have aged out of foster care, although the program is not well known.

Around the country, nonprofit groups are experimenting with a variety of innovative approaches to the housing problem, including supportive landlord settings, host homes, shared housing, subsidies, supervised transitional living residences, mentor homes, and scattered-site housing. For instance, in Portland, a partnership of public, private, and faith-based organizations called Powerhouse provides a range of housing options, from community houses (with or without resident staff) to subsidies to homeowners to scattered-site apartments. The organization also helps youth who have aged out of care pay application fees and deposits and provides mentoring and case coordination. In Cincinnati, Lighthouse Youth Services provides a continuum of transitional housing options ranging from group homes to scattered site apartments. Residents must complete life-skills training, meet with a counselor once a week, and work or go to school. And in Alameda County, California, the First Place Fund for Youth uses a master-lease arrangement to assure housing for sixty former foster youth. Participants receive help with start-up costs, rent subsidies, and a host of supportive services.

Through either formal efforts like the ones cited above or through informal supports provided by individuals, businesses, and community organizations, communities should look for ways to help young people find, apply for, and establish housing. Despite the new programs that have sprung up since passage of the Chafee Act, the supply of targeted housing for youth who have aged out of foster care is still much smaller than the demand.

Ideally, communities with a large number of youth emancipating from care each year will develop comprehensive housing plans that provide a flexible continuum of options, from more structured to less structured, with the possibility of temporary returns to more structured settings if necessary. Short of that, there are still many direct actions that communities or individuals can take.

Help young people meet start-up needs.   Many young people who come out of foster care can't count on moms and dads and aunts and uncles to provide them with hand-me-down appliances and furniture. When Giselle John got her first apartment, friends helped her paint it and members of her church showered her with used appliances and housewares so that she wouldn't use up her savings buying them. Theresa Salazar, one of the women who befriended Alfonso, solicited donations of household goods from people in the community.

Help them maintain their housing.   Young people who have lived in foster or group homes are unlikely to understand the logistics of maintaining a household and could benefit from mentoring on issues like energy conservation, hidden phone charges, security, and maintenance. In San Antonio, the Salvation Army's Scattered Site Apartment Program provided Monica Romero not only with a subsidized furnished apartment but also with a case manager who met with her monthly to help her with budgeting and housekeeping issues.

Health Care

For too many young people, emancipating from foster care means going from fully covered medical care to *no* medical care. Many young people are still being discharged from foster care without copies of their medical records and with no clear idea of how to obtain medical care.

One study found that almost half of emancipated youth in Wisconsin reported being unable to get needed medical care because of the cost. A major problem was lack of access to mental health treatment, especially for depression, adjustment disorders, stress, and substance abuse, problems that often stem from their placement in foster care. Only 21 percent of the sample reported receiving mental health treatment after leaving foster care, compared with 47 percent of a sample of youth still in care.[18]

Only a few states have taken advantage of the option in the Chafee Act to cover youth who have aged out of care through their Medicaid programs. Among the obvious reasons for the disappointing response are the weak condition of state finances and the strain that Medicaid is already placing on state budgets.

But in most states, this is a very small and definable group of people, and extending coverage to them would cost very little. Young people, in general, are low utilizers of health care services. When Arizona extended coverage in 2000 to those age eighteen to twenty-one who had aged out of care, the annual cost was less than $1,000 per person.

To improve medical care for young people who have aged out of care, individuals and community organizations should do the following.

Advocate for Medicaid coverage.   The Wisconsin study found that 90 percent of emancipated youth had received no help arranging for insurance coverage. In the states that have not yet elected to cover this population with Medicaid, young people who have aged out of foster care could benefit from advocacy by community organizations and individuals for coverage. In those states that do offer coverage, young people who have aged out of care may require assistance signing up for it, since coverage is rarely automatic.

Link young people to free or low-cost care. Community volunteers can help youth obtain their medical records and connect them with affordable health care providers in their communities. For instance, in San Francisco, Larkin Street Youth Services operates a free health clinic that serves homeless youth and young people who have aged out of foster care. In Denver, Urban Peak, a community-based nonprofit, collaborates with area hospitals and health care providers to provide a full range of medical services to homeless youth. In Nashville, young people who hold Opportunity Passports receive discounted dental and eye care from local providers.

Personal and Community Engagement

Facilitating a permanent, family-like connection to an adult is the single most important thing anyone can do to make a difference in the life of a youth in or leaving foster care. But we can't just require someone to have a relationship or issue one in voucher form. As a focus group participant once put it, "It sounds like you're trying to give us mail-order brides."

While there are some effective programmatic ways of fostering connections, the larger question is how to expand the opportunities for contact with responsible adults and peers in as diverse a variety of settings as possible. These can range from recreational or cultural events to job shadowing, from structured meetings to informal social gatherings. We are confident that with just a little thought, local communities can come up with creative ideas about how to expand opportunities for young people to establish social connections and networks.

Two particular strategies for fostering connections merit mention.

Mentoring. At its simplest, mentoring is one-on-one interaction—a single contact, an episodic or periodic set of contacts, or a full-fledged relationship. It can be informal and social or highly structured and purposeful. Lamar Williams benefited from a mentoring program, whereas his two brothers did not, which was surely one of the factors contributing to their widely varying outcomes. Reflecting back on his mentors at the institution where he spent his teen years, Lamar says, "They really believed in me, which is one of the most important things anyone can do for a youngster."

There are a great many mentoring models, some not worthy of the name and others legitimately proud of their successes. A 2002 review of mentoring research by Child Trends concluded that "mentoring relationships of short term do more harm than good" and that the most successful were augmented with other services, such as academic support."[19]

Youth engagement.   By "youth engagement" we mean involving young people in the creation of their own destinies. At the social-work level, this means genuinely involving them in case planning and encouraging them to advocate for themselves. Not being taken seriously is a complaint we hear over and over from youth in care. In focus groups that were conducted in 2001 for the Jim Casey Youth Opportunities Initiative, many of the participants said they felt that those in charge of their lives devalued their opinions and desires and had low expectations for their success. The advice they gave was virtually unanimous: "Nothing about us without us." As we all know from our own life experiences, when we have a role in shaping our lives and futures, then our odds of succeeding rise.

Engaging youth at the community level requires that we show them that we value their innate talents, intellect, capabilities, and worldviews; recognize that every young person has something to contribute, and look for opportunities to involve them. For some young people, for instance, Lamar Williams, natural talent and affability lead almost automatically to opportunities for engagement in the community. For others such as Giselle John and Casey-Jack Kitos, involvement in religious institutions provides such opportunities. But many other young people will engage in community life only if we use specific youth engagement strategies to draw them in.

Among the strategies being used around the country with promising results are youth organizing, youth advisory boards, youth councils, youth grant-making boards, youth conferences, and youth-written pub-lications, such as *Foster Care Youth United* in New York City and *Mocking-bird Times* in Seattle. Giselle John's story makes it clear how much her involvement with *Foster Care Youth United* contributed to her personal development and her ability to navigate the world.

Implications for Policy and Practice

Tweaking Policy

The Foster Care Independence Act of 1999, also known as the Chafee Act, provides the framework for providing services to youth transitioning from foster care, as well as a modest amount of public funding. Within that framework, states have wide latitude in deciding the service mix and subpopulations they will serve.

As of mid-March 2006, it is still too early to tell how well Chafee is working. It is particularly worrisome that nearly seven years after the law's enactment, the Department of Health and Human Services has yet to issue the regulations necessary to build the mandated National Youth in Transition Database or to begin to collect the data needed to evaluate Chafee's effectiveness, a failing for which the General Accounting Office had chided it in November 2004. As the National Foster Care Coalition wrote HHS officials in March 2006: "Without this important data, policy makers, advocates, program providers, child welfare professionals, and researchers cannot accurately assess the impact of the Chafee Program, determine whether federal funds have been used appropriately, and most importantly, gather objective information regarding outcomes for youth aging out of the foster care system."[20]

The Chafee Act requires states to engage youth directly in the planning process for implementation, which gives us hope that the services being of-fered to young people are better than before. Also, the law emphasizes measuring outcomes, which at a minimum should help us understand bet-ter what works. In short, the Chafee law holds great promise.

Already, however, it is clear that not all eligible youth have access to or take advantage of the programs; in fact, in many states, it is probably a minority who are benefiting. (For example, a year into their new transition programs, Florida and Iowa each reported serving only 28 percent of eligible youth age eighteen to twenty-one.)[21] Although the funding increase that came with the Chafee Act was welcome, it still amounts to well under $1,000 per year for each eligible youth (those younger teens likely to stay in care until eighteen, plus those age eighteen to twenty-one who have already aged out). In addition, some states have been slow to figure out how to spend their new federal dollars productively. In the first year they received Chafee money, ten states failed to spend their entire allocations; in none of these states would anyone argue that the money wasn't spent because of lack of need.

Also worrisome is that only about a dozen states have extended Medicaid to youth who have aged out of care. Slightly more have provided tuition waivers or special scholarships at their state universities and community colleges. A few, such as Connecticut and Massachusetts, even help with the costs of private universities.

As Congress monitors Chafee's implementation and its impact on the next generation of youth to age out of foster care, we hope it will consider converting the Medicaid option into a mandate, as it has with other options in the past.   Given the growing body of research on the benefits to young people of voluntarily staying in foster care past eighteen, we also urge Congress to consider providing federal funds for their upkeep. States should not be expected to foot the entire bill.

Strengthening Practice

This book is aimed at the general public rather than at those who work in the child welfare system. However, implicit in our recommendations for individual and community action are opportunities and responsibilities for caseworkers, foster parents, residential-care providers, and judges. Although it is important for communities to help youth acquire life skills, establish relationships, and fully engage in the management of their lives, the involvement of "the system players" is not only desired but is natural and obvious. They have the added imperative of legal responsibility for the safety and well-being of children in care.

Our vantage point is not that of system professionals but of people with long experience in the field who have talked with many youth about this issue and have given it considerable thought. (As noted before, Gary Stangler was the guardian of record for 12,500 children when he was director of social services for Missouri. And Martha Shirk has written about these issues for twenty years.) With that caveat, we offer these suggestions for improvements in foster care practice.

Facilitate relationships.   The Chafee Act *requires* states to promote connections between youth in care and mentors or other "dedicated" adults. This is tricky both because of its inherent difficulty and the lack of effective practice models. Relationships and connections are not just items on a service menu that can be delivered to someone. This area of professional practice requires serious attention and collaboration with community organizations.

Involve youth in planning their futures.   The Chafee Act *requires* youth participation and engagement in case planning. We understand this is a difficult process, given the natural tension between the caseworker's legal responsibility for a youth's safety and the desire of almost all youth to have control over their lives. But the payoff is that when treated this way, youth are more likely to feel "ownership" of the plan, increasing the likelihood of follow-through. Think about how much more engaged Giselle John was than Alfonso Torres in planning for the future and how much her sense of ownership over her plans contributed to her success.

Minimize moves.   The number and duration of placements correlate highly with such outcomes as graduation from high school, likelihood of pregnancy, and adjustment disorders. Was Alfonso's difficulty adjusting to life after care predictable, given his frequent moves while in foster care? Evidence is growing that reducing the number of disruptions improves the child's prospects in life. In recent years, many foster care systems have moved in this direction by placing more children with relatives or in sub-sidized guardianships (although both arrangements can make the children ineligible for many transition benefits). A number of successful demonstration projects are underway that emphasize placements within a child's neighborhood of origin, which facilitates continuity of schooling and contact with relatives.

Minimize school changes.   Stability is a strong predictor of success in many areas, but education is clearly one of the most important. Dealing with a new home environment is traumatic enough without having to ad-just to a new school as well. Records rarely follow a student in a timely matter, which can lead to lengthy absences or inappropriate class choices. For each move, there is a commensurate loss in school progress. Placing children in foster homes in the same school-attendance area as their pre-vious homes or arranging for transportation so that they can remain in the same schools can make a big difference in school performance.

Raise your expectations.   Agency-based independent living programs usually focus on high school graduation or GED attainment as the goal. In today's complex economy, neither is sufficient to guarantee a living wage or entrance to a career path. From an early age, independent-living programs should work with youth in care to help them become viable candidates for college or specialized skills training after emancipation.

Recognize the pull of family.   Many youth who age out of foster care maintain relationships with their families, and quite a few even return to them (among our small sample here, Patty, Casey-Jack, Jeffrey, and Mon-ica all did, and Raquel, Alfonso, and Reggie yearned to). Yet there is little federal or state money available for reunification and post-reunification services, and many young people report continued problems at home af-ter they return. Foster care systems must recognize the pull of family and the need for permanency and to provide more help to families before and after reunification. Among the promising strategies are intensive family reunification services and wraparound services.

Provide vital records.   All young people who age out of care should receive copies of their birth certificates, Social Security cards, and medical histories and be informed about their importance. Because of the increasing reliance on photo IDs, caseworkers should also make sure that young people obtain state identification cards or driver's licenses before leaving care.

Make life skills training meaningful.   When it comes to figuring out how to navigate the real world, book learning isn't enough. Youth in care must receive frequent opportunities to practice life skills. It's particularly important to make sure that they are financially literate and understand the importance of accumulating assets and avoiding credit problems, which can haunt them for life.

Recruit partners.   Improving education and employment outcomes have not traditionally been areas of expertise for state or county child welfare agencies, yet the Chafee Act requires them to pursue these goals. Although the child welfare system alone has the legal responsibility to prepare children in foster care for independence, it clearly can't do it alone. To maximize the chances for success of the young people in their care, it will be necessary to aggressively seek collaboration opportunities with philanthropic, education, workforce development, business, and community players.

The Jim Casey Youth Opportunities Initiative

The Jim Casey Youth Opportunities Initiative is a national effort to help young people make successful transitions from foster care to adulthood. Formed by two of the nation's leading foundations focused exclusively on child and youth well-being, the Annie E. Casey Foundation and Casey Family Programs, the Initiative strives to bring together the people and resources to help young people make the connections they need to education, employment, health care, housing, and permanent, family-like relationships.

The Initiative is a private foundation that is focusing most of its work on a demonstration project in up to a dozen states across the United States. Funding from the foundation supports community partnerships, youth boards, and incentive funds for the Opportunity Passport. The Opportunity Passport is a tool designed to organize resources to create opportunities—financial, educational, vocational, health care, entrepreneurial, and recreational—for young people leaving care.

The goals of the Opportunity Passport are to help youth leaving foster care become financially literate; gain experience with the banking system; amass assets for education, housing, health care, and a few other specified expenses, and gain streamlined entry to educational, training, and vocational opportunities.

The Opportunity Passport has three distinct components:

- A personal debit account, to be used to pay for short-term expenses.
- A matched savings account, also known as an Individual Development Account (IDA), to be used for medium- and long-term asset building (such as post-secondary education, rent deposits, down payments on homes, or the purchase of a car).
- Door Openers, opportunities to be negotiated on a local basis. (For example, in Nashville the Tennessee Housing Development Authority has set aside ten Section 8 vouchers for Opportunity Passport holders, who also receive expedited services at the Nashville Career Advancement Center, discounts on health care, and consideration for openings at the Hospital Corporation of America.)

As of mid-2006, community partnerships and youth boards were operating in Atlanta, Denver, Des Moines, Hartford/Bridgeport, Nashville, Providence, San Diego, Detroit and a ten-county area of northern Michigan, and the state of Maine. In addition, in Indianapolis and Tampa, the Initiative is partnering with other foundations to integrate the Opportunity Passport into the Connected by 25 demonstration project.[22]

The opinion survey cited earlier found solid support for the approach of the Opportunity Passport. Ninety-two percent of those polled said they would favor having a program like this in their communities. Two-thirds said they would be likely to include a program like this in their charitable giving plans. And more than one-half (58 percent) said they might volunteer a few hours a month to a program like this.

The Opportunity Passport is not an antidote to all of the problems that young people face as they leave foster care, but it should greatly enhance their opportunities. The Opportunity Passport is a unique demonstration, customized to individual youth and designed to maximize youth engagement and community collaboration. It is a new way of doing business, with clear goals that are easily measurable. The project will be rigorously evaluated, and if it proves successful, the Initiative hopes it will impact policies and systems around the country.

If there is a Jim Casey Youth Opportunities Initiative Opportunity Passport project in your city, please contact the community partnership that administers it about getting involved.[23] The local partner can help you learn about the particular challenges that face youth in your community as they exit foster care and how you can help.

The Next Step

What determines whether a youth who ages out of foster care ends up on the street or educated, employed, and happy?

Sometimes, it's a matter of luck, something that public policy has little influence over. But as we hope these stories have shown, often it's a matter of access to opportunity, which as a nation we can do something about.

We hope that these stories will motivate you to take action to help the thousands of young people who are already on their own in the world, as well as those whose time to go out on their own is fast approaching. Why?

Because we should. Few of us push our children out the door when they reach the age of majority. As citizens of states that assumed legal custody of these young people until they were eighteen, we have at least a moral obligation to help them through their transitions to adulthood.

Because we can. The number of young people who can benefit from our direct action is manageable. In nearly half of the states, youth who age out of care each year number in the low hundreds.

And because small efforts will make big differences. In the stories you've just read, you've seen that very often the line between success and failure was a connection with a single adult or a few life lessons that stuck. By better preparing young people for independence, helping them establish connections with caring and knowledgeable adults, and engaging them in forging their own futures, we can prevent not only personal heartache but also immense societal costs.

We hope we have given you some specific ideas about how to make a difference in the lives of one or more of the many young people who are in foster care or have recently aged out. Among your own children's classmates, there may be youth in care who could benefit from being welcomed into your home, as Lamar Williams did when a friend's aunt and uncle included him in family gatherings. "They took us in like their own kids," he said. "It was like I was a normal kid." For children, having a family is at the top of the list of what it means to be "normal." As both our intuition and own experiences tell us—and these stories clearly demonstrate—all children need families, and they need them for life.

As a society, we are legally responsible for children in foster care. That so many are still being discharged each year with no families to count on is an indictment of what kind of job we are doing. We must redouble our efforts to assure a permanent, stable family or family-like relationship for each of the 523,000 children currently in foster care. No child should ever leave foster care without a family to call his own.

EPILOGUE, MARCH 2006

Since *On Their Own* was first published in 2004, much has happened in the lives of the young people profiled here.

One of them has become a father, and, as this is written, another is about to. One has married and separated. Two have been promoted at work. One has earned a GED, another a bachelor's degree, and a third a master's degree. One has spent more time in jail than out.

In addition, much has happened on the post–foster care research, policy, and practice fronts. The enactment of the Foster Care Independence Act in 1999 (the so-called Chafee Act) launched a flurry of public and private efforts to improve outcomes for youth who age out of foster care. After several years of fits and starts, many states have finally figured out how to take advantage of the flexibility in the law—and the additional federal money appropriated to fund it—to improve the prospects of many youth. More former foster youth are receiving assistance with the costs of housing, higher education, and health care than ever before.

Yet there is a growing consensus, as well as increasing evidence, that we, as a society, are not doing nearly enough. Good legislative intentions and a little extra money by themselves can't compensate for the lingering negative effects of abuse, neglect, abandonment, and, it must be admitted, the foster care experience itself.

Whatever Their Age, Youth Need Families

The area of child welfare practice in which improvement is most needed is in applying the permanency mandate in the 1997 Adoption and Safe

Families Act to those youth who are about to age out of foster care, as well as those young people who are in their first few years out of care. For too many years, the child welfare system considered independent living a permanency option and focused on teaching independent living skills to older youth in care rather than on helping them build enduring family or family-like relationships. A studio apartment, however nicely furnished, is not a family. Fortunately, many child welfare professionals now recognize the importance of permanency for older youth in foster care and they are bringing a new sense of urgency to the mission of assuring it.

Since shortly after the passage of Chafee, the California Permanency for Youth Project has played an important role in showcasing innovative permanency practices, as well as helping establish a consensus in the field for what permanency really means. In the child welfare field, it is now widely acknowledged that achieving permanency requires:

- The involvement of the youth as a participant or leader in the process;
- A lifelong connection to a family, or a committed adult, which is defined as someone "who provides a safe, stable and secure type of parenting relationship; love; unconditional commitment; and life-long support in the context of family reunification, legal adoption, guardianship or some other form of committed lifelong relation-ship;" and
- The opportunity for the youth to maintain contacts with important people in his life, including siblings.[1]

Eighteen is Too Young

As Chafee has been implemented, it has become clear to many players in the child welfare field that eighteen is simply too young to send youth out into the world without a safety net. We don't push our own children out the door at eighteen, and we shouldn't do it to other people's children.

The widely varying post–foster care experiences of the youth whose profiles you've just read make the case for allowing youth to choose to stay under the protection of the child welfare system for a few more years. Two of our subjects—Lamar Williams and Giselle John—took advantage of the option available in New York to retain foster care eligibility until each turned twenty-one. Two others—Patty Mueller and Monica Romero—received extensive financial and personal support from their private foster care agencies well into their twenties. Not coincidentally, we believe, three of these four have received college degrees (including one master's degree), and all have begun promising careers.

In contrast, the youth who were pushed out the foster care door soon after turning eighteen—Raquel Tolston, Casey-Jack Kitos, Alfonso Torres, and, Reggie Kelsey—all struggled. Three of them, Raquel, Alfonso, and Reggie, experienced long periods of homelessness, and Casey-Jack evaded homelessness only because of the generosity of a friend's parents. Unfortunately, fewer than half the states currently permit youth to stay in care past their eighteenth birthdays, and only a handful of states actually encourage it.

The ten young people whose stories are featured here comprise a small sample of former foster youth. But early results from the first longitudinal study of youth who have aged out of care since the enactment of Chafee substantiate our anecdotal findings and provide persuasive evidence of the benefit to individual youth of staying in foster care beyond age eighteen.[2]

Beginning in May 2002, researchers at the University of Chicago's Chapin Hall Center for Children interviewed 736 seventeen- and eighteen-year-old youth in Illinois, Iowa, and Wisconsin as each was entering his or her final years in foster care. Two years later, the researchers reinterviewed 603 of them. (The rest couldn't be found, an ominous finding in itself.) By the second interview, the subjects were all either nineteen or twenty. Two hundred and eighty-two (47 percent) were still in foster care (mostly in Illinois, where eligibility extends to age twenty-one), and 322 (53 percent) had been discharged, usually at eighteen. The researchers compared their situations with those of the nineteen-year-olds who had taken part in the National Longitudinal Study of Adolescent Health. The differences are sobering.

> In summary, youth making the transition to adulthood from foster care are faring worse than their same-age peers, in many cases much worse,

across a number of domains of functioning," the researchers report. "Relatively few of them appear to be on a path that will provide them with the skills necessary to thrive in today's economy. They are less likely to be employed than their peers, and earnings from employment provide few of them with the means to make ends meet. This is reflected in the economic hardships many of them face and the need that many of them have for government assistance. A large number continue to struggle with health and mental health problems. Too many of them have children for whom they cannot provide a home. They are much more likely than their peers to find themselves involved with the criminal justice system.[3]

Among the study's specific findings:

- More than one-third of the former foster youth had not graduated from high school or earned a GED, compared with fewer than 10 percent of the youth in the national Adolescent Health study.
- Former foster youth were twice as likely as the national sample to report being unable to pay their rent or utility bills, one and a half times as likely to have had their phone service disconnected, and four times as likely to have been evicted.
- Only 46 percent had a bank account, compared with 82 percent of the national sample.
- Nearly half of the females and a quarter of the males had received one or more government benefits tied to low incomes.
- Thirty-four percent had been arrested, compared with 21 percent of those who stayed in foster care.
- One-quarter were judged to be "food-insecure," based upon nationally accepted measures.
- One in seven reported having been homeless at least once since they left foster care.
- Nearly half of the females had been pregnant, compared with 20 percent in the national sample.

The study's most promising finding was that those young people who chose to remain in the care of the child welfare system after they turned eighteen experienced better outcomes than those who left care at eighteen, either because they chose to or were forced to by state law. The young adults who left care at eighteen were more than 50 percent more likely to be unemployed and out of school—what sociologists term "disconnected"—than those still in care.

Just what is it about staying in foster care for a few more years that contributes to better outcomes? The researchers suggest several possibilities.

> Young adults still in care had received more independent living services to help them with the transition to adulthood than those who had left care," they wrote. "They had progressed further in their education. They were more likely to have access to health and mental health services. It is still too early in our analyses to say much about how remaining in care confers these advantages. Perhaps the availability of stable housing allows young people to better cope with other responsibilities associated with this period in their lives. Remaining in care may also keep young people in contact with child welfare services professionals who can help provide access to services and supports that they need as they move towards adulthood. In any case, our findings call into question the wisdom of federal and state policies that result in foster youth being discharged from care at or shortly after their eighteenth birthday.

We agree.

Fortunately, there is some progress on this front. As this was written, legislation was under consideration in California, Iowa, and Vermont to permit some foster youth to remain in foster care until they turn twenty-one. And in late March, Washington governor Christine Gregoire signed into law the Foster Youth Achievement Act, which allows youth to voluntarily remain in foster or kinship care after age eighteen while attending high school, college, or a vocational training program. "This is truly landmark legislation that places Washington in a select group of states that recognize the need for youth to continue to receive what youth from intact families typically receive—emotional support, safe housing and health care insurance while pursing an education and career," says Jim

Theofolis, founder and executive director of the Mockingbird Society, which advocated for the change.

Updates on the Youth Profiled in *On Their Own*

In May 2006, we caught up with many of the youth whose stories you've just read and asked them how they're doing. To satisfy publication deadlines for the first edition, each of their stories had to come to an artificial end in the spring of 2004. Two years later, there is much to report.

The Williams Brothers

Lamar Williams has learned a lot about the fast-food business since he and a college buddy opened Totsy's Seafood Heaven in Villa Rica, Georgia, in April 2004 with the goal of developing a fast-food chain. The bottom line: operating a successful restaurant is a lot more complicated than they thought.

"Basically, we were running before we learned to walk," Lamar says. "Myself and my partner pretty much put them [the restaurants] up and let them run on their own. We didn't do enough advertising and marketing to keep the business in the air. We were at home, when we should have been in the stores. We learned some stuff."

The partners closed their first two outlets in December 2005, but early in 2006 they opened a new Totsy's in Kennesaw, Georgia, with a new concept—an all-you-can-eat seafood buffet. "The new restaurant seats sixty, and there's a vacant spot next to the store that we may be able to expand into," Lamar says. "We've got a chef with thirty years experience. I feel confident about this one." They still hope to sell franchises.

Lamar and his wife, Andrea, became the parents of a baby boy, Taz, on May 18, 2005. "It's the best thing in the world, to be honest with you," Lamar says. "I can't tell how smart he's going to really be, but as a father he seems pretty darn smart to me." The couple is expecting their second child in September 2006.

"I'm very happy with life in general right now," Lamar says. "I still have a dream, and a dream ain't a dream unless you try to make it come true. I really want to be somewhere in life, and I know how to get there. Me working hard is going to do it. Even if I don't become a millionaire, I'll still have my big heart and my wife and my kid and my sanity."

There have been major developments in Jeffrey Williams's life, too. After serving twelve and a half years in some of New York's toughest prisons, Jeffrey went before the New York State Parole Board on June 14, 2005. "As I was sitting there waiting my turn, I had doubts, but I told myself I was going to make it because the original charge wasn't so serious," Jeffrey recalls. The board considered seventeen petitioners for parole; seven got it, including Jeffrey.

Jeffrey gave most of his possessions to his friends in prison before boarding a bus to New York City and then catching a flight to Atlanta. As Lamar had promised, he put Jeffrey up for three months and gave him a job managing one of his restaurants and a janitorial service he had started. "I went right to work," Jeffrey says. "I couldn't relax. I cooked and I cleaned and I told people what to do."

Jeffrey is trying to make up for lost time on the relationship front, too. He and his girlfriend, who works for a client of the janitorial service, were expecting a baby in May 2006.

After being locked up for almost thirteen years, Jeffrey isn't quite used to the outside world yet. After all, he entered prison as an eighteen-year-old and emerged as a thirty-one-year-old. "The world is moving so fast," he says. "I kind of feel like I was left behind. But if I put my mind to it, I can make it."

Lamar knows that it takes a lot of support for parolees to make it, and he's happy to provide it to Jeffrey. "This year I really want to see him get a house," he says. "I've got to be patient with him and hang with him. It's going to take him a couple years to get acclimated."

Patty Mueller

Patty Mueller has earned her master's degree in education from Simmons College. "She's doing very well, finally making some good money and having a very good life," her former caseworker, Ginny McConnell, reports.

Alfonso Torres

Over the last two years, Alfonso Torres has been in and out of jail in three Florida counties—Broward, Miami-Dade, and Palm Beach. In fact, he's probably spent more time in jail than out. The charges have varied little from arrest to arrest. Grand theft auto. Burglary to a vehicle. Burglary of an unoccupied conveyance. Possession of burglary tools.

Each time Alfonso was jailed, his mug shot was posted on the county sheriff's Web site. Viewed in sequence, the photographs document the steady deterioration over two years of a once-optimistic young man. In the most recent picture, taken on March 28, 2006, not a glimmer of hope remains in his eyes. He looks unwell.

As this was written in early May 2006, Alfonso, twenty-one, was in a Broward County jail in connection with three felony charges related to auto theft.

"I feel a lot of sadness about Alfonso," says Bernie Perlmutter, the director of the Children & Youth Law Clinic at the University of Miami School of Law School. (Perlmutter is the attorney who helped Alfonso apply for the Road to Independence Scholarship after he aged out of care.) "In retrospect, his life might have taken a different course if he hadn't had to languish in the system so long, if he'd had the good fortune, like his younger brothers, of finding an adoptive home. The fact that he stayed in the system until he turned eighteen was the kiss of death in terms of his prospects. Anything remedial that the Road to Independence Act made available was essentially too little, too late."

Since Alfonso aged out of foster care in December 2002, Florida has been tinkering with its system of supports for former foster youth. Perlmutter says that some of the changes have been good, but that the system makes benefits too hard to get and serves too few youths.

"One of the nice new things, at least on paper, is the mandate to state and private agencies to intensively staff and plan that critical last year of transition, from age seventeen to eighteen," he says. "There are all sorts of mandates about what the agencies in charge of these kids' lives are responsible for. Unfortunately, they're not being complied with."

In 2004, criticism of the Road to Independence Scholarship led the legislature to drop some of its academic requirements, including a GPA of 2.0 and graduation from high school within two years of turning eighteen. Child advocates had argued that many youth with disabilities were unable to qualify and found themselves with no way to continue in school or even house themselves.

In another amendment to the law, the legislature in 2004 permitted scholarship recipients to apply to stay in their foster or group homes after being discharged from care, a hoped-for antidote to the homelessness that some scholarship recipients were reporting. But in practice, Perlmutter says, that option hasn't worked out for many youth. "It reduces the foster parent/young adult relationship to a landlord/tenant relationship rather than a nurturing parent/child relationship," he says.

In 2005, the legislature gave juvenile courts the power to extend jurisdiction to age nineteen, at a youth's request, so as to monitor whether the state was providing appropriate post–foster care services. "Nominally, on paper, it's an improvement," Perlmutter says. "It's critically important to have that additional year to make the agencies accountable to these kids. But kids have to know about it, and they have to know how to get it. In many cases, DCFS [Department of Children and Family Services] actively opposes the court retaining jurisdiction."

In February 2005, DCFS came under criticism from the Florida auditor general for its handling of the state's $17.3 million independent living services program. The auditor general reported that in only half of the cases he reviewed could the agency document that teens in foster care had received federally mandated life-skills assessment and training. He also faulted the department for sloppiness in its administration of the Road to Independence Scholarship and other services for transitioning foster youth.

Florida continues to end Medicaid coverage for youth when they are discharged from foster care, except for the 1,000 or so youth who receive Road to Independence Scholarships, about a fifth of the population of discharged eighteen- to twenty-one-year-olds. The others are permitted to buy into Florida's KidsCare coverage for one year, but Perlmutter says few can afford the $110 monthly premium.

As this was written, the Florida legislature was considering several bills that would affect the services youth receive after aging out of care. But none of the legislative proposals would substantially improve the state's support for youth who have been discharged from foster care, Perlmutter says. "To be honest, I just think they wish these kids would go away," Perlmutter says of state policy makers. "They would rather just close the book, close the file, and hope that these kids disappear."

Raquel Tolston

There are signs of maturity and increasing stability in nearly every aspect of Raquel Tolston's life.

On January 27, 2005, at a ceremony organized by Larkin Street Youth Services, Raquel and thirteen other formerly homeless youth donned caps and gowns to receive their General Educational Development diplomas (GEDs). A photograph shows Raquel grinning from ear to ear.

Three days later, Raquel moved into her first apartment, a furnished studio across Ellis Street from the Lark-Inn Shelter for Youth, the homeless shelter where she had lived three and a half years before. For the first time in more than a decade of shuttling among group homes, homeless shelters, and transitional living facilities, Raquel doesn't have to sign in and out when she comes and goes. "It's very small," she says. "But I like it because it's mine. I can lock my door. I have my own mailbox. I don't have to worry about leaving my things around."

Soon after the move, Raquel started a new job after months on General Assistance. From February through October 2005, she worked up to thirty hours a week as an HIV counselor for the California Prevention and Education Project. She struggled financially during three months of joblessness, but since January 2006 has been working as a telephone interviewer for Field Research Corp., which conducts health services satisfaction surveys. "With the overtime, it's really good money, and it's really interesting work," she says. "I'm talking to regular people just like me and you about what kind of experiences they had as patients."

Raquel has not totally weaned herself from supportive services and probably won't for a long time, given the cost of housing in San Francisco and her limited earning power without a college degree. She lives in a subsidized apartment in the Ellis Street Apartments, a building developed jointly by Larkin Street Youth Services and the Tenderloin Neighborhood Development Corporation to provide permanent housing for formerly homeless youth. She pays 30 percent of her income in rent, with the rest subsidized by the federal Section 8 program.

Raquel continues to try to build relationships with her relatives, particularly on her father's side. She recently learned that she has several half-siblings in the South. "I'm trying to come up with some money because I really want to go visit them next summer," she says. "My father's side of the family is having a family reunion in Madison, Mississippi, and my uncle's wife invited me. She told me, 'It's really important for you to know who your family is.'"

As for her mother, she says, "I would like to see her, but I don't want to push her. When she's ready, I'm here. She knows how to get a hold of me."

Meanwhile, a Midwestern family has taken Raquel into its fold, giving her her first real experience with family life. The connection arose when Raquel attended a media-training workshop in Washington, D.C., in the summer of 2004 and met Carla Owens, director of communications and public affairs for the Jim Casey Youth Opportunities Initiative. When they saw each other again in October at a foster care conference in Sacramento, Owens asked Raquel what she was doing for Christmas. "Probably nothing," Raquel told her. Owens invited Raquel to spend the holidays with her family in Kansas City.

Owens says of her spontaneous invitation: "I had been hearing a lot of talk about how lonely it gets for foster youth around the holidays, and I started to think about what I could do to make a difference for at least one of them. My parents have always reached out to kids in need, and I knew they would welcome Raquel into the family."

Raquel spent Christmas 2004 with Owens's extended family in Kansas City, Kansas, and in July, Owens flew Raquel to St. Louis, where she lives, for a summer vacation. Raquel returned to Kansas City in December for another Christmas celebration with the Owens family. Raquel calls Owens's parents, Chester and Lillie Owens, "Grandpa" and

"Grandma," and telephones them weekly. "They already had two grand-sons, and now they feel like they have a granddaughter," she says.

And Raquel feels as though she's found a surrogate family. "I've never felt as comfortable talking with people about certain aspects of my life as I do with them," she says. "I really feel a connection."

From Carla Owens, whom Raquel calls "Mom," Raquel is learning how to present herself to the world. "She helped me pick out some really nice girly clothes and taught me to put on makeup, the kind of things a mother is supposed to do," Raquel says. "And she's taught me so much more, too, how to dress for the job that I want, not the job that I have, how to budget and set priorities, the kind of stuff you don't learn grow-ing up in group homes."

Owens has also helped Raquel understand that she needs to con-tinue her education. Later in 2006, Raquel hopes to return to San Fran-cisco City College to finish the requirements for certification as an HIV/STD educator. "Eventually, I want to get a college degree, even if it's just an associate's," she says. Her goal is to work for an organization like Larkin Street Youth Services. "They helped me get on my feet and get it together, so I figure why not give back and help somebody who was like me?"

There are still days when Raquel flounders, but far fewer than a few years back. "Every now and then I might not have enough money to get a bag of potatoes or a dozen eggs," says Raquel. "I would like to be pro-gressing faster. But I'm very content right now. I've worked really hard, and I had to go through a lot to get where I am. I'm feeling pretty good about my life."

Raquel says the prospect of turning twenty-five this year made her get serious about her life. "I finally got myself together and cut out the BS—the laziness, the rebelliousness, the not following through with things, the not listening to people when all they're trying to do is help me," she says. "I wouldn't say I hit rock bottom, but I saw what the bot-tom pit was like, and I didn't want to go there. I realized that if I didn't get myself together, by the time I was twenty-five I was going to be truly homeless. I really buckled down and devoted myself to getting what I want out of life."

Casey-Jack Kitos

After much equivocating about whether Ottawa University was the right place for him, Casey-Jack Kitos is now deeply engaged in college life and on track to graduate in 2007.

By January 2006, Casey-Jack had improved his grades enough to get off academic probation. He is majoring in professional communications, with an emphasis on broadcasting and public relations. "That means I can go in one of several directions when I get out," he says. "I can be on the radio or do PR for a big company."

Casey-Jack's consuming passion is his work at the college radio station, KTJO 88.9, where he is special projects coordinator and music director and co-host of "High Voltage," a four-day-a-week drive time show.

"I play alternative music, but I also do a lot of talking," he says. "I'm not exactly a shock jock, but I rant and I rave. The goal of the show is to stir up controversy and provoke people to get active on campus. I'm all about free speech." During the winter, he also provides play-by-play and color commentary for the school's basketball games.

Casey-Jack's other passion is theater. He designs sound for school productions, and he appeared in an Ottawa University production of "Two for the Seesaw" at the regional competition of the Kennedy Center American College Theater Festival in early 2006. "I didn't place, but that was fine," he says. "My dream was to go up and perform."

After accumulating $7,000 in consumer debt in the first few years after he was discharged from foster care, Casey-Jack says he's now living within a budget. The majority of his college-related expenses are covered by several private scholarships, a Pell Grant, a stipend from the Kansas Department of Vocational Rehabilitation, and a federal Education and Training Voucher (ETV) targeted at young people who have aged out of foster care. (His eligibility for the ETV was to end in June 2006 when he turns twenty-three.) Getting off academic probation qualified him for some additional financial aid, which means that he no longer has to borrow money to pay his school expenses. "I finally realized that if you do good at school, they reward you," he said.

Through a work-study program, Casey-Jack gets paid for up to ten hours a week of radio work. He also works up to fifteen hours a week at the school's snack bar. The income from those jobs keeps his 1990 Ford pickup truck on the road and pays his cell phone bills. He shares an inexpensive off-campus house with two other guys.

One thing lacking in Casey-Jack's life is relationships with supportive adults. He gets some moral support from a woman who had once been his sister's foster mother (he refers to her as his godmother.) But the adults who threw him a high school graduation party and played a major role in his life—Jerry and Renita Freeman—have moved across the state, and he can no longer count on them for a home-cooked meal or an emergency loan. "I don't really have anyone to give me advice, but that's OK, because I'm usually the one giving other people advice," he boasts.

"I'm optimistic mostly," Casey-Jack says of the future. "Yes, I have had a hard life. But I have become stronger and more motivated to do more to make my presence known to the world. I've still got lots of things going on in life, but I'm able to keep my head above water. I know what I want, and I know what I need to do to get what I want—out of life, out of school, out of work."

Monica Romero

Monica Romero, who turns twenty-five in September 2006, faces the same challenges as any upwardly mobile single mother with too much to do and too little time to do it. "Right now, I'm going to school fulltime and working fulltime, so I'm pretty busy," she says. "It's a lot to juggle. "It can get tiring and frustrating, but I'm content."

Monica has progressed steadily in her job at USAA, a national insurance agency, and is now a salaried general agency representative. "I love everything about my job, and I want to move up in the company," she says. In 2006, she qualified for a performance bonus as well as $5,000 in educational assistance, which she used to take classes at San Antonio College. She earned a computer help desk certification and is now working on an associate's degree in human resources. Eventually, she hopes to transfer to the University of the Incarnate Word in San Antonio and complete a bachelor's degree.

Monica's finances are in order, and she's saving money so she can buy a house. She drives a 2005 Mazda Tribute, which she bought new.

"Amber loves it because it has a built-in DVD and she can catch movies while we're driving," Monica notes.

Monica and her boyfriend married in September 2004, but separated after fifteen months. "Our marriage wasn't what I pictured it being," Monica says, with obvious regret. "So it's just me and Amber again." Amber will enter first grade in the fall of 2006.

After the split from her husband, Monica and Amber moved into Monica's grandmother's house. With Monica's sisters all living elsewhere, her grandmother welcomes Monica's company and her financial help. She babysits for Amber after school and on any weekend days that Monica has to work.

Monica's relationships with her mother and Amber's father have stabilized enough that Monica now feels comfortable about letting Amber spend time with each of them. "Everything's going pretty good," she says.

Monica continues to receive career counseling, moral support, and a little financial support from Casey Family Programs, her old foster care agency. When she can carve out the time, she takes part in a support group for young single moms at Casey's Community Transition Services Center. "She provides a lot of the moms with a lot of support," says Liz Cruz, Monica's case manager and the group's facilitator. "She's giving, but also she's getting something out of it."

Cruz is proud of what Monica has become. "I think she's ahead of the ball game for a twenty-four-year-old," Cruz says. "She's worked consistently for the same company for a few years. She's saving for her future. She's a wonderful mother and support to her whole family. Not very many twenty-four-year-olds are doing all the things she's doing."

Reggie Kelsey

Reggie Kelsey's death shocked Iowans into confronting deficiencies in the state's system of supports for youth who have aged out of foster care. In the five years since Reggie died, many improvements have been made, particularly in Polk County, the county with the largest number of older youth in foster care.

"What happened to Reggie has been a catalyst for lots of changes in policy and practice related to transition in Iowa," says Carol Behrer, founder and executive director of the Youth Policy Institute, which coordinates the Iowa Aftercare Services Network for the Iowa Department of Human Services. Some of the changes were already in the planning stages as a result of the mandates in the Chafee law, she notes. But "Reggie's case added some urgency to the planning and implementation of the post-eighteen services," she says.

The summer after Reggie's death, the local office of the Iowa Department of Human Services, which had had custody of him for six years, took the lead in setting up the Polk County Transition Work Group, a collaboration of more than twenty community agencies involved with transitioning youth. (It has since been renamed the Transition to Adulthood Community Partnership Board.) The group's initial mandate was to determine ways to better coordinate resources and develop protocols to plan for the transition of youth in care. Once the protocols were developed, the board was given responsibility for reviewing the transition plans for all youth in care in the county, beginning at age sixteen.

Using Chafee funds, Iowa launched the statewide Iowa Aftercare Services Network in April 2002, which contracts with private agencies to offer self-sufficiency support and limited financial assistance to eighteen- to twenty-one-year-olds who have aged out of foster care. In Polk County, the primary provider of these services is Iowa Homeless Youth Centers, the nonprofit agency whose employees tried to help Reggie in the months after he left care.

The state also provided partial funding for the Chapin Hall Center's longitudinal study of youth in transition in Iowa, Illinois, and Wisconsin. Midstudy results suggest that the Iowa nineteen-year-olds who have aged out of care are faring much worse than their peers in Illinois, where they are permitted to stay in foster care until they turn twenty-one.

In 2004, the Iowa Department of Human Services gave $150,000 of its Chafee funding to the Iowa Finance Authority to create a rent subsidy program for former foster youth. The funds assist about forty youth each year with their housing costs.

Since Reggie's death, the legislature has passed laws:

- Mandating the involvement of adult services systems in developing transition plans for foster youth who qualify for such services, as Reggie did.
- Requiring the Iowa Department of Human Services to create local transition teams to review and approve transition plans for individual youth.
- Ordering the redesign of Iowa's child welfare system based on a results accountability framework. The redesigned system emphasizes family strengthening approaches and calls for more community-based supports for youth transitioning to adulthood.

There have also been numerous agency- or court-initiated changes in practice:

- The former Independent Living placement option, which Reggie got thrown out of for bad behavior, has been redesigned as Supervised Apartment Living, and the county's transition team reviews all referrals for their suitability.
- The Juvenile Court is taking a more active role in overseeing transition planning.
- Youth who left foster care at age eighteen are now allowed to return to care before they turn twenty in order to complete high school or obtain a GED.
- With a federal grant, two private agencies are now providing transition assistance for youth who age out of State Training Schools for delinquents.
- With a grant from the Jim Casey Youth Opportunities Initiative, more than 125 Polk County youth have been enrolled in the Opportunity Passport program, which helps them save money for education, housing, medical care, transportation, or work tools.
- In the spring of 2006, foster and adoptive parents received training in how to facilitate permanent family or family-like connections for youth in foster care.

As this was written, Iowa governor Tom Vilsack was about to sign a bill, approved by the legislature, that would permit youth to voluntarily remain in foster care until their twenty-first birthdays if they are employed or attending school. In addition, the legislation would extend Medicaid coverage to age twenty-one for all youth who age out. The legislation has widespread support from service providers and children's advocates.

"While increasing the age when youth are forced out of Iowa's foster-care system will not solve all these problems, it is an essential step in improving outcomes for these youth," Behrer says.

Giselle John

On June 3, 2005, Giselle John received a bachelor's degree in deviant behavior and social control from John Jay College of Criminal Justice. Because she was simultaneously going to school and working full time (sometimes in more than one job), it took Giselle seven years from start to finish, which made her accomplishment all the more rewarding. "I thought I was going to be in school forever, so I was really happy," says Giselle, who turned twenty-seven two months after receiving the degree.

Rather than move directly into a master's program, Giselle decided to take some time off from academics. Eventually, she hopes to enroll in a master's program in social work or licensed case management. "A B.A. has become like a high school diploma, so I know I definitely want to be back in school," she says.

Earning her bachelor's degree also earned Giselle a promotion at Voices for Youth. In the summer of 2005, she became program director of the New York office. Two part-time staff members and an intern report to her. The office's mission is to give youth in the foster care system the tools to become voices for change, as well as to teach other programs strategies for involving youth in their work. "I love my job," she says.

Giselle also takes pride in having shepherded her sister through high school and into college. Roxanne graduated from high school in June 2004 and completed two semesters at Briar Cliff College before the tuition proved prohibitive. Roxanne is planning to transfer to a campus of the City University of New York in the fall of 2006.

In 2005, the girls' mother joined them in New York City. She works as an aide in a retirement home, and the three share a two-bedroom apartment in Queens.

Giselle's relationship with her childhood friend did not work out, and she broke off her engagement early in 2005. She is now involved with a young man whom she had dated previously when she was in her early twenties. They had lost touch for five years, but he tracked her down last year through her church. He lives in Bridgeport, Connecticut, so they see each other only on weekends.

Giselle is proceeding cautiously in her new relationship. Her childhood and foster care experiences make her wary of commitment. "I don't want to let my guard down," she says. "I spend my life keeping my defenses up to protect myself."

APPENDIX A
Adoption and Foster Care Analysis
and Reporting System (AFCARS) Report*

How many children were in foster care on September 30, 2003? 523,000

TABLE A.1 What Were the Ages of the Children in Foster Care?

| Mean Yrs. | 10.2 | |
| Median Yrs. | 10.9 | |

Under 1 Yr.	5%	25,070
1–5 Yrs.	25%	129,470
6–10 Yrs.	21%	108,500
11–15 Yrs.	30%	154,970
16–18 Yrs.	18%	93,810
19 or More Yrs.	2%	9,690

TABLE A.2 What Were the Placement Settings of Children in Foster Care?

Pre-Adoptive Home	5%	24,650
Foster Family Home (Relative)	23%	121,030
Foster Family Home (Non-Relative)	46%	239,810
Group Home	9%	45,700
Institution	10%	51,370
Supervised Independent Living	1%	5,570
Runaway	2%	10,560
Trial Home Visit	4%	19,700

*U.S. Department of Health and Human Services, Administration on Children, Youth and Families, Children's Bureau (http://www.acf.hhs.gov/programs/cb).
Preliminary FY 2003 Estimates as of April 2005.
SOURCE: Adoption and Foster Care Analysis and Reporting System (AFCARS) data submitted for FY 2001, October 1, 2000, through September 30, 2001.

TABLE A.3   What Were the Lengths of Stay in Foster Care?

Mean Months   31
Median Months   18

Less than 1 Month   5%   23,950
1–5 Months   18%   93,900
6–11 Months   16%   84,110
12–17 Months   12%   63,640
18–23 Months   9%   45,850
24–29 Months   7%   35,860
30–35 Months   5%   27,030
3–4 Yrs.   12%   64,810
5 Yrs. or More   16%   93,920

TABLE A.4   What Were the Case Goals of the Children in Foster Care?

Reunify with Parent(s) or Principal Caretaker(s)   48%   246,650
Live with Other Relative(s)   5%   24,090
Adoption   20%   103,460
Long-Term Foster Care   8%   43,250
Emancipation   6%   31,370
Guardianship   3%   15,470
Case Plan Goal Not Yet Established   10%   48,530

TABLE A.5   What Was the Race/Ethnicity of the Children in Foster Care?

AI/AN Non-Hispanic   2%   10,260
Asian Non-Hispanic   1%   3,280
Black Non-Hispanic   35%   184,480
Hawaiian/PI Non-Hispanic   0%   1,540
Hispanic   17%   91,040
White Non-Hispanic   39%   203,920
Unknown/Unable to Determine   3%   13,360
Two or More Races Non-Hispanic   3%   14,310

NOTE: Using U.S. Bureau of the Census standards, children of Hispanic origin may be of any race. Beginning in fiscal year 2000, children could receive more than one race designation.

TABLE A.6   What Was the Gender of the Children in Foster Care?

Male	53%	274,820
Female	48%	248,150

How many children entered foster care during FY 2003? 297,000

TABLE A.7   What Were the Ages of the Children Who Entered Care During FY 2003?

Mean Yrs.	8.4
Median Yrs.	8.3

Under 1 Yr.	14%	42,910
1–5 Yrs.	26%	77,820
6–10 Yrs.	20%	58,490
11–15 Yrs.	29%	85,310
16–18 Yrs.	11%	32,350
19 or More Yrs.	0%	140

TABLE A.8   What Was the Race/Ethnicity of the Children Who Entered Care During FY 2003?

AI/AN Non-Hispanic	2%	6,750
Asian Non-Hispanic	1%	2,640
Black Non-Hispanic	27%	80,300
Hawaiian/PI Non-Hispanic	0%	1,110
Hispanic	17%	51,180
White Non-Hispanic	46%	137,340
Unknown/Unable to Determine	3%	7,830
Two or More Races Non-Hispanic	3%	9,010

NOTE: Using U.S. Bureau of the Census standards, children of Hispanic origin may be of any race. Beginning in fiscal year 2000, children could receive more than one race designation.

How many children exited foster care during FY 2003? 281,000

TABLE A.9   What Were the Ages of the Children Who Exited Care During FY 2003?

Mean Yrs.	9.9	
Median Yrs.	10.0	
Under 1 Yr.	5%	12,630
1–5 Yrs.	28%	79,790
6–10 Yrs.	21%	59,540
11–15 Yrs.	24%	66,790
16–18 Yrs.	20%	55,790
19 or More Yrs.	2%	6,200

TABLE A.10   What Was the Race/Ethnicity of the Children Who Exited Care During FY 2003?

AI/AN Non-Hispanic	2%	5,720
Asian Non-Hispanic	1%	2,620
Black Non-Hispanic	29%	82,420
Hawaiian/PI Non-Hispanic	0%	970
Hispanic	16%	45,890
White Non-Hispanic	46%	127,680
Unknown/Unable to Determine	3%	7,260
Two or More Races Non-Hispanic	3%	8,080

NOTE: Using U.S. Bureau of the Census standards, children of Hispanic origin may be of any race. Beginning in fiscal year 2000, children could receive more than one race designation.

TABLE A.11   What Were the Lengths of Stay of the Children Who Exited Foster Care During FY 2003?

Mean Months	21.7	
Median Months	11.9	
Less than 1 Month	18%	51,120
1–5 Months	16%	45,810
6–11 Months	16%	44,870
12–17 Months	12%	33,720
18–23 Months	8%	23,290

(continued on next page)

(Table A.11 continued from previous page)

24–29 Months	6%	16,770
30–35 Months	5%	12,650
3–4 Yrs.	10%	27,770
5 Yrs. or More	9%	24,110

TABLE A.12   What Were the Outcomes for the Children Exiting Foster Care During FY 2003?

Reunification with Parent(s) or Primary Caretaker(s)	55%	151,770
Living with Other Relative(s)	11%	30,570
Adoption	18%	49,340
Emancipation	8%	21,720
Guardianship	4%	10,700
Transfer to Another Agency	2%	6,420
Runaway	2%	4,070
Death of Child	0%	570

NOTE: Deaths are attributable to a variety of causes, including illness, accidents, and homicide.

How many children were waiting to be adopted on September 30, 2003?

119,000

NOTE: Waiting children are children who have a goal of adoption or whose parental rights have been terminated, or both. Children sixteen years old and older whose parental rights have been terminated and who have a goal of emancipation have been excluded from the estimate.

How many children in foster care had their parental rights terminated for all living parents? 68,000

How many children were adopted from the public foster care system in FY 2003? 50,000

NOTE: The number of adoptions reported here includes adoptions of some children who were not in foster care but who received other support from the public agency. In addition, states have historically underreported adoption discharges. In contrast, states tend to more accurately report the adoptions to the AFCARS.

APPENDIX B

Exits to Emancipation, Fiscal 2000

TABLE B.1 Exits to Emancipation, Fiscal 2000

	Entry Age 12 Years or Under		Entry Age 12 Years or More		Total*
	Number	%	Number	%	Number
Alabama	63	61%	40	39%	103
Alaska	9	19%	39	81%	48
Arizona	104	23%	346	77%	450
Arkansas	25	15%	147	85%	172
California	1,556	35%	2,933	65%	4,489
Colorado	47	19%	205	81%	252
Connecticut	14	26%	39	74%	53
Delaware	5	11%	40	87%	46*
District of Columbia	5	20%	20	80%	25**
Florida	293	33%	606	67%	900*
Georgia	16	29%	40	71%	56
Hawaii	19	16%	102	84%	121
Idaho	9	20%	35	80%	44
Illinois	506	37%	840	62%	1,360*
Indiana	110	37%	182	62%	294*
Iowa	45	18%	204	82%	249
Kansas	29	19%	120	81%	149
Kentucky	32	14%	200	86%	232
Louisiana	147	49%	151	51%	298
Maine	4	27%	11	73%	15**
Maryland	78	34%	152	66%	230
Massachusetts	135	24%	422	76%	557
Michigan	135	24%	426	76%	564*
Minnesota	113	21%	413	78%	527*
Mississippi	22	35%	40	65%	62
Missouri	279	47%	321	54%	600

*Because of missing data on age of entry, the total number of the youth who emancipate in each state is sometimes more than the sum of the two columns.

**Missing data make these figures suspect.

	Entry Age 12 Years or Under		Entry Age 12 Years or More		Total†
	Number	%	Number	%	Number
Montana	17	19%	73	81%	90
Nebraska	1	50%	1	50%	2**
Nevada	1	50%	1	50%	2**
New Hampshire	26	46%	31	54%	57
New Jersey	92	30%	215	70%	307
New Mexico			26	100%	26
New York	721	46%	845	54%	1,568*
North Carolina	79	29%	198	71%	277
North Dakota			43	100%	43
Ohio	231	22%	795	77%	1,028*
Oklahoma	15	28%	37	69%	54*
Oregon	62	42%	85	58%	147
Pennsylvania	217	32%	471	68%	688
Rhode Island	14	17%	67	82%	82*
South Carolina	102	38%	169	62%	271
South Dakota	5	22%	18	78%	23
Tennessee	106	18%	490	82%	596
Texas	193	53%	172	47%	365
Utah	18	10%	154	90%	172
Vermont	18	28%	47	72%	65
Virginia	162	30%	379	70%	542*
Washington	101	30%	231	69%	333*
West Virginia	30	34%	57	66%	87
Wisconsin	41	16%	200	79%	254*
Wyoming	5	14%	31	86%	36
Total	6,057	32%	12,910	68%	19,011*

SOURCE: U.S. Department of Health and Human Services: Administration for Children and Families; Administration on Children, Youth, and Families; Children's Bureau; Adoption and Foster Care Analysis and Reporting System (AFCARS). Data as of October 2003.

APPENDIX C
State Allocations for John Chafee
Foster Care Independence Program

TABLE C.1   **Fiscal 2005 Allotments**

Alabama	$1,563,344	Montana	500,000
Alaska	524,629	Nebraska	1,553,057
Arizona	1,991,020	Nevada	587,636
Arkansas	771,514	New Hampshire	500,000
California	25,012,729	New Jersey	3,298,993
Colorado	2,251,277	New Mexico	540,060
Connecticut	1,733,849	New York	11,585,958
Delaware	500,000	North Carolina	2,451,871
Dist. of Col.	1,091,992	North Dakota	500,000
Florida	7,889,242	Ohio	4,969,320
Georgia	3,506,787	Oklahoma	2,364,432
Hawaii	763,027	Oregon	2,412,523
Idaho	500,000	Pennsylvania	5,598,104
Illinois	5,556,956	Puerto Rico	2,124,039
Indiana	2,288,567	Rhode Island	600,238
Iowa	1,288,685	South Carolina	1,258,597
Kansas	1,486,707	South Dakota	500,000
Kentucky	1,773,196	Tennessee	2,439,784
Louisiana	1,358,131	Texas	5,706,887
Maine	771,257	Utah	522,829
Maryland	2,962,870	Vermont	500,000
Massachusetts	3,242,415	Virginia	1,812,029
Michigan	5,497,293	Washington	2,161,782
Minnesota	1,887,123	West Virginia	1,046,430
Mississippi	723,166	Wisconsin	2,012,108
Missouri	3,090,942	Wyoming	500,000

Total $144,033,280

SOURCE: U.S. Department of Health and Human Services: Administration on Children, Youth, and Families; Administration for Children and Families; Children's Bureau.

APPENDIX D
Jim Casey Youth Opportunity
Initiative Opportunity Passport Sites

Atlanta, Georgia
The Community Foundation for Greater
    Atlanta, Inc.
The Hurt Building
50 Hurt Plaza, Suite 449
Atlanta, GA 30303
(404) 588-3185

Denver, Colorado
Mile High United Way
2505 18th St.
Denver, CO 80211
(303) 561-2340

Des Moines, Iowa
Youth Policy Institute of Iowa
7200 Hickman Road, Suite 202
Des Moines, IA 50322
(515) 727-4220

Detroit and Northern Michigan
Michigan Family Independence Agency
1341 North Lamkin Drive
Harbor Springs, MI 49740
(231) 526-1047

Hartford, Connecticut
Connecticut Voices for Children
33 Whitney Ave.
New Haven, CT 06510
(203) 498-4240, ext. 120

Indianapolis, Indiana
United Way of Central Indiana
3901 North Meridian Street
P.O. Box 88409
Indianapolis, IN 46208
(317) 921-1278

Nashville, Tennessee
Vanderbilt Child and Family Policy Center
Institute for Public Policy Studies
1207 18th Ave. South
Nashville, TN 37212
(615) 343-9905

Providence, Rhode Island
Casey Family Services
1268 Eddy Street
Providence, RI 02905
(401) 781-3669

San Diego, California
Access, Inc.
2612 Daniel Avenue
San Diego, CA 92111
(858) 560-0871

State of Maine
Edmund S. Muskie School of Public
    Service
University of Southern Maine
29 Baxter Blvd.
P.O. Box 9300
Portland, ME 04104
(207) 780-5867

Tampa/Clearwater, Florida
The Eckerd Family Foundation
100 North Starcrest Drive
Clearwater, FL 33765
(727) 446-2996

APPENDIX E

Resources on Foster Care, Youth Transition, and Development

Annie E. Casey Foundation
701 St. Paul St.
Baltimore, MD 21202
(410) 547-6600
http://www.aecf.org

Casey Family Programs
1300 Dexter Ave. North, Floor 3
Seattle, WA 98109-3542
(206) 282-7300
http://www.casey.org

Casey Family Services
127 Church St.
New Haven, CT 06510
(203) 401-6900
http://caseyfamilyservices.org

Child Trends
4301 Connecticut Ave. NW, Suite 100
Washington, DC 20008
(202) 572-6000
http://www.childtrends.org/

Child Welfare League of America
440 First St. NW, Third Floor
Washington, DC 20001-2085
(202) 638-2952
http://www.cwla.org

Connect for Kids
1625 K St. NW, 11th Floor
Washington, DC 20006
http://www.connectforkids.org

Corporation for Enterprise Development
777 N. Capitol St. NE, Suite 800
Washington, DC 20002
(202) 408-9788
http://www.idanetwork.org

FYI3
http://www.FYI3.com

FosterClub
http://www.FosterClub.com

Hunter College/National Resource Center for Family-Centered Practice and Permanency Planning
(212) 452-7053
http://www.hunter.cuny.edu/socwork/nrcfcpp/

Jim Casey Youth Opportunities Initiative
222 S. Central Ave., Suite 305
Clayton, MO 63105
(314) 863-7000
http://www.jimcaseyyouth.org/

National Clearinghouse on Child Abuse and Neglect
(301) 608-8098
http://www.nccanch.acf.hhs.gov/

National Clearinghouse on Families & Youth
(301) 608-8098
http://www.ncfy.com.

National Foster Care Coalition
1776 I St., NW 9th Floor
Washington, DC 20006
(202) 756-4842
www.natlfostercare.org

National Independent Living Association
4203 Southpoint Blvd.
Jacksonville, FL 32216
(904) 296-1038
http://www.nilausa.org/

The National Mentoring Partnership
1600 Duke St., Suite 300
Alexandria, VA 22314
(703) 224-2200
http://www.mentoring.org/

National Network for Youth
1319 F St. NW, Suite 401
Washington, DC 20004-1106
(202) 783-7949
http://www.nn4Youth.org

National Resource Center for Youth Development
The University of Oklahoma
College of Continuing Education
4502 E. 41st St., Building 4W
Tulsa, OK 74135
(918) 660-3700
http://www.nrcys.ou.edu/

National Service Resource Center
http://www.nationalserviceresources.org/epicenter/

Pew Partnership for Civic Change: Spotlight on Solutions
5 Boar's Head Lane, Suite 100
Charlottesville, VA 22903
(434) 971-2073
http://www.pew-partnership.org/

Promising Practice Network for Children, Families, and Communities
c/o Rand Corporation
1700 Main St.
Santa Monica, CA 90401
(310) 393-0411, ext. 7172
http://www.promisingpractices.net/

Public/Private Ventures
2000 Market St., Suite 600
Philadelphia, PA 19103
(215) 557-4400
http://www.ppv.org

Vera Institute of Justice
233 Broadway, 12th Floor
New York, NY 10279
(212) 334-1300
http://www.vera.org

APPENDIX F
Resources Mentioned in *On Their Own*

Chapter 1: Lamar, Jeffrey, and Jermaine Williams

Community Justice Center
1825 Park Ave., Suite 604,
New York, NY 10035
(212) 427-4545

Work Appreciation for Youth (WAY)
c/o Children's Village
Echo Hills
Dobbs Ferry, NY 10522
(914) 693-0600
http://www.childrensvillage.org/way.html

Chapter 2: Patty Mueller

Casey Family Services
127 Church St.
New Haven, CT 06510
(203) 401-6900
http://www.caseyfamilyservices.org

Chapter 3: Alfonso Torres

Covenant House
733 Breakers Ave.
Ft. Lauderdale, FL 33304
(954) 561-5559
http://www.covenanthouse.org/about_loc_ftlaud.html

Children & Youth Law Clinic
University of Miami School of Law
1311 Miller Drive, Suite F305
Coral Gables, FL 33124
(305) 284-3123
http://www.law.miami.edu/cylc/clinic.html

Miami Bridge
2810 N.W. South River Drive
Miami, FL 33125
(305) 636-3526
http://www.miamibridge.org

Chapter 4: Raquel Tolston

The Ark House
2500 Market St.
San Francisco, CA 94414-1915
(415) 255-7948

California Youth Connection
604 Mission St., 9th floor
San Francisco, CA 94105
(415) 442-5060
http://www.calyouthconn.org/

Guerrero House
899 Guerrero St.
San Francisco, CA 94410
(415) 550-4478

Job Corps
U.S. Department of Labor
200 Constitution Ave. NW
Washington, DC 20210
(202) 693-3900
http://jobcorps.doleta.gov/

Larkin Street Youth Services
1138 Sutter St.
San Francisco, CA 94109
(415) 673-0911
http://www.larkinstreetyouth.org

Chapter 5: Casey-Jack Kitos

Appleseed
727 15th Street, NW
11th Floor
Washington D.C. 20005
(202) 347-7960
http://www.appleseeds.net/

National Youth Sports Program
201 South Capitol Ave., Suite 710
Indianapolis, Indiana 46225
(317) 829-5777
http://www.nyscorp.org

O'Connell Youth Ranch
Box 3589
Lawrence, KS 66046
(785) 842-9356

Chapter 6: Monica Romero

Community Transitions Services Center
Casey Family Programs, San Antonio
   Division
2840 Babcock
San Antonio, TX 78229
(210) 616-0813

Project QUEST, Inc.
301 S. Frio, Suite 400
San Antonio, TX 78207-4446
(210) 270-4690
http://www.questsa.com/

Salvation Army Scattered Site Apartment Program
Leonard J. Goslinowski Social Services
   Center (Hope Center)
910 N. Flores St.
San Antonio, TX 78212
(210) 352-2020
http://www.salvationarmysatx.org/text/
locations.html

Salvation Army—Stepping Forward
2801 W. Ashby Place
San Antonio, TX 78201
(210) 734-8055
http://www.salvationarmysatx.org/text/
locations.html

Chapter 7: Reggie Kelsey

Buchanan Transitional Living Center
Iowa Homeless Youth Center
1219 Buchanan St.
Des Moines, IA 50316
(515) 265-1222

Golden Circle Behavioral Health Services
515 28th St., Suite 104
Des Moines, IA 50312
(515) 241-0982
http://www.bhrci.org/TCM&SCL.htm

Iowa Lutheran Hospital
700 E. University Ave.
Des Moines, IA 50316-2302
(515) 263-5612

Westminster House
940 Cummins Parkway
Des Moines, IA 50312
(515) 277-7933
http://www.bhrci.org/whoisBHR.htm

Youth & Shelter Services, Inc.
P.O. Box 1628
Ames, IA 50010
(515) 233-3141
http://www.yss.ames.ia.us/programs
.html#YouthService

Chapter 8: Giselle John

Public Allies
633 W. Wisconsin Ave., Suite 610
Milwaukee, WI 53203
(414) 273-0533
http://www.publicallies.org

Voices of Youth
224 W. 29th St., 2nd Floor
New York, NY 10001
(212) 279-0708, ext. 150
http://www.swkey.org/programs.asp#
voices

Youth Communication
224 W. 29th St., 2nd Floor
New York, NY 10001
(212) 278-0707, ext. 102
http://www.youthcomm.org

Conclusion

Americorps
c/o Corporation for National and
    Community Service
1201 New York Ave. NW
Washington, DC 20525
(202) 606-5000
http://www.americorps.org/

Campus Peer-Mentoring Project
Community College Foundation
http://www.communitycollege.org/Hdys/
youth/campus.htm

Chapin Hall Center for Children
1313 East 60th St.
Chicago, Illinois 60637
(773) 753-5900
http://www.chapinhall.org

Court-Appointed Special Advocates
100 W. Harrison, North Tower, Suite 500
Seattle, WA 98119
(800) 628-3233
www.nationalcasa.org

Early Start to Emancipation Preparation (ESTEP)
Community College Foundation
(916) 418-5100
http://hdys.communitycollege.org/estep
/index.htm

First Place Fund for Youth
1755 Broadway, Suite 304
Oakland, CA 94612
(510) 272-0979
http://www.firstplacefund.org

Guardian Scholars Program
(714) 619-0200, ext. 233
http://www.orangewoodfoundation.org

Lighthouse Youth Services
1501 Madison Rd.
Cincinnati, OH 45206-1776
(513) 221-3350
http://www.lys.org

MDRC
16 East 34 St., 19th Floor
New York, NY 10016-4326
(212) 532-3200
http://www.mdrc.org

Mockingbird Times
3302 Fuhrman Ave. East, Suite 107
Seattle, WA 98102
(206) 323-KIDS
http://www.mockingbirdsociety.org

Orphan Foundation of America
Tall Oaks Village Center
12020-D North Shore Drive
Reston, VA 20190-4977
(571) 203-0270
http://www.orphan.org

Our Piece of the Pie
Southend Community Services
427 Franklin Ave.
Hartford, CT 06114
(860) 296-5068
http://www.scservices.org/opp/index.html

Powerhouse
3531 NE Freemont Ave., Suite #C
Portland, OR 97212
(503) 287-6083

Project Paycheck
Wyoming Department of Employment
1510 East Pershing Blvd.
Cheyenne, WY 82001
(307) 777-3722
http://dwsweb.state.wy.us/dwsnews/
releases/pepnet.asp

Quantum Opportunities Program
c/o Opportunities Industrialization
    Centers of America, Inc.
1415 N. Broad St.
Philadelphia, PA 19122
(212) 236-4500, ext. 251
http://oicofamerica.org/programs.html

School-to-Career Partnership
c/o Jim Casey Youth Opportunities
    Initiative
222 S. Central Ave., Suite 305
Clayton, MO 63105
(314) 863-7000
http://www.jimcaseyyouth.org/

Social Advocates for Youth
538 Valley Way
Milpitas, CA 95035
(408) 956-8034
http://www.sayscc.org

Treehouse
2100 24th Ave. South, Suite 200
Seattle, WA 98144-4632
(206) 767-7000
http://www.treehouse4kids.org/index.htm

Urban Peak
1630 S. Acoma St.
Denver, CO 80223
(303) 777-9198
http://www.urbanpeak.org

Youth Conservation Corps
http://www.fs.fed.us/people/programs/
ycc.htm

Youthbuild USA
58 Day St.
P.O. Box 440322
Somerville, MA 02144
(617) 623-9900
http://www.youthbuild.org

NOTES

Introduction

1. Throughout the book, we use the term *foster care* to refer to the full panoply of court-ordered, out-of-home placements for abused and neglected children, including family foster homes, relatives' homes, group homes, and residential treatment facilities.

2. Data for this list come from the following sources: Ronna Cook, *A National Evaluation of Title IV-E Foster Care Independent Living Programs for Youth: Phase 2 Final Report* (Rockville, MD: Westat, Inc., 1991), and Mark Courtney et al., "Foster Youth Transitions to Adulthood: A Longitudinal View of Youth Leaving Care," *Child Welfare* 80, no. 6 (2001), pp. 685–717.

3. Except where noted, statistical data in this chapter come from the AFCARS report, issued by the Department of Health and Human Services, April 2005, http://www.acf.hhs.gov/programs/cb/stats_research/afcars/tar/report10.htm; see also, "Child Welfare Outcomes Annual Report: 2002" (Washington, DC: Department of Health and Human Services, 2005), http://www.acf.hhs.gov/programs/cb/pubs/cwo02/. Selected data are included in Appendix A.

4. In a small number of cases, parents voluntarily place teenagers in care because of incorrigibility.

5. "Child Maltreatment 2003" (Washington, DC: Department of Health and Human Services, 2005), http://www.acf.hhs.gov/programs/cb/pubs/cm03/.

6. Ibid.

7. "Child Welfare Outcomes 2002" (Washington, DC: Department of Health and Human Services, 2005), http://www.acf.hhs.gov/programs/cb/pubs/cwo02/.

8. Richard Wertheimer, "Youth Who 'Age Out' of Foster Care: Troubling Lives, Troubling Prospects," *ChildTrends Research Brief* (Washington, DC: Child Trends, December 2002), http://www.childtrends.org/PDF/FosterCareRB.pdf.

9. It must be mentioned that we don't know whether those who return to their families in their teens have the supports in place to promote successful transitions to adulthood, though there is little reason to be optimistic, given that most of these youth were removed from their families only a few years before. Adding to their

gloomy prospects are the dearth of services to prepare these young people or their families for reunification and to remedy the deficits that caused the removal.

10. "Child Welfare Outcomes 2002."

11. An increasing number of states permit young people to stay in foster care until they turn twenty-one if they are attending school or vocational training.

12. Barbara Needell et al., "Youth Emancipating from Foster Care in California: Findings Using Linked Administrative Data" (Berkeley: Center for Social Services Research, May 2002), p. 26, http://cssr.berkeley.edu/childwelfare/pdfs/youth/ffy_entire.pdf.

13. "Child Welfare Outcomes 2002."

14. The $70 million federal appropriation triggered $25 million in mandatory state matches. In addition, the General Accounting Office estimated in 1999 that states, local governments, and private donors contributed another $36.5 million to independent living services, bringing the total spent annually to $131.5 million. General Accounting Office, "Effectiveness of Independent Living Services Unknown" (Washington, DC: GAO, November 1999), http://www.nrcys.ou.edu/PDFs/gao11599.pdf.

15. Each state is required to put up a 20 percent match to receive Chafee funds, so, theoretically, the $140 million annual federal appropriation triggers $28 million in state spending.

16. It should be noted that these problems are endemic in this age group, not just among youth coming out of foster care.

17. Tom Smith, "Coming of Age in 21st Century America: Public Attitudes Towards the Importance and Timing of Transitions to Adulthood," GSS Topical Report No. 35 (Chicago: National Opinion Research Center, University of Chicago, April 2003), http://www.norc.org.

Chapter 2

1. http://www.ihep.org/Pubs/PDF/fosteryouth.pdf a 2005 report by the Institute for Higher Education Policy.

2. Boston Children's Services merged with The New England Home for Little Wanderers, another nonprofit agency, in 1999. The new agency's name is The Home for Little Wanderers.

3. Casey Family Services, based in New Haven, Connecticut, is the direct-services arm of the Baltimore-based Annie E. Casey Foundation. The agency provides long-term foster care and family-strengthening and adoption services in Baltimore and throughout New England.

4. The name has been changed.

5. The name has been changed.

6. The names have been changed.

Chapter 3

1. "Effectiveness of Independent Living Services Unknown" (Washington, DC: General Accounting Office, November 1999), http://www.nrcys.ou.edu/PDFs/gao11599.pdf.

2. Tony Bridges, "Kids Find State Fails Them," *Tallahassee Democrat,* February 7, 2003, http://www.tallahassee.com/mld/tallahassee/news/special_packages/the_legacy_of_foster_care/5131544.htm.

3. There are no definitive national data on the number of young people involved with both the foster care and juvenile justice systems, but there is a strong correlation between childhood maltreatment and delinquency. A recent study of youth who were about to age out of care in Illinois, Wisconsin, and Iowa found that more than half had been arrested and one-fifth had been convicted of a crime. Mark E. Courtney, Sherri Terao, and Noel Bost, "Midwest Evaluation of the Adult Functioning of Former Foster Youth: Conditions of Youth Preparing to Leave State Care" (Chicago: Chapin Hall Center for Children at the University of Chicago, 2004), http://www.chapinhall.org/PDFDownload_new.asp?tk=1002275&ar=1355&L2=61&L3=130. In addition, 70 percent of youth who appear in juvenile courts report a history of abuse or neglect, as do 70 to 80 percent of adults in prison. (C. S. Widom, "The Cycle of Violence," *Research in Brief* [Washington, DC: U.S. Department of Justice, National Institute of Justice, October 1992], p. 3). And finally, in 1997, the Vera Institute studied the overlap between foster care and juvenile delinquency cases in New York City and found that 15 percent of those twelve to sixteen years old admitted to the two major juvenile detention centers were in foster care, eight times the rate expected based upon their proportion of the population. See http://www.vera.org/publication_pdf/pathways.pdf.

4. Research suggests that few children in foster care in Florida do well enough in school to quality for the Road to Independence Scholarship. A 2003 study by the Broward School Board of 912 children in foster care who were enrolled in district schools found that they were twice as likely as their peers to perform poorly on standardized tests and three times more likely to be held back a grade. Almost one-half qualified for special education because of disabilities or learning disorders. Fifty-four percent scored in the lowest level for mathematics, and 56 percent scored in the lowest level for reading in the 2002 Florida Comprehensive Assessment Test (FCAT). (Beginning in the 2003–2004 school year, Florida students were required to pass the FCAT to advance to the next grade.)

5. In 2005, the Florida legislature enacted a law that permits youth to petition for court oversight until they turn nineteen.

6. The name has been changed.

7. Bridges, "Kids Find State Fails Them." On October 21, 2003, Beth Englander, a DCF official, told the Florida Legislature that the $15.6 million in federal and state transition funds appropriated for the year was falling short of the need. From October 1, 2002, through June 30, 2003, just over 600 young people had received Road to Independence Scholarships, and 536 had received some aftercare or transitional cash benefits. Since the pool of potential eligibles is 4,112, that means that almost three-fourths—2,971 individuals—hadn't received any financial help. Englander testified that the department was projecting a $3.6 million to $6 million deficit in its independent living services budget in the current fiscal year and was considering reducing the monthly scholarships to stay within its budget. Englander said that among the major challenges for emancipated youth were a dearth of services for those with special needs, a lack of health care options (only scholarship recipients receive Medicaid coverage), limited housing and employment resources, and inadequate personal support systems.

Chapter 4

1. Nan P. Roman and Phyllis B. Wolfe, "Web of Failure: The Relationship Between Foster Care and Homelessness" (Washington, DC: National Alliance to End Homelessness, 1995), http://www.endhomelessness.org/pub/fostercare/webrept.htm.

2. Deborah Bass, "Helping Vulnerable Youths: Runaway and Homeless Adolescents in the United States" (Washington, DC: National Association of Social Workers, 1994), p. 9.

Chapter 5

1. See http://www.acf.hhs.gov/programs/cb/cwrp/executive/ks.htm.

Chapter 6

1. Ronna Cook, "A National Evaluation of Title IV-E Foster Care Independent Living Programs for Youth: Phase 2 Final Report" (Rockville, MD: Westat, Inc., 1991), www.Westat.com.

2. See http://www.geocities.com/maggi19/teenpregnancy/statistics.htm.

3. The name has been changed.

4. This was in 1991, when states were just beginning to understand the benefits of using relatives as foster parents (an arrangement typically called public kinship care). By 2000, foster care agencies in all but two states were placing children with relatives whenever possible, and twenty-two states, plus the District of Columbia, were licensing and compensating them. As of fiscal 2001, 24 percent of all children in foster care were living with relatives.

5. In fiscal 2004, the state rate paid to Casey and other private child-placing agencies in Texas was $1,080 per month per child.

6. The names have been changed.

7. The name has been changed.

8. The name has been changed.

9. Casey Family Programs finances Monica's stipend. For young people who have aged out of public agency foster care, Texas uses its Chafee Act funds to provide assistance. As long as they complete at least twenty-five hours of training in life skills and are employed, actively seeking work, or attending school, they are eligible for a transitional living allowance of up to $1,000 and a household supplies stipend of $300. For a limited number of young people, assistance with room and board is also available for up to $500 a month, to a maximum of $3,000. Texas also waives the tuition at public universities and provides Medicaid coverage until age twenty-one.

Chapter 7

1. "Effectiveness of Independent Living Services Unknown" (Washington, DC: General Accounting Office, November 1999), p. 11, http://www.nrcys.ou.edu/PDFs/gao11599.pdf.

2. The names have been changed.

3. "Investigation into the Transitioning of Reggie Kelsey out of Iowa's Foster Care System" (Des Moines, IA: Office of the Citizen's Aide/Ombudsman, January 14, 2003), p. 66, http://www4.legis.state.ia.us/cao/Reports/files/DHS%20-%20Kelsey% 20-%20Redacted.pdf.

4. Ibid., p. 67.

5. Hoehne told the Iowa ombudsman's investigator that he had had Reggie sign an application for social services and a waiver of confidentiality and had also left a message for his psychiatrist saying he needed a qualifying diagnosis before the agency could provide services to Reggie. "Investigation into the Transitioning of Reggie Kelsey," p. 67.

6. Clark Kauffman, "Reggie Sought Home, but Found Death," *Des Moines Register*, June 17, 2003, http://www.dmregister.com/news/stories/c4780934/15041469 .html.

7. "Investigation into the Transitioning of Reggie Kelsey."

8. About 225 young people age out of care in Iowa each year, and scores more leave care shortly before their eighteenth birthdays, which means that the pool of those between eighteen and twenty-one who are eligible for aftercare benefits is between 675 and 1,200.

9. "Help for 'aged-out' kids." *Des Moines Register*, May 21, 2004. http://www .desmoinesregister.com/apps/pbcs.dll/artikkel?SearchID=73172973362042&Avis =D2&Dato=20040521&Kategori=OPINION03&Lopenr=405210309&Ref=AR

Chapter 8

1. Talbot Perkins closed in 2001.

2. The names of the family members have been changed.

3. In 2003, the publication was renamed *Represent.*

4. Giselle John, "Would You Place Your Child There?" *Foster Care Youth United* (May–June 1997).

5. Some of Giselle's writings are posted on the Web site of Youth Communication: http://www.youthcomm.org.

6. The agency was renamed the Administration for Children's Services and was given broader powers at about the same time Scoppetta was appointed.

7. A 2000 audit of Giselle's agency by the Administration for Children's Services found that the agency couldn't provide receipts for $44,571 in clothing allowances that it had received for the children in its foster homes. See http://216.239.51.100/ search?q=cache:6Uz5o8lKcZIC:www.comptroller.nyc.gov/bureaus/audit/PDF_ FILES/Annual2001.pdf+%22Talbot-Perkins+Children%27s+Services%22&hl= en&ie=UTF8.

Conclusion

1. Susan Bales, "Reframing Youth Issues for Public Consideration and Support" (Washington, DC: FrameWorks Institute, 2001), http://www.frameworksinstitute.org/ products/reframing.pdf.

2. Chris Mooney, "Breaking the Frame," *American Prospect* (April 2003), http:// www.prospect.org/print/V14/4/mooney-c.html.

3. National public opinion poll of 1,121 adults conducted by Lake Snell Perry & Associates for the Jim Casey Youth Opportunities Initiative in January 2003, http://www.jimcaseyyouth.org/docs/poll1.pdf.

4. Robert Ivry and Fred Doolittle, "Improving the Economic and Life Outcomes of At-Risk Youth" (New York: MDRC, Spring 2003), http://www.mdrc.org/Reports2003/at_risk_concept_ppr/at_risk_2003.pdf.

5. The most recent research found that youth on the verge of aging out of foster care were twice as likely as other youth to have been held back a grade, twice as likely to have been suspended from school, and four times as likely to have been expelled. Mark E. Courtney, Sherri Terao, and Noel Bost, "Midwest Evaluation of the Adult Functioning of Former Foster Youth: Conditions of Youth Preparing to Leave State Care" (Chicago: Chapin Hall Center for Children at the University of Chicago, 2004), http://www.chapinhall.org/PDFDownload_new.asp?tk=1002275&ar=1355&L2=61&L3=130. In an earlier study, Washington State found that 37.9 percent had qualified for special education, 36.2 percent had repeated a grade, and 67.6 percent had attended three or more different elementary schools. M. Burley and M. Halpern, "Educational Attainment of Foster Youth: Achievement and Graduation Outcomes for Children in State Care" (Olympia: Washington State Institute for Public Policy, 2001), http://www.wsipp.wa.gov/childfamily/pdf/FCEDReport.pdf.

6. Peter J. Pecora et al., "Assessing the Effects of Foster Care: Early Results from the Casey National Alumni Study" (Seattle: Casey Family Programs, 2003), http://www.casey.org/NR/rdonlyres/CEFBB1B6–7ED1–440D–925A-E5BAF602294D/148/casey_alumni_studies_report.pdf.

7. Ronna Cook, "A National Evaluation of Title IV-E Foster Care Independent Living Programs for Youth: Phase 2 Final Report" (Rockville, MD: Westat, 1991), http://www.westat.com.

8. Pecora et al., "Assessing the Effects."

9. Katherine Kortenkamp and Jennifer Ehrle, "The Well-Being of Children Involved with the Child Welfare System: A National Overview" (Washington, DC: Urban Institute, 2002), http://www.urban.org/url.cfm?ID=310413.

10. The Community College Foundation's Campus Peer-Mentoring Project operates at Mt. San Antonio College and Los Angeles City College. See http://www.cccf.org/Hdys/youth/campus.htm.

11. Robert M. Goerge et al., "Employment Outcomes for Youth Aging Out of Foster Care. Final Report" (Chicago: Chapin Hall Center for Children, March 2002), http://aspe.hhs.gov/hsp/fostercare-agingout02/.

12. Mark Courtney et al., "Foster Youth Transitions to Adulthood: A Longitudinal View of Youth Leaving Care," *Child Welfare* 80, no. 6 (2001): p. 12.

13. Barbara Needell et al., "Youth Emancipating from Foster Care in California: Findings Using Linked Administrative Data" (Berkeley: Center for Social Services Research, May 2002), p. 76, http://cssr.berkeley.edu/childwelfare/pdfs/youth/ffy_entire.pdf.

14. Pecora et al., "Assessing the Effects."

15. The School-to-Career Partnership, which was started by the Annie E. Casey Foundation, operates in Baltimore; Hartford; New York City; Oakland; Portland, Maine; Providence; San Antonio, and San Diego. The program is an example of a "dual-customer" approach to workforce development: The youth benefit from getting jobs with an average wage of $7.83 per hour, and the employers benefit from a higher retention rate than they experience with other new hires.

16. Cook, "A National Evaluation of Title IV-E Foster Care Independent Living Programs for Youth: Phase 2."

17. Pecora et al., "Assessing the Effects."

18. Courtney, "Foster Youth Transitions to Adulthood," pp. 685–717.

19. Richard Wertheimer, "Youth Who 'Age Out' of Foster Care: Troubled Lives, Troubling Prospects," *ChildTrends Research Brief* (Washington, DC: Child Trends, December 2002), http://www.childtrends.org/PDF/MentoringBrief2002.pdf.

20. The Urban Institute and its partners—the Chapin Hall Center for Children and the National Opinion Research Center—are evaluating selected programs funded through the Chafee Act to determine whether they have achieved the act's goals: increased educational attainment, higher employment rates and stability, greater interpersonal and relationship skills, reduced nonmarital pregnancy and births, and reduced delinquency and crime rates. In addition, the General Accounting Office is studying states' progress in implementing the Chafee program.

21. Presentation by Beth Englander, director of Child Welfare/Community-Based Care, to the Committee on the Future of Florida's Families, Florida House of Representatives, October 21, 2003; progress report by the Iowa Aftercare Services Network.

22. A community partnership board and a youth board, intended to work in partnership, run each of the local projects. All members of the youth boards are youth who are currently or were formerly in foster care. Each has a special responsibility to recruit peers to serve on the board and enroll in the Opportunity Passport. Youth board members earn stipends for their service on the board and may also receive funds for leadership training and other activities. All incentive payments and payments for service are split equally between the personal debit account and the savings account. This allows the young person access to money to fulfill immediate needs while simultaneously building a savings account balance.

23. See Appendix D for contact information for the community partnerships.

Epilogue

1. California Permanency for Youth Project. http://www.cpyp.org.

2. Mark E. Courtney, Amy Dworsky, et al. "Midwest Evaluation of the Adult Functioning of Former Foster Youth: Outcomes at Age 19." Chicago: University of Chicago Chapin Hall Center for Children, 2005. http://www.chapinhall.org.

3. Ibid.

REFERENCES

AFCARS Report: Current Estimates (Preliminary FY 2003 Estimates). Washington, DC: Department of Health and Human Services, April 2005. http://www.acf.hhs.gov/programs/cb/stats_research/afcars/tar/report10.htm.

"All Grown Up, Nowhere to Go: Texas Teens in Foster Care Transition." Austin, Texas: Center for Public Policy Priorities, 2001.

Armstrong, M. L. "Adolescent Pathways: Exploring the Intersections Between Child Welfare and Juvenile Justice, PINS, and Mental Health." New York: Vera Institute, May 1999. http://www.vera.org/publication_pdf/pathways.pdf.

Baker, Amy, Carolyn Mincer, and David Olson. "The WAY to Work: An Independent Living/Aftercare Program for High-Risk Youth." Washington, DC: Child Welfare League of America, 2000.

Bales, Susan. "Reframing Youth Issues for Public Consideration and Support." Washington, DC: FrameWorks Institute, and Los Angeles: Center for Communications and Community, 2001. http://www.frameworksinstitute.org/products/reframing.pdf.

Bass, Deborah. "Helping Vulnerable Youths: Runaway and Homeless Adolescents in the United States." Washington, DC: National Association of Social Workers, 1994.

Bridges, Tony. "Kids Find State Fails Them." *Tallahassee Democrat*, February 7, 2003. http://www.tallahassee.com/mld/tallahassee/news/special_packages/the_legacy_of_foster_care/5131544.htm.

Burley, M., and M. Halpern. "Educational Attainment of Foster Youth: Achievement and Graduation Outcomes for Children in State Care." Olympia: Washington State Institute for Public Policy, 2001. http://www.wsipp.wa.gov/childfamily/pdf/FCEDReport.pdf.

"Chafee Foster Care Independence Act—Frequently Asked Questions." Washington, DC: National Foster Care Awareness Project, 2000. http://www.casey.org/documents/adv_faq_booklet.pdf.

"Chafee Foster Care Independence Act—Frequently Asked Questions II." Washington, DC: National Foster Care Awareness Project, 2000. http://www.casey.org/documents/adv_faq2_final.pdf.

"Child Maltreatment 2002." Washington, DC: Department of Health and Human Services, 2004. http://www.acf.hhs.gov/programs/cb/publications/cm02/.

"Child Welfare Outcomes Annual Report: 2000." Washington, DC: Department of Health and Human Services, 2003. http://www.acf.hhs.gov/programs/cb/publications/cwo00/.

"Child Welfare Outcomes Annual Report: 1999." Washington, DC: Department of Health and
    Human Services, 2002. http://www.acf.dhhs.gov/programs/cb/publications/cwo99/.

Cook, Ronna. "A National Evaluation of Title IV-E Foster Care Independent Living
    Programs for Youth: Phase 2 Final Report." Rockville, MD: Westat, Inc., 1991.

Courtney, Mark, Irving Piliavin, Andrew Grogan-Kaylor, and Ande Nesmith. "Foster
    Youth Transitions to Adulthood: A Longitudinal View of Youth Leaving Care." *Child
    Welfare* 80, no. 6 (2001).

Courtney, Mark E., Dworsky, Amy, et al. "Midwest Evaluation of the Adult Functioning of
    Former Foster Youth." Chicago: Chapin Hall Center for Children at the University of
    Chicago, 2005. http://www.chapinhall.org/.

"Effectiveness of Independent Living Services Unknown." Washington, DC: General
    Accounting Office, November 1999. http://www.nrcys.ou.edu/PDFs/gao11599.pdf.

Eilertson, Christine. "Independent Living for Foster Youth." Denver: National Conference
    of State Legislatures, 2002. http://www.ncsl.org/programs/pubs/bkfoster.htm.

Ferber, Thaddeus, and Karen Pitman. "Adding It Up: Taking Stock of Efforts to Improve
    State-Level Youth Policies." Washington, DC: The Forum for Youth Investment,
    November 2001. http://www.forumforyouthinvestment.org/fyi/addingitup.pdf.

Finkelstein, Marni, Mark Warmsley, and Doreen Miranda. "What Keeps Children in
    Foster Care from Succeeding in School?" New York: Vera Institute of Justice, 2002.
    http://www.vera.org/publication_pdf/169_280.pdf.

"Foster Youth Proposals to Improve Mental Health Services: The Consumer's Perspective."
    San Francisco: California Youth Connection, 2000.

"Fostered or Forgotten: A Special Report on Foster Teens in Transition." *AdvoCasey*, Fall
    2001. Baltimore: Annie E. Casey Foundation. http://www.aecf.org/publications/data/
    advocasey_fall2001.pdf.

Goerge, Robert M., et al. "Employment Outcomes for Youth Aging Out of Foster Care. Final
    Report." Chicago: Chapin Hall Center for Children, March 2002. http://aspe.hhs.gov/
    hsp/fostercare-agingout02/.

Guzman, Lina, Laura Lippmann, and Kristin A. Moore. "Public Perception of Children's Well-
    Being: Working Paper." Washington, DC: Child Trends, 2002. http://www.childtrends.org/
    PDF/PublicPerPaper.pdf.

"In the Wake of Childhood Maltreatment." Washington, DC: OJJDP Juvenile Justice
    Bulletin, August 1997. http://www.ncjrs.org/pdffiles1/165257.pdf.

"Investigation into the Transitioning of Reggie Kelsey out of Iowa's Foster Care System."
    Des Moines, IA: Office of the Citizen's Aide/Ombudsman, January 14, 2003. http://
    www4.legis.state.ia.us/cao/Reports/files/DHS%20-%20Kelsey%20-%20Redacted.pdf.

"It's My Life *(Es mi vida):* Summary of a Framework for Youth Transitioning from Foster
    Care to Successful Adulthood." Seattle: Casey Family Programs, 2001.
    http://www.casey.org/documents/its_my_life_book.pdf.

Ivry, Robert, and Fred Doolittle. "Improving the Economic and Life Outcomes of At-Risk
    Youth." New York: MDRC, Spring 2003.
    http://www.mdrc.org/Reports2003/at_risk_concept_ppr/at_risk_2003.pdf.

John, Giselle. "Would You Place Your Child There?" *Foster Care Youth United*
    (May–June 1997).

Kauffman, Clark. "Reggie Sought Home, but Found Death." *Des Moines Register,* June 17, 2003. http://www.dmregister.com/news/stories/c4780934/15041469.html.

Kessler, Michelle. "The Transition Years: Serving Current and Former Foster Youth Ages Eighteen to Twenty-One." Tulsa: National Resource Center for Youth Services, 2004. http://www.nrcys.ou.edu/PDFs/Monographs/Transitions.pdf.

Kortenkamp, Katherine, and Jennifer Ehrle. "The Well-Being of Children Involved with the Child Welfare System: A National Overview." *New Federalism, Series B,* No. B-43. Washington, DC: The Urban Institute, January 2002. http://www.urban.org/Uploaded PDF/310413_anf_b43.pdf.

Lake Snell Perry & Associates. National public opinion poll of 1,121 adults conducted for the Jim Casey Youth Opportunities Initiative, January 2003. Summary of results: http://www.jimcaseyyouth.org/docs/poll1.pdf.

Miller, Carol Marbin. "Advocates: Law Hurts Older Foster Kids." *Miami Herald,* January 20, 2003.

Mooney, Chris. "Breaking the Frame." *American Prospect,* April 2003. http://www.prospect.org/print/V14/4/mooney-c.html.

Needell, Barbara, et al. "Youth Emancipating from Foster Care in California: Findings Using Linked Administrative Data." Berkeley: University of California Center for Social Services Research, May 2002. http://www.cssr.berkeley.edu/childwelfare/pdfs/youth/ffy_entire.pdf.

Nixon, Robin, and Maria Garin Jones. "Improving Transitions to Adulthood for Youth Served by the Foster Care System." Washington, DC: Child Welfare League of America, 2000.

Pecora, Peter J., Jason Williams, Ronald C. Kessler, A. Chris Downs, Kirk O'Brien, Eva Hiripi, and Sarah Morello. "Assessing the Effects of Foster Care: Early Results from the Casey National Alumni Study." Seattle: Casey Family Programs, 2003. http://www.casey.org/NR/rdonlyres/CEFBB1B6-7ED1-440D-925A-E5BAF602294D/48/casey_alumni_studies_report.pdf.

"Pembroke Pines Police Hunt Owners of $20,000 in Stolen Goods." *Ft. Lauderdale Sun-Sentinel,* September 19, 2003.

"Policy Counts: Setting and Measuring Benchmarks for State Policies." Washington, DC: Center for the Study of Social Policy, 2002. http://www.cssp.org/major_initiatives/policy_counts.html.

"Promising Practices: School to Career and Postsecondary Education for Foster Care Youth." Brooklyn, NY: Workforce Strategy Center, March 2000. http://www.workforcestrategy.org/publications/promisingpractices2.pdf.

"The Road to Independence: Foster Care Alumni Study." New Haven: Casey Family Services, 2001.

Roman, Nan P., and Phyllis Wolfe. "Web of Failure: The Relationship Between Foster Care and Homelessness." Washington, DC: National Alliance to End Homelessness, 1995. http://www.endhomelessness.org/pub/fostercare/webrept.htm.

Straka, Doreen, et al. "Supportive Housing for Youth." New York: Corporation for Supportive Housing. http://www.csh.org/2003.

Wertheimer, Richard. "Youth Who 'Age Out' of Foster Care: Troubled Lives, Troubling Prospects." *ChildTrends Research Brief.* Washington, DC: Child Trends, December 2002. http://www.childtrends.org/PDF/FosterCareRB.pdf.

Widom, C. S. "The Cycle of Violence." *Research in Brief*. Washington, DC: U.S. Department of Justice, National Institute of Justice, October 1992.

Wolanin, Thomas R. "Higher Education Opportunities for Foster Youth: A Primer for Policymakers." Washington: The Institute for Higher Education Policy, December 2005. http://www.ihep.org/Pubs/PDF/fosteryouth.pdf.

Wulczyn, Fred, Kristen Brunner-Hislop, and Robert Goerge. "Update from the Multistate Foster Care Data Archive: Foster Care Dynamics 1983–1998." Chicago: Chapin Hall, 2000. http://www.chapinhall.org/article_abstract_new.asp?ar=1322&L2=61&L3=130.

INDEX

ABOUT THE AUTHORS

Martha Shirk is a freelance journalist who specializes in social issues. She is coauthor of *Lives on the Line* (Westview, 1999) and *Kitchen Table Entrepreneurs* (Westview, 2002). She was a reporter for the *St. Louis Post-Dispatch* from 1975 to 1997, and she now lives in Palo Alto, California.

Gary Stangler is the founding executive director of the St. Louis–based Jim Casey Youth Opportunities Initiative, which seeks to enhance opportunities for youth who are making the transition from foster care to adulthood. For eleven years, he served as the director of Missouri's Department of Social Services, which gave him legal responsibility for the welfare of all children in foster care in the state. He lives near Columbia, Missouri.

For a **Reader's Guide to** *On Their Own*, visit http://www.jimcasey youth.org.

The authors can be reached by email at info@jimcaseyyouth.org.